RELIGION AND NATIONALISM IN IRAQ:
A COMPARATIVE PERSPECTIVE

Religion and Nationalism in Iraq:
A Comparative Perspective

edited by David Little and Donald K. Swearer

with Susan Lloyd McGarry

Center for the Study of World Religions
Harvard Divinity School
Cambridge, Massachuetts
Distributed by Harvard University Press
2006

Grateful acknowledgement is made to the United Nations Cartographic
Section for permission to reprint the following maps:
Iraq Map No.3835 Rev 4 January 2004
Sri Lanka Map No.4172 Rev 1 January 2004
Sudan Map No.3707 Rev 7 May 2004
Bosnia and Herzegovina Map No.3729 Rev 5 June 2004

Library of Congress Cataloging-in-Publication Data

Religion and nationalism in Iraq : a comparative perspective / edited by
    David Little and Donald K. Swearer ; with Susan Lloyd McGarry.
    p. cm.
    Includes bibliographical references.
    ISBN-13: 978-0-945454-41-0 (pbk. : alk. paper)
    1. Religion and politics—Case studies. 2. Nationalism—Case studies.
    3. Religion and politics—Congresses. 4. Nationalism—Congresses.
    I. Little, David, 1933-   . II. Swearer, Donald K., 1934-   .
    BL65.P7R4265 2006
    201'.72—dc22
                                                    2006029193

Contents

Preface

Neo-Marxist and neo-Darwinian predictions of the withering away of organized religion in the face of secular political transformation or the individualism of modernity have proved to be at least premature if not patently false. The mixture of religion, ethnic, and communal identity, and the modern nation-state has created explosive and seemingly intractable conflicts around the globe, particularly in the Middle East. It was to explore four of the most violent, contested situations that the Center for the Study of World Religions at the Harvard Divinity School convened a conference on April 22–23, 2005 that brought together 25 experts from different fields who are authorities on Iraq, Bosnia, Sri Lanka, and Sudan.

We had not intended to produce a conference volume, but the overriding importance of the topic and the value of the presentations and ensuing discussions argued otherwise. Not only the named authors but many of the participants contributed greatly to the strength of this volume through their incisive comments during the discussions. The result is this collection of conference presentations, summary discussions, and brief country summaries, co-edited by David Little and Donald Swearer, that constitute *Religion and Nationalism in Iraq: A Comparative Perspective*.

I am particularly indebted to David Little, the Dunphy Professor at Harvard Divinity School. The conference would not have been possible without his extensive comparative knowledge of the topic and his leadership at the conference. I am also indebted to Susan Lloyd McGarry, the CSWR Manager of Planning and Special Projects, for the many hours she devoted to editing and organizing the diverse contributions that constitute this volume. The volume would not have come to fruition without her collaboration.

Donald K. Swearer
Director, Center for the Study of World Religions
Harvard Divinity School

Editors' Note about Transliteration and Special Characters

Given the comparative nature of this volume, its appeal to generalists as well as specialists, the many differing linguistic areas that it covers, and the diversity of its authors, we have chosen to omit diacritics and special characters such as the ayn and hamza in Arabic to increase the volume's readability. While recognizing regional differences, we have tried to transliterate consistently within those constraints.

Introduction

David Little and Donald Swearer

Whatever else is true about it, present-day Iraq represents a potentially volatile mixture of the forces of religion and nationalism. As a result of the countrywide elections of January and December 2005, the three largest groups—the Shiites, Sunnis, and Kurds—are locked in a sharply divided contest over the definition of national identity and the distribution of national power, as well as over the control of territory. The nationalist contest looks all the more ominous, of course, against the backdrop of a relentless insurgency and the continuing threat of civil war. The Shiites, who comprise some 60 percent of the population, were big parliamentary winners in the elections. They have advanced various versions of a religious agenda and have encouraged a divisive debate over, among other things, the place of religion in Iraqi national life. That development has, in turn, tightened the connection between ethnic identity and religious outlook in respect to all three of the groups and, as a consequence, has intensified ethnoreligious sectarianism throughout Iraq. These divisions have been played out recently in the complicated processes of drafting a new constitution and forming a government. They are also evident in the increasing violence, which is escalating toward civil war.

Because the situation in Iraq exhibits some of the standard symptoms of religious nationalism, it seems appropriate to compare it to other cases, like Bosnia and Herzegovina (henceforth B&H), Sri Lanka, and Sudan, where the impulses of religion and nationalism have also come together—in those places in a highly lethal way. Such an enterprise can be of value, both from an academic and a policy perspective. Scholars are anything but agreed about the causes and character of nationalist conflicts, or about the meaning and role of religious and ethnic identity. Careful efforts by noted students of such conflicts to think together comparatively might yield interesting and informative results. Certainly, the endeavor would be worth trying, if only better to learn where similarities and uniformities among the various examples begin and end.

By the same token, policymakers, particularly in a place like Iraq, need all the help they can get. It is reasonable to conclude that more attention to the ethnic and religious history and dynamics of the country, particularly when compared to other cases, might have helped to avoid or mitigate some of the more egregious policy errors that have occurred since the invasion of Iraq in March 2003. Moreover, what can be learned from a comparative consideration of attempts to manage and resolve nationalist conflicts, like those in B&H, Sri Lanka, and Sudan, may hold promise for improving similar efforts in Iraq, and in particular for reducing the appalling degree of destruction and loss of life too often associated with nationalist conflicts.

These were the general assumptions behind convening a conference to examine Iraq in comparative perspective, held April 22-23, 2005 at the Harvard Divinity School's Center for the Study of World Religions, whose proceedings and conclusions this volume is intended to summarize. The conference drew together some 25 scholars, most with special expertise in one of the four cases, but several with more generalized interests. Professor Juan Cole of the University of Michigan led off the conference with a public talk entitled "The Rise of Religious and Ethnic Mass Policies in Iraq." Subsequently, other participants provided brief introductory comments on each of the four cases, which were followed by open discussion designed both to update awareness of the present state of affairs in Iraq, B&H, Sri Lanka, and

Sudan, and to draw common lessons that might be of special relevance to the situation in Iraq.

Inevitably, by the time this book is read, each of the country situations will have changed—in some cases, dramatically. In the course of editing and producing this volume, we have provided some brief updates in the introduction up until February 2006. The value of this volume is not in its immediacy, but in thick description, deep background, rich comparison, and cogent analysis.

Religion and Nationalism: Current Thinking

Before getting to the findings of the conference, it may be valuable to review briefly some of the current thinking on the connection of religious and ethnic factors to nationalist conflicts. There is at present considerable scholarly controversy in this area. If the idea of "nation" is understood as "a relatively large grouping of people who conceive themselves to have a communal past, including shared sufferings and shared achievements, from which...is derived a common culture...uniting past[,]...present and...future,"[1] and the idea of "nationalism" is taken, at a minimum, to mean a claim by one or more "nations" to political authority over the inhabitants of a given territory, a "nationalist conflict" is a contest, sometimes violent, between two or more groups claiming the "right to rule" within a given territory based upon competing conceptions of nationhood. In short, nationalist conflicts are contests over which national ideal will prevail in a given nation-state. In common parlance, such conflicts are often described as "ethnic" or "religious," or as "ethnoreligious," because it is assumed that the competing ideals of nationhood are shaped or strongly influenced by considerations of ethnic or religious identity or both.

There are two points of serious controversy about this way of characterizing nationalist conflicts: one, terminological and the other, theoretical or causal. The terminological problem is raised by the fact that in discussions of nationalism the conceptual differences and connections between "ethnic" and "religious" are not usually made clear. "Ethnic" denotes "origin by birth or descent," but it also denotes, in a more archaic but still potent usage, "a person not of the Christian or

Jewish faith," as in "heathen,"[2] or "gentile"—namely, a spiritual alien or outsider.

Consequently, "ethnic" can mean different things. It may designate membership in a group determined by inherited characteristics (genealogical lineage, language, manners and mores, etc.) that are not necessarily "religious" in the sense of reflecting adherence to a sacred authority, or other indicia commonly accepted as identifying a religion.[3] At the same time, "ethnic" may also and often does take on a distinctly "religious" connotation, a condition by no means restricted to Christianity or Judaism. In that case, groups are distinguished and evaluated depending on the degree to which they exhibit faithful adherence to a preferred religion. In combination with religion, then, genealogy, language, inherited manners and mores, and other ethnic characteristics all assume a strongly normative tone reflected in widely employed terms like "chosen people."

The widespread tendency of ethnic groups in all cultural contexts to authenticate themselves religiously lends plausibility to the term, "ethnoreligious." The tendency also explains why, in particular cases, it is artificial to try to distinguish too sharply between religious and non-religious ethnic attributes. In those instances where religious identity becomes ethnically salient, language, customs, and even genealogy take on strongly religious overtones.

Furthermore, it is the central role of ethnic and religious impulses in forming the identity of a people or "nation" that directly ties these matters to discussions of nationalism and nationalist conflict. Though ethnic groups or "peoples" do not necessarily need a religious reason to seek to preserve and promote their identity by achieving political sovereignty, a claim of religious legitimacy is likely to strengthen and intensify such a campaign.

Still, with all this appropriate and generally not well appreciated emphasis on the conceptual distinctions and connections between ethnicity and religion, an important proviso should be emphasized. It is that significant "trans-ethnic" impulses exist in religious traditions alongside "pro-ethnic" ones. For example, there are references in the New Testament to the requirement of forsaking family and ethnic group in the name of new, higher obligations, as well as to the superiority of celibacy to marriage. Indeed, the whole idea, essential to Christianity, of being "born again" as a member of a "new family," a "new people" in the sacrament of baptism, underscores this trans-ethnic dimension.

A belief in the superiority of "spiritual" to "natural" relations, including sexual relations, is, of course, central to all celibate monastic movements, not only in Christianity, but in other religions such as Buddhism and Hinduism. That belief obviously represents a direct challenge to the priority of biological heredity. A different form of the same emphasis can be found in all religions of conversion since, ideally, personal voluntary commitment to fundamental religious tenets supersedes the status of birth or ethnic membership. This would apply in general to Islam, even though "origin by birth" does bestow special status on certain direct descendents of Muhammad. The contrast and tension between pro-ethnic and trans-ethnic religious impulses, sometimes within the same religion, is occasionally an important dimension of nationalist disputes over the meaning of national identity.

The theoretical or causal problem is raised by the claims of social scientists and others that nationalist conflicts are either not about ethnicity and religion at all, but rather about economic and political matters, or that they are at bottom more about ethnic than religious issues. As to the first claim, Paul Collier, the World Bank economist, has famously argued that national civil wars are basically the product of "greed, not grievance," presumably including ethnic and religious grievances.[4] Economic conditions (such as low national income connected with slow economic growth and accelerated population increase) together with unscrupulous entrepreneurs make countries susceptible to nationalist conflicts. "Where rebellions happen to be financially viable, wars will occur."[5] Charges of cultural, economic, or political mistreatment by one or another party to a conflict are of no causal significance for the onset of violent conflict, except, Collier concedes, in multiethnic societies where one ethnic or ethnoreligious group constitutes between 45 and 90 percent of the population—"enough to give it control but not enough to make discrimination against a minority pointless."[6]

The problem with Collier's argument, and with similar arguments by others,[7] is that they do not prove what they set out to prove. First, the exceptions are so large that they make the argument irrelevant to much of the world's conflicts. Collier himself admits what turns out to be a huge and very consequential exception to his argument when he excludes countries where one ethnic group constitutes between 45 and 90 percent of the population: all of the ethnoreligious majorities in the four cases we are considering—the Sinhala Buddhists in Sri Lanka, the Arab Muslim northerners in Sudan, the Serbs in the former Yugoslavia, and the Shiite Arabs in Iraq—constitute between 45 and 90 percent of the relevant populations. Thus they have reason to institute discriminatory policies against minority populations that, on Collier's own terms, would significantly affect the causes of violent conflict. In other words, Collier's thesis, by his own admission, has no explanatory power in regard to four of the most notable current nationalist contests!

But beyond that, Collier also admits that during the course of even unexceptional national civil wars, grievances (presumably including ethnic and religious grievances)—and not just greed—do become potent in influencing the direction and outcome of the war. He emphasizes the importance of a "sense of injustice," and a perception of discrimination in legitimating an insurgency, and in rallying recruits to its cause, and he explicitly mentions that grievances concerning areas such as equitable government provision for education and health must be taken into account in any sustainable peace settlement.[8] If that is so, then it is not simply economic factors that must be addressed in resolving national conflicts, as his thesis about the priority of greed over grievance would seem to imply. Again, it appears that, even in regard to the conflicts to which Collier believes his thesis does apply, ethnic and religious grievances, undoubtedly along with other concerns, eventually become very salient when considered in relation to the overall course of a national conflict.

Another scholar, Ted Robert Gurr,[9] while assigning substantially more significance to grievance as a cause of national conflict than does Collier, nevertheless plays down the causal importance of religion in contrast to the ethnic factor. The difficulty is that some of his own data and arguments do not support this conclusion. In *Peoples versus States* he writes: "The only conclusion drawn here [about the effects of group type on political action] is that religiously defined communal groups are not a relevant factor in a risk model of ethnorebellion."[10] But later, Gurr turns around and draws some large, ominous conclusions about the global risks of what he calls "ethnorebellion" in a revealing comment about intolerant Islamist political leaders. "Probably the greatest threats to [peaceful ethnonational relations] come from predatory, hegemonic elites who use the state as an instrument to protect and promote the interests of their own people at the expense of others. These and other sources of communal warfare and repression remain in many corners of the world and will continue to cast up challenges to those who would contain ethnic violence."[11] As the reference to the Islamist leaders suggests, religious identity appears, after all, on Gurr's own accounting, to be relevant to the risks of nationalist conflict in regard *both* to minorities and to dominant state structures.

Essential Themes

In the course of reflection on the conference, four themes emerged as essential for understanding nationalist contests with a religious cast, such as the ones before us, as well as for identifying specific implications for Iraq. All four themes are touched upon to a greater or lesser degree in the commentary, discussions, and background papers: the salience of religious and ethnic identity; the significance of history; the perils of self-government; and the place of international involvement.

1. The Salience of Religious and Ethnic Identity

What is most striking about the commentary and discussion among the experts at the April conference is the degree to which it confirms, with virtually no dissent, the salience of ethnic and religious identity in regard to the four nationalist contests—Sri Lanka, Sudan, B&H, and Iraq—taken up for comparative consideration. Of course, no one argued, or assumed, that these contests were just about ethnicity or religion. All participants presupposed that the contests are, after all, essentially nationalistic in character, which already sets them in the context of politics, or, better said, of political economy. The sort of struggle they all exhibit—for Sri Lanka, Sudan, and B&H a severely violent struggle, for Iraq one increasingly so—concerns at bottom the distribution and legitimation of political, military, economic, and territorial control. Ethnicity and religion come into it in regard to defining the national ideals that compete in all these cases over what ought to be accepted as the legitimate distribution of national control.

When the 9/11 al-Qaeda terrorists attacked the World Trade Center and the Pentagon they chose targets that symbolized America as the cosmic "Other," the world's dominant economic and military superpower perceived by them as a threat to the very being of the Islamic world. Analogously, although the conflicts in Iraq, Sri Lanka, B&H, and Sudan are nationalistic in character and reflect a struggle over political, military, economic, and territorial power and control, their undeniable ethnic and religious dimensions point in another direction as well, namely, as a virulent symptom of a perceived threat to communal identity, symbolized by religious and cultural institutions as well as political ones. The violent intensity of ethnonationalism in B&H, Sri Lanka, Sudan, and Iraq has many causes, but among its roots is a fear of domination by an Other who threatens the integrity or purity of a particular communal or group identity. The 1998 Tamil Tiger suicide bombing at the sacred Temple of the Tooth in Kandy; the rampage of Sinhala police in Jaffna in 1981 that destroyed thousands of culturally irreplaceable Tamil manuscripts in the Jaffna Public Library; the Serb military destruction of all of the mosques in the northeast Bosnian town of Zvornik in 1992; and hundreds of similar acts of violent destruction are intended not only as political intimidation but as a direct attack on the Other symbolized by venerated religious shrines and sites central to a community's cultural, historical, and religious identity. Similarly, Sunni terrorist raids on Shiite mosques in Iraq, while having the political aim of disrupting the creation of a constitution and formation of a democratic government, are acts by a formerly privileged religious minority who fear domination by a previously persecuted Shiite majority. The perceived threat of the Shiite majority looms even larger because of Iraq's Shiite neighbor, Iran; likewise Sinhala Buddhists see their identity being overwhelmed by an imagined alliance between Sri Lankan and Indian Tamils.

It is undeniable that religion works to define identity, differentiating insider from outsider in terms of belief, ritual practice, and symbolic cultural markers; moreover, religion functions to motivate, promulgate, and sanction ethnonational claims. The examples of Sri Lanka and B&H illustrate the point. In the case of Sri Lanka, Buddhist ethnonationalists appeal to a sacred text, the sixth century CE *Mahavamsa*, to legitimate an imagined Buddhist state on the island of Sri Lanka. During three visits to the island, the Buddha drives out malevolent demons, converts benevolent *nagas* to the true religion (*sasana*), visits places that become sacred sites, most notably Sri Pada (also known as Samantakuta and Adam's Peak), and prepares the island for the arrival of Vijaya, the founding ancestor of the Sinhalas. From a union between Vijaya and the demoness, Kuveni, issue the Veddas, the island's indigenous hunter-gatherers. Vijaya also marries a princess from Madurapura, the Tamil region of south India. These and other aspects of this charter myth highlight the theme of incorporation but also exemplify fluid boundaries between ethnicities and religions— Sinhalas, Veddas, Tamils, Buddhists, Hindus, animists. This same fluidity finds expression in the eclectic nature of Sinhala Buddhism as it evolved over time—a blending of Buddhist, Hindu, Brahmanical, and animistic elements. Sinhala Buddhist ethnonationalists, however, selectively retrieve those aspects of the tradition that denigrate the Other. The *Mahavamsa* becomes a proof text legitimating the violent subjugation of the Tamils (Hindu) by the Sinhalas (Buddhist), in particular, the text's focal story of Duttugamani's slaughter of the Tamil king, Elara, and his army. They imagine the land as sanctified from time immemorial as the place of the Sinhalas (*Sinhaladipa*), the protectors of the true religion (*Dhammadipa*).

In Eastern Europe, the area of Bosnia and Herzegovina has been a battleground of Catholic Croat and Orthodox Serb ethnic nationalisms and militant religious ideologies. Beginning in 1992, Serb and Croat armies engaged in the wanton destruction of cultural and religious centers in Sarajevo. The Serb army destroyed the National Library and the National Museum housing an irreplaceable collection of Islamic and Jewish manuscripts and artifacts, and dynamited over six hundred mosques. The Croat army destroyed mosques and Orthodox churches in the territory they controlled. Between them Serb and Croat ethnonationalists attempted to efface all evidence of Bosnian Muslim life, even destroying graveyards and birth records.[12]

In Kosovo, Serb ethnonationalists instigated genocidal attacks on Muslims aimed at nothing short of cultural eradication. Michael Sells identifies the religious ideology of "Christoslavism," which first emerged in the nineteenth century, as motivating and justifying the bloodshed and violence.[13] A cardinal feature of this ideology was a mythologized antagonism between the Serbs and Slavic Muslims read back to the beginning of time from the Battle of Kosovo fought in 1389 in which Prince Lazar died fighting the Ottoman Turks. In the nineteenth century Lazar was portrayed as a Christ figure as a strategy to rally national sentiment against the Ottoman Turks, and the story was revived in an extreme form in the 1980s. In 1989 Slobodan Milosevic, militant bishop-politicians, and others used the performance of the ritual of remembrance of Prince Lazar's death as a grand passion play to galvanize ethnonationalistic sentiment against Muslims in Kosovo. The ritual contemporized a mythic time for a million people gathered for the event, generating an emotional group psychology that turned against Muslims as the alleged killers of Lazar-cum-Christ.[14] Mark Juergensmeyer characterizes such instances of religious ethnonationalism as a "cosmic war," a struggle in defense of identity so basic that losing it would be unthinkable.[15] In the face of an imagined threat to communal identity—as in the Bosnian and Sri Lankan cases—religion both motivates and sanctions radical group violence.

The relationship between ethnicity and religion is, to be sure, complex. Together with language, they constitute major building blocks of communal and personal identity; however, they are not isomorphic—they interrelate and overlap in different ways in particular historical situations and contexts. Michael Sells argues that the term "ethnic" in the ethnic cleansing of Muslims by Serbs in B&H was but a euphemism for religious: "It entail[ed] a purely extrinsic definition of the victim in terms of religious identity."[16] The Other may be of a different religion and ethnicity as in the case of animist and Christianized tribal groups in the southern Sudan and Arab Muslims in the North; or of the same ethnicity but different religion/sectarian tradition as with the Sunnis and Shiites in Iraq. In the former Yugoslavia, Croat and Serb ethnonationalists carried out genocidal violence against Muslims but they also engaged in destructive acts against Orthodox and Catholic churches respectively. As we know from Northern Ireland, intrareligious violence can be as persistently malignant as interreligious violence.

Coupled with the complex interrelationship between ethnicity and religion within a given historical and cultural context is a tendency to reify ethnoreligious identities. Media stereotypes of today's politically motivated Sunni-Shiite conflict in Iraq largely overlook the historical and cultural multiplex and multilevel relationships between them. In the case of Sri Lanka to equate being Sinhala with being Buddhist ignores the historical fact that there were probably Tamil Buddhist communities on the island and that Sri Lankan Buddhist monks traveled on pilgrimage or to study at Buddhist centers in the Tamil region of south India. Furthermore, when the political discourse about national identity focuses on the dominant ethnoreligious antagonists, minority groups such as Christians in Iraq or Muslims in Sri Lanka are largely overlooked.

A historical perspective on today's ethnoreligious nationalist conflicts cautions against hypostatizing them as mere instances of a primordial or age-old antagonism. Rather, early sensibilities of difference that defined communal identities within a given geopolitical environment become increasingly intractable in response to political change. In the case of B&H under Ottoman rule, religious and ethnic differences created obvious tensions; however, today's Orthodox Serbs, Catholic Croats, and Muslims of B&H are not "direct descendants through stable ethnoreligious communities of ancient Orthodox, Catholic, and Muslim ancestors."[17] Rather, different loyalties in B&H were complex and shifting with mutual conversion occurring among religious communities. Although very real tensions existed among different religious groups, a culturally and religiously pluralistic society flourished for five centuries. As discussed in other sections of this introduction and in the B&H case study, various political factors contributed to the rise of more extreme religious ethnonationalist sentiments that eventually led to the militant assertion of ethnoreligious communal identities culminating in the ethnic cleansing campaigns of the 1980s and 1990s.

A similar trajectory with important variations can be applied to Sudan, Sri Lanka, and Iraq that, broadly speaking, superimposes an imagined centralized nation-state on ethnoreligious communal identities. The much contested shape of the nation-state, some form of federalism versus the authority and power of a central government, entails not only political, economic, and military considerations but also the question of identity. The degree of violence among ethnoreligious communities stems, as least in part, from a fear of a hated Other perceived as a threat to the very existence of a people. In Sudan, although ethnoreligious nationalism has its roots in earlier periods, British colonial rule (1898–1956) significantly exacerbated the ethnic, religious, and cultural boundaries between the North and South by governing the country as two essentially separate colonies. As discussed later in this introduction, subsequent Khartoum regimes instituted programs of increased Islamization-Arabization. As Ann Mayer observed in her conference paper, the Islamization project imagined a nation that "could only grow strong via crushing diversity and adopting a common culture and religion."

In Sri Lanka the conjoining of place, ethnicity, and religion to which the sixth century *Mahavamsa* and the fourteenth century *Pujavaliya* bear witness arose out of historic circumstances that threatened the imagined Sinhala Buddhist community. For example, the *Pujavaliya* was written soon after an invasion of the island by Magha of Kalinga (Orissa) in 1214 and the migration of Sinhala civilization from Anuradhapura to the southwest.[18] Mahanama, the author of the *Mahavamsa*, recounts the story of the heroic king, Duttugamani, defender of the heritage of the Buddha and Vijaya in the third century, but he imagined that history from his own sixth-century contested situation. Although the *Mahavamsa* has become an icon of today's Buddhist ethnonationalism, the compiler "was not interested in creating the 'national' identities" but, rather, textualized a set of identities that "enable[d] the rise of nineteenth-century nationalism."[19]

Gananath Obeyesekere contends that the chronicle depiction of Sri Lanka as a land of the Sinhala Buddhists cannot account for the rise of Buddhist ethnonationalism in the modern period, which he attributes to Western colonialism. The Portuguese, Dutch, and above all, the

British, became the hated Other. Otherness until this time had not meant a total exclusion but rather a series of identity boundaries that tended to be fuzzier in some periods of history than others.[20] After independence the hated Other then became the Hindu Tamils.

In regard to Iraq, as Juan Cole observed in his opening plenary address, the ethnic divisions among the Kurds, Shiites, and Sunnis that were evidenced in the January 2005 election when virtually every Iraqi who voted did so on ethnic grounds were an "unfamiliar world" when compared to the past history of the region. In ancient times the term, "Iraq" referred to a fertile, green region in the midst of arid landscape, and in the nineteenth century what is now Iraq was three or four provinces under the Ottoman Empire. Nor was Iraq any more "Islamic" in the imagined sense of the term than it was a nation. Islamization and nation building emerge in the early twentieth century with the British colonial incursion which set in motion the forces of ethnoreligious communal confrontation resulting from sectarian and cultural differences and exacerbated by a long history of separation. These realities, deepened even further during Saddam Hussein's Baathist regime, underlie the conflict over Iraq's constitution.

We conclude from these examples that ethnoreligious boundaries in the cases addressed by the conference on religion and nationalism were relatively fluid prior to the period of state formation in the late nineteenth and twentieth centuries but that conflict among ethnic communities becomes increasingly violent when confronted with incorporation into a centralized nation-state that threatens the diverse self interests of ethnic enclaves. The 2005 Sudanese peace agreement, which respects the ethnic and religious integrity of the southern tribes, guarantees a significant degree of independence, holds out the promise of autonomy in six years, and offers one type of solution to this confrontation.

Of utmost importance in any consideration of ethnoreligious nationalism is the crucial role of individual leaders, religious as well as political. Although religious leaders are capable of promoting tolerance and understanding of other ethnoreligious communities, "too many...continue to pursue narrow sectarian or ethnic agendas...and fail to oppose the demonization of the other. As long as this is the case, religion will remain a disrupter of peace, and a source of violence."[21] In B&H by 1992, Serbian church leaders such as Metropolitan Amfilohije (Radovic) and Bishop Vasilije fanned the flames of ethnoreligiosity by charging a worldwide Islamic conspiracy against the Serbian Orthodox Church, and Slobodan Milosevic's genocidal Christoslavism was endorsed and promoted by the majority of Orthodox clerics with a few outstanding countervailing voices.[22] In Iraq the Grand Ayatollah Ali al-Sistani, who was instrumental in creating a coalition of Shiite groups that dominated the 2005 elections, has been a consistent voice of non-violence and moderation in the face of more radical Shiite clerics such as Muqtada al-Sadr whose militias have clashed not only with U.S. occupation forces but with rival Shiite brigades as well. In Sudan, Hassan al-Turabi founded the National Islamic Front (NIF), a faction of Muslim Brotherhood, and used violent, draconian means to create an Islamic state. In Sri Lanka since 1956, Buddhist monks have been a prominent force in promoting a chauvinistic ethnoreligious national-ism culminating in the formation of the Pure Sinhala National Heritage party in 2004.

The Ayatollah Sistani stands out as a voice of moderation and rec-onciliation in an increasingly fractious Iraq. However, there are many less well-known, countervailing religious voices that have advocated peaceful, democratic nonviolent resolutions to sectarian violence in each of these countries: in 1994 Catholic church leaders such as Cardinal Kuharic of Zagreb courageously spoke out against Croatian army attacks against Bosnian Muslims; since 1983 A. T. Ariyaratna's Sarvodaya Shramadana movement has organized over 150 peace walks and mass meditations to demonstrate for a nonviolent resolution to the civil war in Sri Lanka; in B&H, Michael Sells points to the International Forum Bosna, an attempt by Bosnians of all religious persuasions to reconstruct Catholic, Orthodox, and Islamic monuments as symbols of a common heritage; and in Sudan, an ecumenical initiative, the New Sudan Council of Churches, has organized a series of People-to-People Peace Meetings.

The religious dimension in ethnonationalism, as Mark Juergensmeyer argues, has given divine, cosmic sanction to violent confrontation with the Other: the religious imagination has the "propensity to absolutize images of cosmic war," and at this moment in history to "cry out for absolute solutions."[23] It is also true, however, that while religious teachings are used to justify ethnoreligious nationalisms, they also challenge narrow, chauvinistic identities, both religious and political. Peace advocates in Sri Lanka, for example, appeal to the Buddhist principles of nonviolence (*ahimsa*) and nonkilling to challenge injustice and violence. The founder of the U.S.-based Muslim Peace Fellowship grounds an international Islamic program of peace and justice in the terms "Islam" and *"jihad."*[24] Islam, etymologically linked to *salaam* (peace), is the Way of Peace, and *jihad*, popularly translated as "holy war" and associated with "jihadist" suicide bombings, in the Quran means struggle or effort especially in the establishment of justice.

Students of religion are quick to point out that historically the world's religions fall far short of the ideals of peace, love, and justice to which they appeal. Scott Appleby contends that they can only become operative in the life of a community through education and intentional formation. He proposes that in situations of interreligious and interethnic conflict, religious nongovernmental organizations (NGOs) be formed to pursue the goal of peacebuilding. As an example, he cites the Interreligious Council of Bosnia-Herzegovina founded to exercise a constructive influence in local and regional affairs that would affect not only the particular concerns, rights, and responsibilities of specific religious bodies but the common good as well.[25] The Interreligious Council is affiliated with Religions for Peace, which has a similar mission and is active in more than 55 countries.

2. The Significance of History

It is a remarkable coincidence that three of the four countries under consideration were—in different combinations—influenced, respectively, by the Ottoman and the British empires. For significant periods of time Bosnia, part of Iraq, and Sudan, were under Ottoman control; Iraq, Sri Lanka, and Sudan were under British control. Two of the countries, Iraq and Sudan, were at times ruled by both empires. Sri Lanka was also under the colonial dominion of the Portuguese and the

Dutch before the British took over. After World War II, Bosnia was threatened first by fascist rule supported by the Germans and the Italians, then fell briefly under Soviet control, until it became part of the breakaway communist dictatorship of Josep Broz Tito (1948–1980).

While there should be no suggestion that colonial control or other historical factors predetermined what would happen to the four cases, or that the actions and policies undertaken in the postcolonial period were not critically important, it is clear that the historical background is significant in shaping the context within which postcolonial actions and policies were worked out.

In varying degrees, the colonial legacy in all four cases influenced the kind of ethnoreligious nationalism that developed after the different countries gained independence. In the cases of B&H, Sri Lanka, and Sudan, ethnoreligious nationalism eventually culminated in violent civil war. As to Iraq, British actions laid the foundations for the rise of a form of "authoritarian nationalism" under the control of the Baath party, which, in turn, has had a crucial effect on the nationalist struggle currently taking place in that country. The policies of the Ottomans and the British, despite certain positive contributions, either did not encourage, or actively retarded the development of lasting, robust institutions that might work to modify and mediate among what would become potent ethnic and religious divisions in these countries. In some circumstances, particular Ottoman and British policies tended to exacerbate the divisions.

Ottoman rule had the effect of sometimes tolerating, sometimes strengthening religious and ethnic divisions. Such divisions could be encouraged by means of the famous *millet* system, according to which local communities were granted a significant degree of political and religious autonomy beneath the overarching tissue of Ottoman control. Consequently, religion was at once politicized and "ethnicized." Not only was the political role of local religious leaders expanded, but, in addition, religious identity became increasingly entangled with ethnic membership. As a result, ethnoreligious distinctions between Muslim and non-Muslim groups were sharpened, just as they were among different communities within the same religion, as, for example, between Eastern Orthodox and Roman Catholic Christians. It should be added that in regard to former Yugoslavia as a whole, of which Bosnia was a part, the Hapsburg or Austro-Hungarian Empire, which included Slovenia, Croatia, and eventually Bosnia, also helped to entrench ethnoreligious divisions in the region by preserving the Roman Catholic character of Slovenia and Croatia.

All this helps explain the communal character of ethnic and religious consciousness in Bosnia, a territory under Ottoman rule from the fifteenth to the nineteenth century, as well as of neighboring communities including those that would make up Yugoslavia. The familiar markers of the various major groups in Yugoslavia—Serbian Orthodox, Croatian Catholic, and Bosnian Muslim—illustrate the inseparability of religion from the community of birth or ethnic membership.[26] It also explains the readiness with which ethnoreligious ideals are translated into demands for political and territorial control, as they were in the Bosnian war, and still continue to be in the post-conflict setting.

If Bosnia endured 400 years of Ottoman control, Sudan's experience was much briefer. The Ottoman Empire manifested its control there in the form of a special Turko-Egyptian administration that lasted from 1821 until 1885, known as the Turkiyya. The general outcome was to deepen the divide between the predominately Arabic peoples of the North and the black Africans of the South.[27] Apart from undertaking slave-trading ventures and ineffective pacification efforts, the Turkiyya left the South pretty much to its own devices. On the other hand, it consolidated the sense of Islamic and Arab distinctiveness and superiority on the part of the North, thereby adding to the tensions between the two sections of the country that would afflict Sudan thereafter.

At the same time, and in some contrast to the legacy of divisiveness, the Turkiyya also provoked a nationwide drive for unity and independence among the Sudanese, thereby laying the foundations for Sudanese nationalism. As a whole, the Sudanese people came to resent the exploitation of natural resources, severe taxes, and the forced recruitment of slave soldiers. Moreover, contrary to the *millet* approach, which partially respected local customs, Ottoman policies in Sudan virtually eliminated local tribal jurisdiction. Finally, the form of Islam that the Ottomans imposed was regarded as alien to the Sufi Islam that predominated in Sudan.

These common grievances provided a basis for the overthrow of the Turkiyya in 1885, led by the charismatic Muslim rebel, Muhammad Ahmed, better known as al-Mahdi, the Islamic messiah. Al-Mahdi traded successfully on widespread anti-Turkish sentiments, and although he did not employ nationalist rhetoric, his campaign had proto-nationalist characteristics: it was undertaken to expel foreign domination in the name of unifying Sudan under an indigenous Islamic regime. The problem was that the thirteen-year experiment failed, and in the process fueled countrywide tensions that would later erupt into civil war. The Mahdist revolt intensified sectarian strife among Muslims in the North, and further antagonized people in the South, who were happy to join the revolt against the Turkiyya, but turned against Mahdist troops when they tried to reinstate northern control, new taxes, and slave raids.

In comparison with B&H and Sudan, Ottoman rule in Iraq was less important in respect to the rise of ethnoreligious nationalism, except perhaps in the sense of fostering a spirit of local group and regional loyalty that might work to retard the development of a comprehensive national identity. Under Ottoman rule, Iraq as we know it today was not a unified territory, but consisted of three or four disjointed, loosely defined provinces (not including the Kurdish region of northern Iraq) that were only very remotely connected to Istanbul. The peoples of the region lacked anything like a common language and religion, and they were made up of shifting collections of inhabitants.

As mentioned earlier in this introduction, more than the Ottomans, it was the British who created the conditions for the rise of ethnoreligious nationalism in Iraq. During World War I they defeated Ottoman forces, and in 1920 they took over the territory that is now Iraq as a mandate of the League of Nations. British influence on the country had the same ambiguous effects as did Ottoman rule in Sudan in the late nineteenth century. On the one hand, the British invasion aroused concerted Iraqi military resistance, thereby inspiring the first signs of a self-conscious indigenous national movement, particularly among the Sunni and Shiite Arabs. For their part, the Kurds mounted their own rebellion against being included in British Iraq, illustrating the fierce sense of sectional independence that was beginning to take shape throughout the country in response to outside intervention.

On the other hand, the British also cultivated the beginnings of "subnational"[28] rivalries within Iraq. For various reasons, the Sunnis were elevated to a position of political dominance, and the Shiites were effectively marginalized. The Kurds, of course, continued to advance their own independent interests, animated by their resentment at having been made part of Iraq in the first place. The British did introduce some important institutions such as a constitutional monarchy and modern schools. They also granted Iraq independence in 1932. However, their subsequent influence in the affairs of the country did little to modify the intergroup antagonism and division they had helped to create.

British rule in Sudan in the form of an Anglo-Egyptian administration lasted from 1898 until 1956 when modern Sudan was given its independence. The British inherited the divisions between North and South from the Turkiyya, but in nearly sixty years did very little to lessen them and a great deal to intensify them. The policy was essentially one of "divide and rule." Attempting to create a buffer against Egyptian hegemony, the British cultivated nationalist sentiments in the North by accentuating the idea of Islamic identity and encouraging development there. At first, the South was effectively ignored except as an area that could, in turn, serve to contain any expansionist pretensions the North might have. Somewhat later, the British devoted more attention to the South and undertook to foster a sense of subnational independence that was critically influenced by the influx of Western Christian missionaries. In that way, the cultural, religious, and linguistic divide between the two sections of the country was deepened enormously.

Though the British emphasized the importance of liberal ideas and institutions, such as modern education and constitutionalism, including separating religious and political authority and discouraging ethnic factionalism in politics, these ideas and institutions had minimal impact on moderating the growing tensions in the country. So long as the British were there, they were relatively successful in containing conflict, but once they left "things fell apart."[29] They failed to establish effective and reliable forms of government and social organization that could provide a basis for national unity and loyalty to mitigate, if not eliminate, the ethnic and religious antagonisms the British themselves had helped to create.

The Sri Lankan experience with British colonial rule from the end of the eighteenth century until 1948 when independence was granted, was remarkably similar to what happened in Sudan and Iraq. The British did introduce a form of democracy based on universal and eventually gender-inclusive suffrage, as well as patterns of education and administration that might, if appropriately designed and instituted, have moderated ethnoreligious tensions in Sri Lanka. However, practice on balance did not match theory.

First, the two constitutions devised by the British prior to independence established a form of democracy that turned out to be seriously defective in the context of a country increasingly divided along ethnoreligious lines. Lacking sufficient safeguards for the Tamils and other minorities, a blatantly majoritarian electoral system favored the interests of the Sinhala community who constituted around 70 percent of the population. Right after independence these interests were expressed at the polls in strongly exclusionary and vindictive ways. The Sinhala community regarded the Tamils as having been unfairly privileged under British rule, and concluded it was time to rectify the inequities. The outcome, made possible by the British legacy, unquestionably sharpened ethnic tensions.

Second, the British introduced social and religious policies that had the effect of inflaming an indigenous Buddhist reaction, a reaction that readily joined forces with a militant Sinhala Buddhist nationalist movement. Predictably, that movement, in turn, provoked a nationalist response on the part of the Tamils, and some of the preconditions were present for an intense, eventually bloody, nationalist conflict.

These preconditions for conflict were enhanced by the fact that the British had succeeded in consolidating the country by introducing modern techniques of transportation, education, commerce, and political and legal administration. By this process, what was once a territory consisting of localized, relatively disjointed communities was transformed into a potential nation-state with all of the consequences for nationalist competition and conflict that that entailed.

As for Bosnia and the rest of Yugoslavia, control by the Ottomans and the Hapsburgs was overturned during World War II, first by the Germans and Italians, and later by Tito's authoritarian communist government. Germany and Italy promoted a fascist government in Croatia, known as the Ustasha, that aimed at encompassing B&H within its borders. Ustasha policies, which included ethnic cleansing, inspired deep antagonism, especially on the part of the Serbs, and thereby added to ethnoreligious friction in the region.

Although Tito, having successfully led a Yugoslavian independence movement against the fascist powers, did not depend on Soviet support after World War II and eventually rejected any Soviet affiliation, the system of government he imposed was in many ways an adapted and localized Soviet replica.

Tito's attitude toward subnationalist movements based on particular ethnoreligious identity was thoroughly in line with Marxist-Leninist orthodoxy. He suppressed any such movements in the name of an inclusive communist ideology of "Brotherhood and Unity," imposing by staunchly authoritarian means a series of federal constitutions which endeavored to restrain and balance the special interests of his Serbian, Croatian, Muslim, Slovenian, Macedonian, and Albanian constituents. As a good communist, Tito was particularly hard on religious commitment and affiliation.

When Tito's health declined in the latter 1970s, the federal institutions he had devised, and which depended solely and completely on his dictatorial authority, degenerated as well. Accordingly, with the death in 1980 of this great oak tree, as he was known, "in the shade of whose immense branches nothing else could grow,"[30] the particular and often conflicting aspirations of the various subcommunities, long repressed, now began to blossom in profusion. Yugoslavia moved closer to the bloody nationalist conflict that would break out in 1992. Of special importance in this regard, was the rise in the late 1970s and 1980s of an aggressive form of religious nationalism, first among the Croatian Catholics, and then in mimetic succession, among the Serbian Orthodox and finally the Bosnian Muslims.[31] This phenomenon helps to explain how religion eventually became so deeply entangled with the war in B&H.

3. The Perils of Self-Government

As we have stressed throughout, the subject of religious nationalism is unavoidably a problem of politics or, as we have put it, of political economy. The nationalist impulse, especially when it arises within
multiethnic societies, involves a contest, and possibly a violent conflict,
over which group or groups' national ideals will become the basis for
the formulation and enforcement of the laws and public policies of a
given society, as well as of the production, distribution, and regulation
of wealth. Ethnicity and religion, as the previous sections have demonstrated, may very well come to play an important role in this process
because of their recurring prominence in helping to articulate and
mobilize a sense of national identity. That is unquestionably the case
with respect to the formative historical circumstances surrounding the
colonial experience of B&H, Iraq, Sri Lanka, and Sudan. Since again
and again questions of ethnoreligious identity bear on the legitimation
or justification of political and economic order, it is not surprising that
these questions would turn up in the context of nationalist campaigns.

In the postcolonial period, after countries like the four we are considering have achieved self-government, nationalist regimes "come
into their own." They begin to determine for themselves, as they have
for so long aspired to do, their own form of political and economic
order, including the way they will manage diverse expressions of religious, ethnic, and national identity within their societies. Of course,
government is not the only concern in these matters. Nongovernmental
educational, religious, civic, and economic institutions and organizations are also highly important in creating and sustaining stable and
equitable, multiethnic and multireligious societies, as is a professional,
impartial media. Nevertheless, the character and efficacy of government, especially in the postcolonial period, is one critical index of success or failure in regard to handling the challenges of ethnoreligious
nationalism.

A common theme that emerges from the record of all four cases
after independence is the importance of establishing "liberal" rather
than "illiberal" forms of government. By "liberal government," we
mean a political and legal arrangement effectively disposed toward
political and civil liberties and rights that ensure open democratic par-

ticipation, as well as equal treatment and impartiality in the public sphere, conditions which help to prevent ethnic and religious discrimination toward minorities and others. By "illiberal government," we mean a political and legal arrangement officially or informally opposed or indifferent to the principles of equal treatment and impartiality in regard especially to ethnic and religious matters. The cultivation of illiberal government is likely to encourage nationalist conflict, perhaps even to the point of violence, whereas the cultivation of liberal government is likely to contain conflict, and reduce the probability of violence. Considerable empirical evidence confirms this general hypothesis,[32] and the evidence presented by the four cases also supports it, most dramatically on the negative side—that illiberal government encourages conflict.[33] Moreover, there is also some support here and there for the positive claim that liberal government encourages peace and tolerant ethnoreligious relations.

We begin with B&H. After the demise of Tito and the collapse of a central government capable of imposing order on the increasingly fractious subnational groups that made up Yugoslavia, the process of governmental restructuring was undertaken. The late Slobodan Milosevic, Serbian leader and long-time communist, was eager to rebuild a neo-Titoist regime. He encountered widespread resistance in the early 1990s from Slovenia, Croatia, and the other republics when he tried to impose his will by military means. Failing that, Milosevic placed increasing emphasis upon Serbian nationalism, fed by the publications of prominent intellectuals, and by his own skillful manipulation of long-standing Serbian resentments and grievances. All of this led to strong support for a new constitution favoring the sovereignty and self-determination of "the Serbian people," "defined in terms of the ethnic nation, not in terms of democratic participation of individuals."[34] Milosevic's authoritarian ways and his domineering military efforts, together with his new-found devotion to Serbian nationalism, stimulated competing nationalist sentiments on the part of the other republics and hastened them in the direction of independence, and the eventual breakup of the former Yugoslavia.

B&H was part of this picture. It gained its national independence in a referendum that took place in the spring of 1992. However, this event proved to be the beginning of a descent into violent nationalist conflict. Prompted by illiberal political principles, as defined above, and aided and abetted for much of the war by their Serbian and Croatian neighbors, the Bosnian Serbs and Croats undertook to divide up B&H territory in keeping with the ideals of ethnoreligious exclusivity. Accordingly, Bosnian Muslims would either be "ethnically cleansed," as they were in large numbers, and much of their cultural heritage destroyed, or they would be subjected to Serbian or Croatian rule. In response to this particularly strident form of ethnoreligious nationalism, the Bosnian Muslims gradually formulated their own ethnoreligious ideals, further complicating the prospects for developing a liberal, ethnically inclusive B&H government.

Instituting such a government was the aim of the Dayton Peace Accords, worked out in late 1995 as the result of the military intervention of NATO forces, and the loss of military advantage on the part of the Bosnian Serbs. However that experiment is evaluated (see the next section), the fact that it had to be imposed coercively marked the distinct failure of self-government on the part of the Bosnians, as well as the disastrous effects of illiberal governance.

Iraq's postcolonial story is a variation on the same theme. According to Juan Cole, the 1950s signaled "the rise of mass politics in Iraq." Urbanization, an expanding oil economy, and the growth of literacy generated support for inclusive ideologies such as communism and Baathism. When the Baath Party gained power by means of a military coup in 1963, it encompassed both Sunnis and Shiites under the banner of Arab nationalism. However, ethnic harmony did not last long. Despite the rhetoric, the Sunni faction set about ridding the party of Shiite influence and shaping the government of Iraq in its own image. Predictably, the Shiites responded in kind, founding the Dawa Party, premised on the ideal of a Shiite Islamic state. That ideal, incidentally, had considerable influence on Ayatollah Khomeini and the Iranian revolution of 1979, and the connection between Iranian and Iraqi Shiism was strengthened after Saddam Hussein took control of the Baath Party in the same year, and promptly began persecuting Shiites.

Indeed, both the domestic and foreign policies initiated by Hussein during the quarter century of his ultra-authoritarian rule consolidated the ethnoreligious rivalries throughout Iraq. He effectively destroyed all national political institutions that might have helped to mitigate and integrate the different factions by privileging the Sunni minority and brutally repressing the interests of the Shiites and the Kurds. It became a crime for Shiites to join the Dawa Party, and many members were summarily liquidated, while Hussein's atrocities toward the Kurds are now legendary.

The war he initiated against Iran in the 1980s further entangled Iranian and Iraqi Shiites; it also advanced the growing sense of Shiite subnational identity. Although most Shiites remained loyal to Iraq, substantial numbers fled to Iran, many of whom Khomeini organized into the Supreme Council for the Islamic Revolution in Iraq (SCIRI). During the war, SCIRI constituted itself as a paramilitary group that carried out raids against Iraq, thereby cultivating the idea of Shiite militias, such as the Badr Corps, which, like the Kurdish militias, still exist and are gaining strength. SCIRI later broadened into a religious political party that, along with Dawa, now exerts significant Shiite influence in present-day Iraqi politics. What the prospects are for creating a stable, liberal government in Iraq will be examined in the next section.

The general record of self-government in Sri Lanka, after independence from the British took effect in 1948, represents still another example of political illiberalism, one in which, like B&H, ethnoreligious differences eventually erupted into a bloody civil war. As hinted above, the British contributed to ethnic tensions by failing to insure constitutional protections for minorities. They also undoubtedly overestimated the capacity of the indigenous leaders they had groomed to keep ethnic divisions under control, in part because the British fostered an elitist attitude toward government that was severely out of touch with the people.

By the national election of 1956, things changed radically. A new political party, led by S. W. R. D. Bandaranaike, swept into office on a wave of virulent ethnoreligious chauvinism. Raised as part of the elite corps of postcolonial leaders, Bandaranaike switched sides in the early 1950s and joined ranks with the fervent promoters of Sinhala Buddhist nationalism that included a strong contingent of Buddhist monks. He and his wife, Sirimavo, who took over the government for two formative terms after her husband was assassinated in 1959, set Sri Lanka firmly on the path toward ethnoreligious conflict.

Whatever else postcolonial political history in Sri Lanka shows, it clearly demonstrates how deeply deleterious are illiberal ethnoreligious policies, whether deliberately discriminatory or simply halfhearted and ineffective in combating ethnoreligious tensions. An example of the former is the "Sinhala Only" policy passed in 1958 that enshrined what has been called linguistic nationalism in Sri Lanka, by making the language of the majority the only official language, and thereby relegating the Tamil minority to second-class status. The latter is illustrated by Bandaranaike's early, very promising concessions to the Tamils that were later revoked under pressure from supporters.

As often happens when politicians attempt either to manipulate fractious interests to their advantage or fail to stand up to them, the chauvinism Bandaranaike unleashed came back to haunt him. He was himself assassinated by an errant monk in 1959, and the policies pursued by his wife, who succeeded him, only served to further entrench the spirit of majority domination. In the 1980s the initiatives of J. R. Jayewardene, allegedly aimed at accommodation and peace, inflamed rather than mitigated minority grievances. Ethnic violence, which had occurred but sporadically in the early years of independence, intensified in 1983. In effect, the civil war had begun.

The civil war pitted the Sri Lankan army, largely composed of Sinhala personnel, against the Liberation Tigers of Tamil Eelam (LTTE). Tamil Eelam refers to the northeastern section of the country claimed as a homeland by the insurgent forces. In 1987, the Indian government, alarmed by a conflict so close to its shores, and feeling particular ties to the Tamil community, brokered an agreement between the two sides and committed to enforcing the peace. As discussed in the next section, the arrangement backfired, and by 1990, the Indian army withdrew leaving the agreement in tatters and the conflict, if anything, more bitter than when the agreement was first adopted.

Since then the ethnic violence has ebbed and flowed as other peacemaking initiatives have come and gone. In 1994, the election of Chandrika Kumaratunga as president, and the start of fresh negotiations, raised hopes, as did a flurry of activity headed by Ranil Wickremasinghe upon his election as prime minister in 2001.

However, these efforts came to nought as the result of a power struggle between him and President Kumaratunga. Another round of peace talks undertaken during the fall and spring 2002-03 again showed promise, but they collapsed as well because of the influence of the "strong nationalists," as Rohan Edrisinha refers to them in his paper in this volume. They are those groups on both sides who favor a weakly confederated two-nation arrangement, rather than an asymmetrical federalist solution that would allow considerable local autonomy on the part of the Tamils living in the northern and eastern sections of the island under an otherwise central government. The presidential election, which occurred in November 2005, and resulted in the narrow victory of Mahinda Rajapakse over Ranil Wickremasinghe, appears to have reduced the chances for reviving the peace process. Rajapakse identifies strongly with the cause of Sinhala Buddhist nationalism, and, like former President Kumaratunga, has sharply criticized Wickremasinghe for conceding too much to the LTTE. He has pledged to take a hard line during resumed negotiations. After a period of escalating violence, both sides met in Geneva in February 2006 and reaffirmed their support for the 2002 ceasefire. However, each vociferously accused the other of massive violations of that ceasefire.

According to Edrisinha, the political situation in Sri Lanka is especially worrisome because of the current rise of strong nationalism, and the accompanying intensification of illiberalism, among both the Sinhalas and the Tamils. For the Sinhalas, this trend represents a reemphasis on majoritarian privilege, including Sinhala religious and cultural preeminence, and a corresponding indifference to minority rights and protections. For the Tamils, it means an analogous insensitivity to minority religious and ethnic interests. Overall, the recent trend confirms once more how potent and extensive are the forces of ethnocentrism in the kind of societies we have before us, and how profoundly they complicate the tasks of self-government.

The postcolonial record of Sudan is generally consistent with the other cases. It is true that as of January 2005, an agreement between the Khartoum government and the Sudanese People's Liberation Movement was achieved under international auspices. The agreement may hold promise for peace, though its terms remain quite controversial. As of this writing, there is the additional obstacle of the continuing strife in Darfur, located in the western section of the country, which presents a major obstacle to the lasting and just resolution of conflict in Sudan. Time will tell whether this bloodiest and costliest of civil wars can actually be brought to an end.

As mentioned, in 1956, at the time of independence, Sudan was deeply divided. At first, there was some tinkering with liberal constitutionalism, but strong calls by southerners for a federal system built around regional and cultural pluralism were first ignored by the North and then brutally repressed. All this was prologue to a campaign to "nationalize" Sudan under the banner of Islam and Arabism that was instigated by General El Ferik Ibrahim Abboud, after a coup in 1958. Abboud's authoritarian government lasted until 1964, during which time a liberation movement and an incipient insurgency took shape in the South.

Between 1964 and 1969, Abboud's successors, Muhammad Ahmed Mahjoub and Sadiq el-Mahdi, continued the pattern of northern domination, further polarizing the country in respect to ethnoreligious identity. Constitutional conventions were convened from time to time, but the results mostly ignored southern interests—most blatantly, when Sudan was declared an Islamic state.

The pattern was temporarily interrupted after Jaafar Muhammad al-Nimeiri seized power in 1969 and turned Sudan into a socialist state. His initial instincts were to exceed his predecessors in granting at least qualified autonomy to the South under a de facto federal system. The Southern Provinces Regional Self-Government Act, which was agreed to in Addis Ababa in February 1972, and which lasted until Nimeiri abrogated it in 1983, created a unified southern government responsible for internal security and for the local administration of social, cultural, and economic matters. Arabic remained the official language, but English was accepted as the primary language in the South, and southern schools were allowed to teach indigenous languages. Remarkably, Sudan was described as having a dual Arab and African identity, and to be based on common respect for Islam, Christianity, and "noble spiritual beliefs," presumably including those of indigenous African religions. Beyond that, the agreement reversed a tradition of legal inequality between northern and southern citizens, together with discriminatory practices in regard to participation in the legislature and the executive. Without question, the Addis Ababa Accords, as they came to be known, were a significant step, at least on paper, in the direction of liberal federalism and the improved prospects for peace.

For several reasons, however, the accords failed. The provisions for southern self-rule, particularly in regard to taxing capacity and central government support, were inadequate. Because of his own mismanagement and distraction, as well as the discovery of oil in the South in 1978, Nimeiri lost interest in southern autonomy, and intervened increasingly in ways that undermined the agreement. In addition, the South itself was afflicted by internal rivalries. Finally, and most important, Nimeiri officially revoked the accords after embracing radical Islam in 1983, and imposing *sharia* law throughout the country as a way of disabling growing Islamic opposition. The most notorious single action of the new regime was the public execution for apostasy of Mahmoud Muhammad Taha, an outspoken advocate of a tolerant, pluralist version of Islam. By such behavior, Nimeiri conclusively ended the experiment with federalism, and reverted to conventional northern illiberalism. In response, the Sudanese People's Liberation Army (SPLA) was formed in the South, under the leadership of John Garang, and the next phase of the Sudanese civil war began in earnest.

Although he was overthrown in 1985, Nimeiri's domineering policies were not reversed. After a brief and partially moderate interlude, a group known as the National Islamic Front, under the leadership of General Omar al-Bashir and Hassan al-Turabi, seized power in June 1989, and proceeded to up the ante. Theirs was a heightened form of ethnoreligious nationalism based upon what Ann Mayer referred to in her conference paper as "Arab ethnic and linguistic chauvinism," and an "Islamization project" that is "associated with a barely concealed racism and contempt for Sudan's African minority." This attitude had an enormous impact. Politics, education, economic policy, the status of women, the practice of religion, the dissemination of information, and security measures were all reshaped in accord with this radical form of Arab/Islamic ideology.

Moreover, the "war of visions" between the NIF and the SPLA was intensified, spreading massive suffering and destruction throughout much of the South and in certain parts of the North as well. The continuing rivalries among southern ethnic groups, exacerbated by the Khartoum government, complicated the situation. Massive human rights violations were committed by the NIF government, though the SPLA, together with breakaway insurgent groups in the South, were by no means innocent of substantial violations themselves.

In June 2002, the Khartoum government and the SPLA and its political arm, the Sudanese People's Liberation Movement (SPLM) began a promising process of trying to end the conflict. They met in Kenya and agreed to the Machakos Protocol, sponsored by IGAD (the Inter-Governmental Authority on Development), made up of Sudan's neighboring states and its "friends," the United States, Britain, Norway, Italy, the African Union, and the United Nations. In January 2005 the agreement was formally accepted by the two sides.

The arrangement amounts to a provisional federal settlement according to which the North and South each have their own subsidiary governments, including their own military forces, with authority to regulate much of the administrative, cultural, religious, educational, and economic life within their own region. In keeping with long-standing convictions, the South is to be understood as a "secular" entity, with equal freedom for all, regardless of religion or ethnicity, while the North is regarded as Islamic in character, though the sensitive question of the extent of *sharia* jurisdiction has yet to be worked out. At the same time, both sides agree mutually to submit to certain national power- and wealth-sharing political and economic protocols whereby, for example, the national president shall be from the North and the vice-president from the South, and the proceeds from oil will be shared. The agreement is provisional in the sense that, after a period of six years has expired, there will be a national referendum to decide whether both entities will stay together or separate.

The agreement is publicized as an attempt to move away from illiberal policies and institutions and toward liberal ones, as a basis for reducing the likelihood of continuing violent national conflict. It appears the agreement will hold despite the sudden death in 2005 of the newly appointed Vice-President of Sudan, John Garang.

Of interest is the fact that the agreement is an adaptation of the provisions of two previous documents, both of which endeavored in important ways to outline the conditions for a stable and just peace in Sudan. One is the Declaration of Principles produced by IGAD in 1994. It expresses concern for the unity of Sudan, but only if premised on "a secular and democratic state," with legal guarantees of "complete political and social equalities of all peoples" in the country, as well as "extensive rights of self-administration...to various peoples," the separation of "state and religion," "appropriate and fair sharing of wealth," along with the protection of human rights standards, and provision for an independent judiciary. "In the absence of agreement on the above principles...the respective peoples will have the option to determine their future including independence through a referendum," and specifically, "the right of self-determination of the people of southern Sudan...through a referendum."[35]

The other document is Sudan's Draft Constitution of 1998, as discussed by Ann Mayer in her conference remarks. Though far from perfect, it represents a firm renunciation of many of Sudan's postcolonial policies, especially the fallacy of trying to impose ethnic and religious identity on others. Rather than unifying the country she says in this volume that efforts to Islamize and Arabize minorities only exacerbated Sudan's "fissiparous tendencies, making southerners more acutely conscious that they were not Arabs and not Muslims and that, unless they were willing to forfeit their identity, they had to fight the North."

Instead of reinforcing such dysfunctional practices, the draft constitution enunciates some indispensable foundations of sound government in a multiethnic and multireligious society. Remarkably, there is no claim in the draft that Sudan is either an Arab or an Islamic state. Rather, it is understood as a country comprising a diversity of cultures, languages, and religions, with equal ethnic and religious freedom for all. Islamic law has a limited role. It is mentioned as applying only to Muslims, and is included alongside other factors, like the consensus of the nation and existing customs, as but one of the legitimate sources of law. The reference to custom, according to Mayer, appears in particular to invite respect for African traditions.

While some of the worthy considerations contained in the

Declaration of Principles and the Draft Constitution are partially incorporated into the present peace agreement, important aspects of the agreement—both in regard to substance, as well as the manner in which in was negotiated—have been the subject of criticism. If valid, the enumerated difficulties present serious obstacles toward achieving a stable peace in Sudan based on the principles of liberal government (see next section and the Sudan case study).

4. The Place of International Involvement

International actors have been critically involved in attempting to create conditions of peace in the four countries under consideration after each has gained independence. In the process international efforts have impinged directly on issues of political order, particularly on constitutional questions, including the way the governments in each country work out ethnoreligious relations. The record of international involvement in all the cases is decidedly mixed.

In B&H, the Dayton agreement, signed ten years ago by leaders of B&H, Croatia, and Serbia and Montenegro at the Wright-Patterson Air Force Base outside Dayton, Ohio, was unquestionably an international product. Without the prior pressure of NATO military action, together with the intimate and imposed supervision of the United States, the agreement would never have occurred. Moreover, without continued and extensive international military, political, and economic participation, the agreement could not have held as long as it has. Above all, it is yet another international reality, the attraction of European integration that provides the most significant incentive toward overcoming ethnoreligious chauvinism in B&H as well as in the rest of the former Yugoslavia.

The Dayton agreement successfully terminated a bloody, destructive four-year war in which over 100,000 people lost their lives, more than a million were displaced, and many homes, public buildings, and cultural and holy sites laid waste. As such, the war constituted the most severe outbreak of violence in Europe since World War II.

While it was probably the best deal achievable at the time, the Dayton agreement was severely flawed. To a degree, it ratified the very ethnoreligious segregation that was the objective of the ultranationalist campaign. The resulting ethnic enclaves were coordinated by only the feeblest central authority and institutions. These enclaves further retarded the development of a mature liberal system by making necessary, in the name of effective government, the dominant role of the office of high representative. Appointed by international forces and with powers to impose decisions when government authorities disagreed with each other, that position became, in effect, the vice regency of an international protectorate. Responsibility was taken away from the Bosnians, who were made more passive and dependent, rather than becoming active participants in building a mature democracy. Moreover, the eagerness to hold elections only a year after the agreement was signed worked to entrench ethnoreligious divisions, and made it more unlikely that the objective, affirmed at Dayton, of encouraging the reintegration of the masses of people displaced by the war would be achieved. Because of fundamental constitutional imperfections, subsequent elections have not gone very far to improve things.

However, on November 22, 2005, nine Serbian, Croatian, and Boshniak[36] leaders signed a Commitment to Pursue Constitutional Reform at the U.S. State Department in Washington, D.C., an undertaking aimed at rectifying many of these defects. The dysfunctional tripartite presidency is to be replaced by a single nationally-elected president, and a strong office of prime minister and a reformed parliament are pledged. It is hoped that this new commitment will lead to the creation of other robust, interethnic national institutions, including, most importantly, an integrated military and police force. By overcoming a system dominated by ethnic interests on the one hand, and abject dependency on the international community on the other, B&H could mightily improve its chances for becoming a European partner. "There is so much to be gained along the road to European integration... Bosnian politicians have every reason to wise up and take charge."[37]

It is impossible to understand the present situation in Iraq without taking account of the role of international actors, particularly the United States. The impact of U.S. policy on peace and political order there, including ethnoreligious relations, has been enormous. Because U.S. policy makers were not well acquainted with the history of Iraq and because of their unfounded preoccupation with disposing of unconventional weapons, the task of reforming the government and making peace was considerably more difficult than expected after the invasion. Their focus on eliminating Saddam Hussein as a geopolitical threat also blinded them to the complex realities of Iraq's cultural, religious, and ethnic situation.

In March 2003, the U.S. was not aware that it was entering a society fraught with revolutionary potential. As Juan Cole pointed out in his conference remarks, the effect of the invasion was: "to blow the lid off and tell people now they're free to do as they please. Well, we know what they wanted to do. They wanted to make revolutions." All along the Kurds, Sunnis, and Shiites had their separate agendas with very little in common among them, and with no history of developed national institutions. In the absence of a dominating center, the ethnoreligious forces of the society flew apart. Whether U.S.-led efforts can contain and harmonize these forces by creating an inclusive constitutional democracy and prevent a civil war and wider conflicts in the region, remains uncertain. The U.S. administration seems never to have understood that electoral politics under the wrong conditions can actually exacerbate, rather than reduce ethnic and religious tensions, a fact that is abundantly clear in B&H and Sri Lanka. Whatever the eventual outcome, the direction Iraq is now going, as Cole says, is "not one that bodes well for national unity."

In short, the impact of international involvement on religious nationalism in Iraq is very much a work in progress. If the consequences of outside influence ultimately produce more conflict than peace, it will not be the first time that has happened in the history of the country.

In its effort to overcome the ill effects of chauvinistic nationalism, Sri Lanka has experienced several kinds of international involvement. In 1987, as the conflict between the Sri Lankan government and the LTTE intensified, the Indian government became very concerned about the fortunes of the Tamils because of a special communal attachment perceived to exist at the time between them and the residents of Tamil Nadu in southern India. Taking an active role, Indian prime minister, Rajiv Gandhi, pressured the Sri Lankan president into agreeing to the

Indo-Sri Lanka Accord of 1987, which made a number of concessions to the Tamils. The agreement acknowledged that "Sri Lanka is a multi-ethnic and multi-lingual plural society" where "each ethnic group has a distinct cultural and linguistic identity which has to be carefully nurtured," and it affirmed a society in which "all citizens can live in equality, safety, and harmony." As to the sensitive topic of national language, it stated that "the official language of Sri Lanka shall be Sinhala," but added, somewhat ambiguously, that "Tamil and English will also be official languages."[38] The agreement went on to prescribe the devolution of some administrative power to the northern and eastern provinces, where the majority of Tamils live. It left to a later referendum of inhabitants the question of the political connection of the two provinces. Finally, the agreement called for the disarming of the Tamil guerrillas and the dispatching of an Indian peacekeeping force to implement the agreement.

After some initial enthusiasm, the agreement was rejected both by Sinhala activists and by the LTTE, who were, to their disgruntlement, not included in the negotiations. (The LTTE later vented their wrath definitively by assassinating Rajiv Gandhi in 1991.) Moreover, the efforts of the government to devolve power to the Tamils by creating provincial councils "failed to inspire popular confidence and indeed...contributed to widespread disenchantment with the system, and, as a result, the concept of devolution as well."[39] Eventually, the civil war resumed its full intensity, and the Indian peacekeeping troops came to find themselves in an untenable position, and ignominiously withdrew in 1990.

Despite the rejection of the Indo-Sri Lanka Accord, the proposal of the devolution of power within a federal arrangement as a way of resolving ethnic difference in Sri Lanka made headway as the result of another effort at international mediation in December 2002. That produced the Oslo Agreement, worked out under the auspices of the Norwegians. The agreement, in turn, broke down in April 2003 as the result of fears on the part of the Sinhalas, that too much of the central authority of the government was being given away in the talk of federalism and devolution, and on the part of the Tamils, that not enough autonomy was being granted to them. This fundamental division of opinion was represented in the opposing positions of Rajapakse and Wickremasinghe in the recent presidential election of November 2005. That Rajapakse won (if barely in an election boycotted by the LTTE) on a platform of stronger central government with fewer concessions to federalism and Tamil autonomy, is certainly a temporary setback. Nevertheless, since Oslo, and with continuing Norwegian encouragement, the constitutional debate has concentrated on federalism, "which is itself a significant development. Many people have argued for years that a solution must be based on federal lines."[40]

Finally, there is the role of international intervention and mediation in Sudan. As mentioned above, the January 2005 agreement between the North and the South was the product of international sponsorship by IGAD. IGAD consists of seven East African members, Djibouti, Eritrea, Ethiopia, Kenya, Somalia, Sudan, and Uganda, and in the late 1990s was assisted by a troika of three non-African states, the U.S., Great Britain, and Norway, who became actively involved in the negotiations surrounding the Machakos Protocol and the final agreement. IGAD was founded in 1986 with a very narrow mandate around the issues of drought and desertification, but in the 1990s came to focus on regional security and political dialogue.

While the agreement has been praised for providing the opportunity for ending what is unquestionably the most devastating and destructive civil war in recent history, it has been plausibly criticized in large part because of what is regarded as misguided international influence. A primary concern is that access to the peace process was too exclusively restricted to the National Congress Party, which makes up the government in the North, and the SPLA/M in the South. Consequently, the criticism continues that these groups were allowed to gain an unfair share of political, economic, and military power in the final agreement. It has been suggested, for example, that the decision to exclude representatives from the rebel forces of Darfur has already taken its toll on the stability of the peace agreement. Likewise, further instability could yet occur because of having disregarded the voices of those located in the so-called "marginal areas," like South Blue Nile, the Nuba Mountains, and Abyei. The interests of these communities are not easily comprehended by either of the two principal parties to the agreement. [41]

A related concern is that this imbalance of power provides insufficient provision in the agreement for transparency, equal political and economic participation, and human rights.[42] One prominent example of the apparent denial of human rights is the failure to apply to the North the guarantees of equal religious freedom that are assured to the South. Giving the NCP the authority to dictate its version of *sharia* law for the North would appear to deny "the right of moderate Muslims in Sudan—possibly a majority—to be rid of a *sharia* imposed on them by a government that came to power not through democratic elections, but by overthrowing a democratically elected [one]."[43]

It is argued that the primary focus on the part of IGAD members, and particularly the U.S., is more on geopolitical security and counterterrorism than on improved conditions within Sudan itself:

> While a measured U.S. interest in Sudan has ensured a more balanced approach to the peace process, it has not generated support for dealing with the social and economic inequalities that caused the civil war in the south and Darfur. U.S. support for democracy in Sudan has been ritualistic, and takes the form of support for the so-called Washington consensus restricted to multi-partyism and an open economy. At no time has the U.S. shown sympathy, much less support, for a democratic transformation of Sudan.... Ironically, while the U.S. professes to be leading a war against authoritarian Islamism, it is denying the moderate Moslems in Sudan [the right of religious freedom].[44]

Whether these and similar perceived deficiencies, which appear to bear the marks of strong international influence, will eventually undermine the chances for a just and stable peace in Sudan remains to be seen.

The complexity of the issues at stake in the debates about religion, ethnicity, and nationalism is further compounded when seen within the backdrop of globalization, a process that accelerated under colonialism and greatly intensified after World War II. We have commented on the colonial impact, but contemporary globalization patterns should also be noted. Although a factor in Sudan, B&H, and Iraq, globalization has had especially deleterious consequences in Sri Lanka. There economic inequalities, a deepened poverty, privatization and cutbacks in state welfare services, the dominance of transnational corporations, the influence of consumerism, and Western cultural homogenization have weakened community and local cultural identities, increased a sense of alienation and despair and, as a consequence, have fueled anti-Tamil and anti-Sinhala violence.[45]

Notes

1. Neil MacCormick, "Nation and Nationalism," in *Theorizing Nationalism*, ed. Ronald Beiner (Albany: State University of New York Press, 1999), 191.
2. Oxford English Dictionary, (Oxford: Oxford University Press, 1968) s.v. "Ethnic."
3. We refer to the helpful list of the defining characteristics of "religion" found in William P. Alston's well-known discussion in *Philosophy of Language* (Englewood Cliffs, N.J.: Prentice-Hall, 1964), 8. Alston's list refers to attributes like a belief in supernatural beings and a distinction between sacred and profane reality, along with ritual practices, including prayer; attitudes of reverence and awe; a moral code; and patterns of social organization that are formulated in reference to the sacred beliefs. Alston holds, plausibly, that the list will apply selectively and in different combinations to different religions, but that all religions will be understood to manifest some mixture of the defining characteristics. Although there are of course penumbral cases, the list of attributes works well in general. In various combinations, it certainly characterizes the religions of the four countries under consideration in this report: Western and Eastern Christianity (B&H), Western Christianity (Sri Lanka, Sudan); Sunni Islam (B&H, Iraq, Sri Lanka, and Sudan), Shiite Islam (Iraq); Sufi Islam (Sudan); Theravada Buddhism and Hinduism (Sri Lanka).
4. Paul Collier, "Economic Causes of Civil Conflict and Their Implications for Policy," in *Turbulent Peace: The Challenges of Managing International Conflict*, ed. Chester A. Crocker, Fen Osler Hampson, and Pamela Aall (Washington, D.C.: United States Institute of Peace Press, 2001), 143-62.
5. Ibid., 154.
6. Ibid., 149.
7. See, for example, James D. Fearon and David D. Laitin, "Ethnicity, Insurgency, and Civil War," *American Political Science Review* 97, no.1 (February 2003): 75-90, which emphasizes political over economic deficiencies as causes of national civil wars. Though the authors, like Collier, start out making the same claims about the irrelevance of grievances to the onset of civil war, on careful inspection they introduce along the way a number of qualifications that concede the salience of perceptions of mis-

treatment and injustice on the part of insurgent groups for the direction and outcome of nationalist conflicts.

8. Collier, "Economic Causes of Civil Conflict," 153.
9. See Ted Robert Gurr (with contributors), *Minorities at Risk: A Global View of Ethnopolitical Conflict* (Washington, D.C.: United States Institute of Peace Press, 1993); and *Peoples Versus States: Minorities at Risk in the New Century* (Washington, D.C.: United States Institute of Peace Press, 2000).
10. Gurr, *Peoples versus States*, 232.
11. Ibid., 287.
12. Michael A. Sells, *The Bridge Betrayed: Religion and Genocide in Bosnia* (Berkeley: University of California Press, 1996), 2-3.
13. Ibid., 39.
14. See Sells conference paper in this volume.
15. Mark Juergensmeyer, *Terror in the Mind of God: The Global Rise of Religious Violence*, 3rd ed. (Berkeley: University of California Press, 2003), 164-65.
16. Sells, *Bridge Betrayed*, 15.
17. Ibid., 35-36.
18. Gananath Obeyesekere, *Buddhism, Nationhood and Cultural Identity: The Premodern and Pre-Colonial Formulations* (Colombo: International Centre for Ethnic Studies, 2004), 47.
19. Steven Kemper, *The Presence of the Past: Chronicles, Politics, and Culture in Sinhala Life* (Ithaca: Cornell University Press, 1991), 21.
20. Obeyesekere, *Buddhism, Nationhood and Cultural Identity*, 52.
21. R. Scott Appleby, *The Ambivalence of the Sacred: Religion, Violence, and Reconciliation* (Lanham, Md: Rowman & Littlefield, 2000), 281.
22. Sells, *Bridge Betrayed*, 65.
23. Juergensmeyer, *Terror in Mind of God*, 248.
24. Rabia Terri Harris, "Nonviolence in Islam: The Alternative Community Tradition," in *Subverting Hatred: The Challenge of Nonviolence in Religious Traditions*, ed. Daniel L. Smith-Christopher (Cambridge: Boston Research Center for the 21st Century , 1998), 96.
25. Appleby, *Ambivalence of Sacred*, 300.
26. Srdjan Vrcan, "The Religious Factor in the War in Bosnia and Herzegovina" in *Religion and the War in Bosnia*, ed. Paul Mojzes, (Atlanta, Ga: American Academy of Religion Books, 1998), 115.
27. Francis M. Deng, *War of Visions: Conflict of Identities in the Sudan* (Washington, D.C.: Brookings Institution, 1995), 46.
28. A term taken from Paul Brass and used by Juan Cole in his conference keynote address. The term implies the articulation of group identity that aspires to "national" autonomy, whether as part of a wider federal structure, by secession, or, presumably, by gaining control of a nation-state.
29. Deng, *War of Visions*, 58.

30. Laura Silber and Allan Little, *The Death of Yugoslavia* (New York: Penguin/BBC Books, 1996), 29.
31. See Lenard J. Cohen, "Bosnia's 'Tribal Gods': The Role of Religion in Nationalist Politics," in *Religion and The War in Bosnia*, ed. Paul Mojzes (Atlanta, Ga: American Academy of Religion Books, 1998), 50-51 and Vjekoslav Perica, *Balkan Idols: Religion and Nationalism in Yugoslav States* (New York: Oxford University Press, 2002).
32. See the work of Ted Robert Gurr, especially *Peoples versus States*, above, and Morton H. Halperin, Joseph T. Siegle, and Michael M. Weinstein, *The Democracy Advantage: How Democracies Promote Prosperity and Peace* (New York: Routledge, 2005): "And contrary to the claims that democratization [understood by the authors as 'liberal' in our sense (p.9)] increases fragmentation in ethnically diverse societies, the record shows that democracies do a better job of developing broad social coalitions and balancing multiple, competing interests in diverse cultures," (p 12).
33. For confirmation of the negative proposition that illiberal democracy contributes to a rise in violence, see Jack Snyder, *From Voting to Violence: Democratization and Nationalist Conflict* (New York: Norton & Co., 2000); and Edward D. Mansfield and Jack Snyder, *Electing to Fight: Why Emerging Democracies Go to War* (Cambridge: MIT Press, 2005). The earlier book focuses mainly on internal violence, while the more recent book focuses on external violence.
34. Snyder, *From Voting to Violence*, 212.
35. The quotations, more or less in the order presented, are taken from the account of the Declaration of Principles in Ann Mosely Lesch, *The Sudan: Contested National Identities* (Bloomington: Indiana University Press, 1998), 182.
36. Boshniak or Bosniak are terms for Bosnians of Muslim heritage (see also discussion in note 5 of Paul Mojzes' paper in this volume).
37. Laura Silber, "Dayton, Ten Years Later," *New York Times*, 21 November, 2005, A25.
38. The accord is available from the website for the Sri Lankan Government's Secretariat for Coordinating the Peace Process (http://www.peaceinsrilanka.org/insidepages/Agreement/IndoSriLanka.asp), paragraphs 1.2, 1.3, and two quotes from 2.18.
39. Rohan Edrisinha and Lee Seymour, with Ann Griffiths, "Adopting Federalism: Sri Lanka and Sudan," in *Handbook of Federal Countries*, ed. Ann L. Griffiths (Montreal: McGill-Queen's University Press, 2005), 430.
40. Ibid., 426.
41. See John Young, "Sudan: A Flawed Peace Process Leading to a Flawed Peace," *Review of African Political Economy* 103: 32 (March 2005), 99-113, in particular, 101-02.
42. Ibid., 101.
43. Ibid., 107.
44. Ibid., 105, 107.
45. Asoka Bandarage, "The Sri Lankan Conflict: Broadening the Debate," *Peacework*, October, 2000.

CASE STUDY: IRAQ

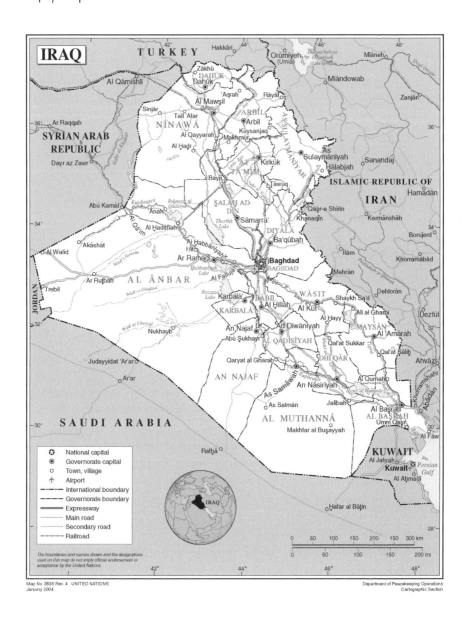

Iraq Map No. 2825 Revision 4, January 2004
Courtesy of United Nations Cartographic Section

The Rise of Religious and Ethnic Mass Politics in Iraq

Juan R. I. Cole[1]

We are trying to catch some history on the run. That is usually the province of journalists—we historians would prefer our subjects safely dead and not in a position to object to our going through their letters and laundry lists. In this paper, I am bringing some historical understanding and historical techniques to the subject of the rise of ethnic and religious politics in Iraq.

The rhetoric of Iraqi nationalism has been widespread in the last several years until recent sectarian violence. In 2004 if you spoke to Iraqis, most Iraqis (with the possible exception of some more nationalistic Kurds) would have said that we are all Iraqis together; the Iraqi nation is what is important; religious divisions do not matter; and foreigners are making them up as a way of dividing us. I respect that point of view. However, when I looked at the January 2005 elections, virtually every single Iraqi who voted voted on ethnic grounds. I do not know of any votes for the Kurdistan alliance in Basra, in the Shiite South, nor of any Kurds who voted for Muqtada Sadr, yet the rhetoric of national unity remains quite powerful. Iraqi nationalism exists as a complicated social and psychological phenomenon, coexisting with what Anthony Smith has called subnationalisms.[2]

This is not an unusual situation in the world. After all, probably most Scots are fairly happy to be in the United Kingdom, but Sean Connery is not, nor are some other Scots. There is a movement for Scottish subnationalism. National identities are very often overlaid by regional and religious and ethnic ones. Even France, which one thinks of as the archetypal modern nation-state, has Alsace-Lorraine where people speak German, especially around non-German-speaking French. It also has Brittany with the Bretons descended from Gaels, and Provence, and the Basque country. Even France is not without its subnationalisms, though they have not usually been expressed in a political way in modern France.

We have to unlearn what we think we know. Modern nationalism configures how we see the past. Historians are particularly aware of this because when we visit the past in archives and letters, we do not find a familiar world. The categories by which we contemporaries organize our world are often insufficient to the past. There was no Iraq in the nineteenth century. There was no Iraqi nation. I can show you books in Arabic on the Iraqi nation through history that begin with the Sumerians in 3000 BC. No Sumerians thought they were Iraqis. Very likely, they did not know they were Sumerians either.

Iraq is an old word, maybe even pre-Arabic with Semitic roots. It has to do with things being green and well-watered. It probably means something like what we mean when we say Fertile Crescent. After all, if you were an Arab Bedouin and came to Iraq, you would be impressed at how green it is. *Iraq Arabi*, mentioned by medieval Arabic geographers, refers to much of what we now call Iraq, so the term is not without historical precedents. However, part of Iran was called Iraq: the area around Isfahan. Thus *Iraq* was probably a generic term meaning a green place.

In the nineteenth century, what is now Iraq was a set of three, sometimes four, Ottoman provinces: Mosul, Baghdad, and Basra. The Ottomans at Istanbul tended to depend on the governor in Baghdad to oversee the governors in Basra and Mosul. Those Ottoman provinces did not look like the areas that have the same name today: Basra extended down the coast into al-Hasa, into what is now Saudi Arabia. The Kurdish region of what is now northern Iraq was often not under

Ottoman rule at all but under Iranian rule or under strong Iranian influence. For example, the Baban clan of the Kurds in the nineteenth century had a strong alliance with the Iranians. Iraq as a nation did not exist.

Nations are not natural. There is no national essence that has existed through history and has always caused a people in a reified sense to have a connection with a particular soil. People move and genes move. Population geneticists suggest that after 50 generations or so, all human beings become related to one another. In the nineteenth century, there was a romantic nationalism, particularly in Germany—an idea of nations as consisting of bloodlines which are pure. This is a complete fantasy, yet a powerful one which persists.

Nationalism is a modern phenomenon. Most nations have come into being in the past two centuries, and most Middle Eastern nations more recently than that. Nations are always constructed by states. The romantic nationalist view is that nations pre-exist states and give rise to them. We recall what happened under Garibaldi in Italy. It was called Italian reunification, as though there had been an Italy before the late nineteenth century that was being reunified—this is simply not the case. In creating a nation, the nation-state standardizes the language and constructs universal schooling, writing textbooks in which ancient peoples and territories are claimed for the nation. Thus, Iraq gets the Sumerians and Italy gets the Romans even though the Romans, and the Sumerians would not have recognized themselves in those ways. Then there are museums and maps. Benedict Anderson has written about the range of ways by which the modern nation is formed.[3]

Our subject here is not so much the formation of the modern Iraqi nation but the formation of subnationalisms as this coincides with nation building. Most nations contain subnations within them which navigate between a local identity and a national one. The worst case scenario is one like Yugoslavia, where the subnationalisms come to the fore and the nation is divided up.

Political scientist Paul Brass wrote an important book in the early 1970s about subnationalist movements in India (*Language, Religion, and Politics in North India*). He examined which ones were successful and which ones were not. None were successful in becoming independent of India with the exception of Pakistan and Bangladesh. But some did succeed in redrawing the provincial boundaries of India. For example, the Sikhs of Punjab succeeded in getting their own province. Initially they were lumped in with Hindus in what is now Haryana. They succeeded through agitation in getting India to create the province of Punjab, in which the Sikhs were the vast majority. On the other hand, there was a group in Bihar called the Maithili who had a distinctive dialect. They mobilized on linguistic grounds to secede from the province of Bihar. Brass points out that the Maithili failed, and the Sikhs succeeded. From the Indian case he extrapolates that two markers of identity provide a more favorable ground for these subnationalist movements to succeed: for example, a distinctive language, as with Punjabi for the Sikhs, and distinctive religious identity, as with the Sikh religion for the Sikhs.[4] By that logic, the Kurds have a shot, the Sunni Arabs, probably not.

None of the ingredients for a nation were there in the Ottoman period. There was low literacy: only the urban areas had anybody who could read. There was little knowledge of formal Islam. What people did in their everyday lives in nineteenth-century Iraq does not look like what we now think of as Islam. From travelers' accounts, Sufis were known to put needles through their cheeks at fairs. We would consider this a kind of carnivalism, but the Sufis who were performing considered it a part of Islam. In 1850, perhaps one third of the people in the provinces of Basra, Baghdad, and Mosul were pastoral nomads. Pastoral nomads are universally illiterate and do not have a strong attachment to soil and nation. A substantial population of marsh Arabs, the Maadan tribes, had their own distinctive way of life in what is now southern Iraq. The formal language of government was Ottoman Turkish. The Ottoman archives in Istanbul are filled with documents on Iraq because the Ottomans were running the place. There were many dialects of spoken Arabic. Many Arabic speakers in Iraq probably could not comprehend one another very well. That is very common before languages are standardized, or national schooling exists. The Kurdish dialects were also characterized by large divergences. Kurmanji and Sorani are the two main Kurdish dialects today. Even within those, there are still many dialects. In premodern times, before languages became standardized, those dialects would not have been well understood across villages.

In the nineteenth and early twentieth century, many travelers provide accounts of the marsh Arabs, who lived in the southern marshes. They were smugglers and fishermen. Some of them did agriculture. In the accounts of those Westerners who knew Arabic, the marsh Arabs do not seem like Muslims. They did not give their children Muslim names, for the most part; marsh Arab names are quite distinctive. They had their own legends and mythology. In fact, the British, who were very Indocentric, even claimed the marsh Arabs were a misplaced Punjabi tribe, which wandered through Iran and got stuck in the marshes. Colonial ethnographers found them very distinct from the rest of the Iraqi population. In the course of the nineteenth and early twentieth centuries, the marsh Arabs converted gradually to Shiite Islam, although probably not to something that most high-powered clerics in Qum in Iran would have acknowledged as Shiite Islam. There has been a process of Islamization in Iraq. As people have gone from being more tribal and more rural to being more urban and more literate, they have conformed increasingly to the standards of urban literate Islam.

However, they did not start out that way. It was a long process whereby they adopt an Islamic identity as something very important to them. Najaf and Karbala are holy cities in Iraq south of Baghdad. From those cities, clerics sent out missionaries in the nineteenth century to the tribal peoples to try to convert them to Shiism. Devotion to the family of the prophet is characteristic of Shiite Islam, particularly mourning the martyrdom in the late seventh century of the prophet's grandson, Husayn at Karbala. The Iraqi popular classes mourned Husayn frequently by flagellation; the clerics, the formal arbiters of Islam, did not approve. Islam in this area of the Middle East at that time was not necessarily the Five Pillars, praying five times a day, going on pilgrimages to Mecca, and the other practices that we associate with highly literate Islam. It was getting up on the tenth day, *Ashura*, and using a whip on your back until you bled. Of course, the clerics were often quite upset with this practice.

So when does Iraq come to be? It was formed, as with many of the nations in the Middle East, initially as a result of the British colonial incursion. The British conquered what is now Iraq in World War I, or you could say that what is now Iraq is what the British managed to conquer in the course of World War I. They sent the British Indian army up from Basra—300,000 British Indian troops. They fought hard campaigns against Ottoman armies, which were led by German high commands detailed to the Ottomans. The first British invasion, in fact, was defeated, and a second one had to be mounted. Not only did the British bring in 300,000 British Indian troops, but they also brought in 300,000 Indian civilian contractors, some of whom were targeted by the Iraqis. There are many resonances from the World War I period today.

The British decided to make Iraq what was then called a mandate by the League of Nations: a kind of colony, but a colony with a term limit. Eventually the mandates would become independent countries, unlike colonies, which might be kept forever. There was a paternalistic language about the mandate: the League of Nations would give to Great Britain the duty of preparing the Iraqis to be citizens of an independent state. When President Bush said that he hoped eventually the Iraqis would be able to take the training wheels off, this was not a new sentiment that the Iraqis were hearing from Westerners. The same language could be heard from Gertrude Bell (an influential British political officer and Oriental Secretary to Iraq) in the 1920s. The Iraqis resented that condescension because Iraqis were characterized by a fairly high degree of urban civilization as Baghdad was a great provincial capital of the Ottoman Empire. The Iraqis rebelled when the British announced that they were not going to give the country independence but, rather, were going to keep it as a mandate in 1920. This rebellion was predominantly a Shiite one, but some Sunnis joined in as well. The 1920s revolts loom large as a moment of indigenous Iraqi unity against the British: there was also a Kurdish rebellion, with the Kurds objecting to being incorporated into British Iraq.

The British saw the Shiites as seditious and pro-Iranian, another resonance of the past century with the current situation. Because the British officials feared the Iraqi Shiites would serve the interests of Tehran, they brought into Iraq a client of theirs, King Faisal. He had helped to lead the Arab revolt. The British rewarded him with Syria. However, they had also given Syria away to the French in the secret Sykes-Picot agreement of 1916. The British hoped that they would be able to put Faisal into power in Syria and did so for two years after they had successfully ousted the Ottoman Empire. The French, having armies and knowing how to land them, decided to take what had been promised. In 1920, they invaded and kicked Faisal out of Damascus.

The British had a rebellious colony without a monarch and they had a monarch without a country, so they put the two together. At the end of the process, Gertrude Bell wrote in her diary, "I shall never again attempt to create a monarchy." It was not easy.

Faisal was a Sunni Arab from Mecca, having nothing to do with Iraq. He depended on the Sunni Ottoman officer corps that had pre-existed him in Iraq. The Sunni notables, the landlord and merchant elite, gravitated towards him. Basically the British put the Sunni Arabs in power in Iraq. The Shiites were relatively marginalized. The British were so weak in Iraq they could not control it. The people kept rebelling against them. In response, the British bombed Iraq almost continuously. Bombing was a blunt instrument, and finally the British had to admit that they were not in control. They gave Iraq "independence" in 1932, although the British continued to have a hand in Iraqi politics from their embassy.

During this period of the constitutional monarchy, some important state institutions and modern schooling began. Baghdad University was founded. These developments affected a relatively small number of people. Most Iraqis remained relatively rural; there continued to be low literacy rates. As time went on, especially into the 1950s, the rise of mass politics in Iraq begins. The first round of mass politics in Iraq tended to center on parties that promoted universal ideologies. Petroleum income started to come in. There were modern factory workers and modern workers on the oil rigs, so a small proletariat began to grow up. The cities expanded. Village youth began to migrate to the cities and receive a modern education, increasing literacy.

Many of these first generation, young intellectuals were attracted to the Communist Party or to the Baath Party, an Arab nationalist party which believed in the brotherhood of all Arabs, as well as espousing socialism and equality. Of course, the Communists focused on the unity of the working classes. Both of those parties emphasized social equity and the irrelevance of ethnic identity. For example, if you were Jewish and Communist, the Muslim Communists would not hold that against you—you would all be Communists together. Similarly, once you were in the Baath Party, your ethnic background became much less important. They were appealing to a universalist identity. This emphasis on social equality was attractive to these young Iraqis, in part because Iraq under the monarchy had become extremely stratified. A few thousand families owned much of the best land of Iraq, including enormous haciendas where landless peasants toiled.

The Baathists ultimately came to power in 1963 with a failed coup that only lasted for eight months, during which they helped to destroy the Communist Party. The military wing of the Baathists, which had a very substantial Shiite component, led the coup. However, it was overthrown by the officers from the previous government, who had in turn overthrown the monarchy in 1958. The Baathist Shiite officers were hunted down and killed, or marginalized. What was left of the Baath Party was the civilian wing that had tended to be dominated by Sunni Arabs, especially from the region of Tikrit.

It is the civilian, Sunni-dominated wing of the Baath Party that came to power in 1968. Now, it did not identify itself as Sunni. The rhetoric of the Baath is Arab nationalism, so Sunni/Shiite does not matter. In fact, ideally, Iraqi/Syrian/Jordanian should not matter. These universal ideologies often get subverted to more ethnic uses. The Baath rhetoric of universalism was subverted for the purposes of enriching and enhancing the power and prestige of the Sunni minority.

As a reaction to the rise of the Baath Party with its universalist identity, traditionalist Shiites began worrying that they were losing the young people of their community. Thus, they began organizing the Dawa Party in the late 1950s. The Dawa Party was modeled, in many ways, on the Communist and Baath Parties. It was a covert party, a revolutionary party with cells. Its aim was a utopian state. But its utopia was not a workers' paradise, as with the Communists; nor an Arab paradise, as with the Baath; but a Shiite paradise or at least an Islamic one in which Islamic law would be implemented and an Islamic state would be attained.

Muhammad Baqir Sadr, the theorist of the Dawa, was the first to put forward this idea of an Islamic state within Shiism. He influenced Ayatollah Khomeini, although Khomeini took his ideas in a different direction. The Dawa Party was not predominantly a clerical party; it was largely lay. Also, about 10 percent of its members were Sunni in the 1960s, in its golden age. Because Muhammad Baqir Sadr had not envisioned clerical rule, he thought there would be a kind of parliament. He did want Islamic law implemented, but he also had a socialist interpretation of Islamic law.

The Iranian Revolution of 1979, as well as trouble between the Baathists and Shiites in 1977 in which there were riots in the shrine cities and in East Baghdad (which had become a Shiite slum), scared the Baath. In 1979, Saddam Hussein had come to power within the Baath in an internal party putsch. Khomeini came out and said that the Iraqi Shiites, who were a majority, should rise up and do to the Baath what the Iranians had done to the Shah. Saddam was determined that that not happen, so he had Muhammad Baqir Sadr killed along with his sister and a number of other prominent leaders in the Dawa Party. Then Saddam made it a capital crime to belong to the Dawa Party. Many of the mass graves we are finding in southern Iraq are full of people who were Dawa Party members. Saddam's secret police had captured the party lists.

Many Dawa Party members fled to Tehran. In fact, many Shiite activists who were working for a Shiite vision of Iraq fled to Tehran. The Iran-Iraq war began. Saddam invaded Iran, thinking that the best defense was a good offense. Most Shiites remained loyal to the Iraqi state. Most fought against the Iranians. They were Shiites, but they were Arab Shiites and Iraqis, and they did not want to be ruled by Persians. However, over time, because of Saddam's repression, 300,000 to 400,000 Iraqi Shiites did go to Iran and became refugees there. About 40,000 troops deserted to Iran. That is a relatively small number, for at the time Iraq had a million-man army. Some Kurds toyed with an alliance with Iran in order to gain greater autonomy from Iraq. In response to that budding alliance, Saddam Hussein gassed the Kurds in the al-Anfal campaign in the late 1980s, one of the great atrocities in modern Iraqi history.

Saddam Hussein based his power on the center of the country where he could get a slight Sunni majority. He marginalized the North and the South. Thus people in the deep South, in al-Hillah and Basra, were marginalized as were those in Kurdistan in the North.

In Tehran in 1982, Khomeini organized the Iraqi expatriates into the Supreme Council for the Islamic Revolution in Iraq (SCIRI), an umbrella group that incorporated many of the Shiite activists who had fled to Iran. The Supreme Council then developed paramilitary capability and sent fighters over to hit Baathist targets. In other circumstances we might call them terrorists. Gradually, SCIRI gained great influence in some parts of Iraq. Fighters would come through the marshes to Basra, and over through eastern Kurdistan areas, and around Diyala Province—all the eastern part of Iraq. Over time eastern Iraq became much influenced by the SCIRI and its Badr Corps fighters who were trained by the Iranian revolutionary guards.

Saddam, having lost the Iran-Iraq War and being deeply in debt, still wanted to be powerful. He invaded Kuwait for its resources so that he could pursue his ambitions. That was stopped by the international coalition under George Bush, Sr. During that war, Bush Sr. called upon the Iraqis to rise up and overthrow Saddam. There was a great rebellion: the Baath Party was kicked out of power in 16 of the provinces. It was a revolution. The Baath Party could only hope to come back if it was allowed to use helicopter gun ships and tanks against this revolution. The United States could have interdicted that, but it did not. The revolution was brutally crushed. Many Shiites still do not forgive the United States for standing by and allowing their compatriots to be killed after Bush Sr. had called for them to rise up.

The aftermath played out differently in the South and the North. The Shiites were killed in very large numbers in Najaf, Karbala, Basra, and other areas of the South. In the North, the Kurds fled up into the mountains. However, they would have died because there was no way to live up there, if no one had intervened. Bush Sr. was presented with the prospect that a million Kurds would starve to death during his watch. Unlike in the Shiite South, Bush Sr. was forced to intervene to save the Kurds. The no-fly zone was established to keep the Baath military from incursions into the far North. Under that no-fly zone, the Kurds organized to establish a semi-autonomous state, with its own parliament, its own tradition of politics, and its own political parties. As quickly as they could, they stopped teaching their children much Arabic. Thus, ethnic subnationalism advanced very substantially in the Kurdish region. Schooling and television began a process of linguistic standardization; many more Kurds can understand each other now than a century ago.

In the Shiite areas, there was a period of quietism, but underneath people were organizing. Many Shiites began turning to clerical institutions for guidance in a way that Iraqi Shiites probably had not done before. A great historian of Iraq, Hanna Batatu, once did a calculation of mullahs per person in Iran and Iraq. He found many more mullahs per person in Iran than in Iraq. Iraqi Shiism was not clerically oriented in the 1960s and 1970s.

In the 1990s, people began turning to the Shiite religious authorities because so much else had been destroyed by Saddam. The leader to whom the majority turned was Grand Ayatollah Ali Sistani. He was a quietist; he did not get involved in politics at that time. He had a competitor (some say initially supported by Saddam, but the two broke) called Muhammad Sadiq Sadr from the same Sadr family mentioned earlier, that of Muhammad Baqir Sadr who was executed by the Baath. Sadiq Sadr argued for something like a Khomeini-style Islamic Republic. He called it a third way between Iraqi Shiism and Iranian Shiism. He organized Friday prayers, when Saddam had forbidden them, out in the slums and tribal areas. He also organized Islamic courts to bypass the Baath. He attracted the Arab tribes of the South to come and study with him. This continued the process of Islamization of the marsh Arabs. They become much more oriented toward clerical Shiism. Sadr's appeal stretched into the North, where there is a minority of Turkmen, about 750,000, with about half of them Shiites. They were heterodox Shiites; they had many myths and were not clerical. Many of them started turning to Sadiq Sadr as well. The heterodox groups within Iraqi Shiism begin being gathered up into what we would call a fundamentalist movement. Muhammad Sadiq Sadr was assassinated by Saddam in 1999, but his young son Muqtada Sadr went underground and continued to keep the movement going, along with some of Sadiq Sadr's disciples.

This was the situation when the United States invaded Iraq. I would argue that Iraq in the 1990s was in a revolutionary situation. The Kurds more or less had made a revolution and had a mini-state of their own. The Shiites had several groups—the Sadr movement, the Dawa Party, SCIRI—trying to make a revolution. When Sadiq Sadr was killed, there were very substantial riots in the Shiite areas, which were not well covered in the Western press. We still do not know enough about those riots. The United States came into that revolutionary situation and blew the lid off of it. Essentially the effect was to tell people that now they were free to do as they pleased. We know what they wanted to do. They wanted to make revolutions.

In the aftermath of the American war, Grand Ayatollah Sistani emerged as a major leader of the Shiites and issued *fatwas* that forced the Americans, quite against their will, to follow through on their promise of moving toward Iraqi democracy. Initially the Bush administration wanted to restrict the electorate to council members that had been picked by the Americans and the British. Sistani said that legitimate government derives from the will of the Iraqi people. Sistani got what he wanted, and open elections were held in January 2005. But Muqtada Sadr emerged as a major leader as well, one who liked to organize militias and engage in thuggish politics. He continued to attract an increasing number of marginal people: slum dwellers, the marsh Arabs, Turkmen. Also, the SCIRI appears to have done significant organizing work, opening offices and getting people on its side. Similarly the Dawa Party has also organized effectively.

The Sunni Arabs were deprived of their main vehicle of politics, the Baath Party, which was dissolved. They saw the Shiites mobilizing on religious grounds and the Shiite clerics coming to the fore as effective leaders. In reaction, the Sunni Arabs, who had been largely secular, seem increasingly in the last few years to have turned to religious parties and leaders to express their subnationalism. Opinion polls and voting patterns show a shift away from secularism towards religious parties such as the Association of Muslim Scholars, a very hardline—what is called Salafi—movement, and the Iraqi Islamic Party descended from the old Iraqi Muslim Brotherhood.

This process whereby the subnationalisms are expressed, which begins in the Saddam Hussein period, comes to fruition in the January 2005 elections in which the Iraqi public, almost to a person, voted along ethnic and subnational lines. Ayatollah Sistani put together a coalition of Shiite religious parties, called the United Iraqi Alliance, and then he endorsed it. The word he used was blessed. He said that there may be other good parties, but this is the one that I know and I bless it. They used his image in their campaigns, and their symbol was a candle. They won big, winning about 53 to 54 percent of the seats in Parliament.

However out in the provinces, SCIRI became the leading party in the Shiite South. The Fadilah or Virtue Party, a splinter of the Sadr movement, maneuvered itself into control of Basra. These provincial victories have long-term consequences because the victorious parties then pack the bureaucracy with their people.

Why are voters voting for the SCIRI, Dawa, and other religiously connected parties in southern Iraq? Because these parties have organizational capacity. These people were organizing in the 1990s while they were trying to avoid domination by the Baath. The Americans had this idea of Iraq as a totalitarian state, but Iraq in the late Saddam period was extremely ramshackle. What do you think would have happened to a Baathist who showed up in East Baghdad in what was then called Saddam City? They would have had their throats slit. It was not possible, in fact, for the Iraqi Secret Police to know everything that was going on in the slums of these Shiite southern cities. It was not possible for them to control the marsh Arabs, for instance, very closely. People formed cliques which, in a broad way, affiliated with Dawa, SCIRI, or the Sadr group.

When the Americans got rid of the Baath and removed the restrictions on organizing, these groups were very good at grassroots organizing because they had already started. There are reports of the Supreme Council sending out emissaries to all the villages around Basra and opening offices. Also, of course, they have money. Some of it probably comes from Iran, but even the remaining Iraqi middle classes who are religious, support these activities substantially. These parties are giving people some jobs and patronage. They are promising them more: if you vote for me, your cousin gets a job in such-and-such a bureaucracy.

Furthermore, in the aftermath of the war, social order broke down in much of Iraq. There was a great deal of looting and crime. There is still a great deal of crime, including waves of kidnapping. In some areas of Baghdad for a while, people stopped driving their cars because they kept getting carjacked. These are law and order parties. They are saying if somebody is a burglar, they should be taken out and shot on the spot. Young girls were being kidnapped. They are saying keep the girls home or veil them—control them in various ways. Liquor stores were doing great business, so they firebombed the liquor stores.

Iyad Allawi and those put into power in the summer of 2004 by the Americans and the United Nations as an interim government tried hard to position themselves as the party for law and order. On the one hand, since they were the government, and since there was not much order, they were blamed for not doing a better job. On the other hand, they never quite understood what the Iraqis meant by law and order. Allawi would get up in the morning and say the Americans need to bomb Fallujah more. That was not what most Iraqis wanted. They wanted him to take control of the situation, not to encourage the Americans to bomb them more. Also, he struck me as having a tin ear when it came to popular politics. In contrast, Muqtada Sadr is someone who knows exactly what to say. He says the American troops should leave immediately. He says the Iraqis can supply their own order.

The Sunni Arabs did not vote in January 2005, for the most part. Only 2 percent of the mostly Sunni Anbar Province voted in the January 2005 elections. The Sunnis only got 17 seats in parliament. They received three of these seats because three Sunnis were on Sistani's list. In the provinces, this tendency toward the politicization of ethnic identity was even clearer. The SCIRI won big in places like Najaf. They even led in some Sunni areas because a very small Shiite minority was coming out and voting. To have the SCIRI win or lead in Sunni Arab areas would have warmed the cockles of Khomeini's heart.

Much of Sunni Arab frustration has been expressed through guerilla war, conducted by Salafi (Muslim revivalists) and by ex-Baathists.

Some of the ex-Baathists themselves turned to political Islam or had begun doing so even in the late Saddam period. Some small number of foreign fighters participated, although their numbers and effectiveness have been greatly exaggerated. In the Fallujah campaign, only 6 percent of the fighters captured were foreigners. It seems clear that most of the violence in the guerilla war has been conducted by the Iraqis and the Arabs—again, increasingly, with religious rhetoric, and even in some cases reaching out towards an al-Qaeda type of Islam. To say that Sunni Arabs from Baghdad, until recently so secular in their outlook, would be talking like bin Laden is incredible, as a datum.

The guerilla movement does not care if people have elections or not; it is trying to destabilize the country, very possibly by fomenting; ethnic violence between the Shiites and Sunnis and between the Arabs and Kurds. The people in it want to make the country ungovernable. At that point the Americans would have to leave. The Baath military people still think in those terms. They lost in 1963 and came back; they think they can do it again. The election does not matter at all in that regard. Those people are going to continue fighting for 10 years or so. I do not think they can win, but they can make life hell in the meantime.

They have resources. There are 250,000 tons of missing munitions in Iraq. There were 600,000 to begin with. The U.S. military has done an excellent job of destroying munitions but they have not gotten all of them. The ex-Baathists are the ones who know where those supplies are. They get money from outside, too, from millionaires in the Gulf who see the Sunni Arabs of Iraq as being under siege. They also smuggle petroleum. The ex-Baathists have resources and determination, and they will go on fighting. If they could, they would take the new government out and shoot it. That is why the new government has not demanded that the Americans leave. They say they wish the Americans would leave, but they do not say it very insistently.

The Kurds came out in large numbers and voted for the Kurdistan Alliance. In January 2005, they elected 75 members to Parliament, disproportionate to their percentage of the total population, even though the election was set up on a national basis with proportionality.

There is concern about what will happen with ethnic conflict and the Kurds. If ethnic conflict in the North can be reworked into ordinary parliamentary politics so that parliamentary compromises are achieved on issues like the disposition of Kirkuk, the oil city which is claimed by the Turkmen, the Kurds and the Arabs, then the situation in Kurdistan is likely to be worked out peacefully. A similar issue is the move to redraw the provincial boundaries of Iraq because the Kurds want a Kurdistan province, an ethnically based super province that would include three present provinces plus parts of another three—in essence, to become more like Pakistan, with Baluchistan and Punjab and ethnically based provinces. If that can be done, as one Shiite politician has suggested, with two Shiite provinces and one or two Sunni provinces, then Iraq has just five or six provinces and the Kurds get Kurdistan. Some political scientists suggest that a country with a small number of ethnically based provinces is less stable: for example, as in Nigeria or the original Pakistan, which included what is now Bangladesh.

If these big issues can be worked out, if there are negotiations on how much of the Kirkuk oil money stays at home rather than going to Baghdad, then you might be able to erect an Iraqi federalism. They talk about the Canada model, which would keep the Kurds in the federation. But much could go wrong: if the Shiites, who remain interlocutors with the Kurds, are insufficiently flexible or if the Kurds are insufficiently flexible—or, if some donkey cart gets turned over in Kirkuk and a riot spreads throughout the city and a lot of Turkmen are killed and the Turks are upset that their Turkmen were killed and they invade, then the whole North might explode. We can not predict whether we can get through the next five years without Kirkuk exploding. It is a tinder box.

There has been some talk of dividing Iraq into three separate countries based on subnationalisms, but there would be severe disadvantages to that approach. The first disadvantage is that Iraqis of differing subnationalisms are located throughout the country. There are about a million Kurds in the Baghdad province, about a million Sunni Arabs in the south of the country. There is intermarriage in Iraq: cross-sectarian, cross-ethnic marriages—more so than in Lebanon, for example. Ghazi al-Yawer, the former president and current vice president, is a wonderful example of how intermixed Iraqis are. He is from the Shamar tribe of Iraq, the majority of whom are Sunni. However, they do have a Shiite branch, so he has Shiite cousins. He took as his second wife, the minister of public works in the first postwar government, Nesereen Barwari. She is a Kurd. They were serving together on the Interim Government Council and fell in love. What would dividing Iraq into countries based on subnationalism do to the Yawer family? With this approach, there would be massive ethnic cleansing. Millions of people would be displaced.

Another disadvantage would be with petroleum revenue. There are probably substantial petroleum reserves all over the country, including near Fallujah. In the short term, the major petroleum producing fields are Rumayla in the South and Kirkuk in the North. Who is going to get those if the country is divided? Obviously the Shiites get Rumayla. That is the good one to have; it is big and will last for a long time. The Kurds might get Kirkuk, but they would have to fight for it because the Turkmen want it. There is also a substantial Arab population in the North that wants it. There would be a lot of bloodshed. Even if the Kurds did get Kirkuk, the Kirkuk fields are going to run dry after 20 to 30 years. If I were an Iraqi, I would want to maintain some connection to the Rumayla field. The Kurds could end up being poor shepherds again when the oil is exhausted.

Finally, there are many geopolitical considerations. The Turks desperately do not want a Kurdish state in the North and have occasionally threatened to invade if that happened. The Iranians do not want it either because they have a substantial Sunni Kurdish minority, which has sometimes had trouble with that regime. The Saudis do not want these divisions: if the Shiite South of Iraq became independent, it might start making claims on the traditionally Shiite eastern province of Saudi Arabia, which has most of the Saudi oil. The Shiites in al-Hasa could hook up with the Sadrs in Iraq and become militant and sabotage pipelines.

For the Saudis, the invasion has been a nightmare. The Saudis are threatened by the politicization of their own 10 percent Shiite minority, which is largely in the oil areas. The Saudis are also afraid of the radicalization of the Sunni Arab population of Iraq, which is not so far from Saudi Arabia. They fear an al-Qaeda type of terrorism spilling back over into Saudi Arabia from Sunni Iraq. The Americans think the Saudis are Wahabis with a strict form of Islam, which they are disseminating and causing trouble. From a Saudi point of view, the Americans went into Baghdad and cleared out secularism and are encouraging terrorism among the Sunni Arabs of Iraq.

Iran is also an important factor in Iraqi affairs: it gave refuge to the Iraqi-expatriate Shiites who were religious activists; the SCIRI was formed under the auspices of Ayatollah Khomeini; the Badr Corps, paramilitary of that army, was trained by the revolutionary guards; and the Dawa Party also had a Tehran branch and was very much beholden to the Iranian state. Jalal Talabani, the Kurdish leader, has often been very close to Tehran.

However, it is more likely that the Iranians will find a way to use the Iraqi Shiites and Kurds against the Americans rather than the other way around. There is some reason to think that that has already been happening. The Iranians were big supporters of holding elections in January 2005. The Iranians were encouraging whatever contacts they had in the Sunni community in Iraq to vote as well. Iran has been a major beneficiary of U.S. foreign policy in the eastern Middle East in the past three years. The Iranian regime had two major enemies: the Taliban and al-Qaeda on one hand, and Saddam Hussein on the other. The United States has removed both. The Iranians had two major allies: the Northern Alliance in Afghanistan, including the Hazara Shiite party in Afghanistan; and the SCIRI. The United States has put both into power.

There are other factors affecting unity in Iraq. Arabic has been a vehicle for Iraqi national unity. The Iraqi state has tried to establish schooling in Arabic throughout the country and to have that be the common language. However, there are linguistic minorities: Turkmen, Kurds, and Aramaic-speaking Chaldeans. In the no-fly zone the Kurds did not educate their children in Arabic nearly as much as had earlier been the case. In fact, I recently heard a report from Mosul on National Public Radio in which it was said that some Kurdish fighters had been detailed to protect the Arab governor of Mosul, but that they do not know Arabic. That is an artifact of the last 15 years. Had fighters been sent down to Mosul from Kurdistan in the 1970s they most likely would have known Arabic. Iraq is probably less linguistically unified now than it was.

Religion can also act as a unifying force. There have been cross-sectarian and religious alliances: Shiites of Najaf sent aid to the Sunni Salafis of Fallujah, and vice versa. There can be a sense of Iraqi national unity that says we are all Muslims together or all Iraqis together: we should cooperate against a common foe. In that regard, the U.S. military presence in Iraq may be a good thing for Iraqi unity. Although those sentiments exist, Iraqis did not vote that way. There is no sign of cross-sectarian unity in the voting patterns. The way they did vote is quite disturbing.

Our experience from Iran would suggest that these religiously based voting blocs may not last for the long term. Khomeini and the clerics were very popular in Iran in the 1980s; in 2005, only 15 percent voted for them. Things can change. The Shiite religious parties may be hurt by their success in the provincial elections because now they are in charge of the provinces. People are going to expect them to provide services and water and electricity. Why would we think they would be able to do that? The Americans could not. There may be a backlash against them eventually.

The evidence that I saw in the press was that the Shiite middle classes voted for Allawi's list in Baghdad and in Basra in January 2005. His 14 percent mainly came from those two places and from that stratum. If unemployment fell under 50 percent and the middle class expanded, there may be a demand for a more secular kind of government. Much of the vote for the Sistani list was coming from poor and lower middle-class neighborhoods. It was a sign of some desperation. We do not know whether this religious Shiite victory will hold together.

On the other hand, the religious Shiite parties do have a majority in Parliament. In 2005, the Iraqi state may have received $17 billion a year in revenue, even with the sabotage from petroleum and other sources. That means the Supreme Council for Islamic Revolution in Iraq and the Dawa Party have billions a year. They control the government; they control the income. That might keep them together, because if they withdraw from the alliance, then they lose those billions. With such a significant amount of money to spread around in patronage, they could continue to do well in national politics.

Religious Shiite parties are probably the key factor in the development of contemporary Iraq for the medium term, five or ten years out. After that, all bets are off. Imagine somebody who is now nine and in school: what will that generation think when they are twenty? We cannot predict. They may be tired of Muqtada Sadr by then. We should be cautious about what the rise of religious parties means for the long term, but, short to medium term, they will persist.

So my conclusion is that the Iran-Iraq war; the crackdown of Saddam on the Shiites and Kurds, partially in connection with that war; the 1991 suppression of the uprising; and then the U.S. war, have all contributed to a heightening of religious-ethnic identities in Iraq. The shunting aside of the secular, universalist Baath ideology with nothing to take its place on a national scale has contributed to this phenomenon. It is very likely that religious and ethnic politics will continue to play an extremely important role as Iraq goes forward. There is some question about whether this kind of associational politics is stable. There could well be unexpected events that could cause Kurdistan to erupt in violence and make it very difficult for it to remain in Iraq, for instance. Some of the southern Shiite provinces are talking about getting together and forming a federation as well. I am not predicting civil war or the breakup of Iraq, but the direction in which Iraq is headed is not one that bodes well for national unity.

Notes

1. Editors' note: This paper has been created from the transcript of Professor Cole's remarks on April 22, 2005.
2. See Anthony D. Smith, *The Ethnic Origins of Nations*, reprint (Oxford and Malden Mass.: Blackwell Publishers, 1999).
3. See Benedict Anderson, *Imagined Communities: Reflections on the Origin and Spread of Nationalism,* rev. ed. (London and New York: Verso, 1991).
4. See Paul R. Brass, *Language, Religion, and Politics in North India* (Cambridge: Cambridge University Press, 1974).

Kurds and Arabs, Sunnis and Shiites: Can an Iraqi Identity be Salvaged?

Phebe Marr[1]

Iraq is undergoing two political struggles:

- a struggle for power (which groups will control the central levers of power in the state and thus be in a position to determine its future direction); and
- a more fundamental struggle for identity (what common values and ties will bind and compel basic loyalty to the state).

The first struggle is important, but not determinative as events since the fall of Saddam Hussein's regime show. The second will be decades in progress and is still uncertain.

For most of its modern history, Iraq has been dominated by the center, defined—geographically and politically—as Baghdad and its environs. At the time of Saddam's fall, greater Baghdad contained almost a third of Iraq's population in a thoroughly heterogeneous mixture of Sunni and Shiite Arabs, Kurds, Turkmen, and Christians. The center housed much of Iraq's government structure—the headquarters of its civil service, army, and security apparatus—employing a large percentage of the population, as well as a disproportionately large share (in quantity and quality) of the country's civil infrastructure (educational establishments, the media, and health facilities). The center also had a concentration of Iraq's middle class, characterized by higher education, higher standards of living, and a high degree of secularism. To a large extent, this middle class had espoused a national identity, reducing tribal, ethnic, and sectarian loyalties to secondary importance. However, by the end of Saddam's rule, this class had been greatly weakened and reduced in size through war, sanctions, and emigration. In the periphery of the country, the Kurdish provinces of the North had escaped Saddam's control while the Shiite South remained underdeveloped and alienated.

With the occupation, the center has now been hollowed out. The occupation authorities have not only removed Saddam and his security forces, but much of the Baath Party apparatus that ran the government, its satellite facilities, and the 400,000 strong military. Looting following the war added untold damage to the physical infrastructure. The political vacuum created by the occupation is gradually being filled by new leaders, many of whom have been exiles and opponents of Saddam, mainly through two elections held in 2005. The control of this new government beyond the center is tenuous. The Kurdish North is virtually self-governing; insurgency dominates areas to the north and west of Baghdad and Baghdad city itself, while the Shiite South is developing new provincial leaders and armed militias.

One of the most important ideological changes in Iraq since the occupation has been a shift away from Iraqi identity to ethnic and sectarian loyalties—the politics of cultural identity. This was made apparent in three national elections in 2005: one a referendum on a new constitution; and the other two voting for a national assembly. In the December 2005 election, which led to a permanent Iraqi government in 2006, over 80 percent of the votes went to ethnic or sectarian tickets (some 45 percent to the United Iraqi Alliance representing Shiites; 19 percent to the two main Kurdish parties, and 16 percent to the Sunni-oriented Iraqi Concord Front). Less than 15 percent went to non-sectarian tickets: 9 percent to the secular Iraqi List and 4 percent to an ex-Baathist group, both essentially representing the old secular middle class. Ethnic and sectarian identity—and parties organized around it—are not new in Iraq. The KDP (Kurdistan Democratic Party) goes back to the end of World War II; the PUK (Patriotic Union of Kurdistan) to 1975. The Shiite Dawa Party has its origins in the late 1950s, while SCIRI (the Supreme Council for the Islamic Revolution in Iraq) was founded in Iran in 1982. In the 1960s and 1970s, these ethnic and sectarian movements grew, but they did not dominate the scene. The strength of these sentiments came to the fore in 1991. The rebellions in the Kurdish North and the Shiite South—but not the Sunni center—revealed different loyalties and foreshadowed current realignments.

Despite this recent trend in politics, Iraqi social reality is more complex. None of its communities are homogeneous. Communal and ethnic identity is intersected by tribal and family ties, by regional and local differences, and historically by identification with ideological movements. However, in the new, rapidly changing political environment, political and religious leaders are using ethnic and sectarian identity to develop constituencies and achieve power—something that recalls other troubled situations, such as the former Yugoslavia.

A question for those interested in nation building, democracy, and religion is whether the current sectarianism is a permanent fixture or a temporary situation. How much of the old middle class is left? Is an Iraqi identity completely gone? Or can it be reconstituted on a different basis?

I have been engaged in a research project at the U.S. Institute of Peace on Iraq's emerging political leadership, that is, the people likely to shape Iraq's future. In addition to acquiring standard information on their backgrounds, careers, and education to indicate the skills and orientations they may bring to the task of governing, I am also attempting to explore their views and their visions for the future of Iraq with a representative sample. The study focuses on five broad dimensions:

- how leaders identify themselves in national, ethnic, and sectarian terms, bearing in mind that they may be prioritizing among overlapping identities;
- their attitude toward democracy and the ways in which they would define that term, including the issue of federalism;
- their attitude toward the role of religion in the state;
- the importance they attach to economic development and the priority they would give it;

- their attitude toward foreign powers (primarily the U.S. and Britain, but also regional neighbors).

These are the issues critical to the future direction of Iraq. I am also interested in where there is convergence and divergence of outlook, where views cut across ethnic and sectarian lines, and where views reinforce differences. Identifying problem areas would help us support policies which bring groups together. I would like to outline what I have found so far with two groups, the Kurds and the Sunnis.

Kurds

In the past 15 years, I have made a number of trips to the Kurdish area and held discussions with numerous Kurdish leaders. My most recent interviews indicate a stronger sense of Kurdish identity than at any time in my experience, which goes back to 1957. In a range of interviews, only one leader identified himself first as an Iraqi and second as a Kurd. The desire for Kurdish independence (expressed most clearly in an unofficial referendum held in 2005 in which voters were overwhelmingly in favor of independence) is strong, although this is tempered by a sense of realism on the part of the leadership about Kurdish ability to realize this aim in the near future. Hence their desire for a Kurdish federal state, expanded to include Kirkuk, Khanaqin, and other Kurdish majority areas within Iraq.

The generation gap is notable. The older, more experienced Kurdish leaders are realistic and willing to compromise. One, in the PUK, told me he did not believe in breaking down larger states into smaller and smaller ethnic units, which were not viable in today's world. But the generation that has come to maturity in the last 15 years and is moving into leadership positions is overwhelmingly Kurdish in identity and orientation. Their knowledge of Arabic is scanty, their familiarity with "Iraq" to the south almost non-existent, and their willingness to participate in the new Iraqi experiment minimal. In addition, there is a new emphasis on ethnic and cultural differences instead of on similarities between Kurds and Arabs that is reinforcing a separate identity.

The reasons for this trend are clear:
- Kurds have been isolated from the rest of Iraq since 1991.

- The security problems which afflict the rest of Iraq are absent in Kurdistan, and the rest of Iraq does not look very attractive to a Kurd.
- The language of teaching at all levels of the school system has gradually become Kurdish; it will be difficult for younger Kurds to communicate with ease in Arab areas. The second language Kurds want to learn is English.
- Civic textbooks have been rewritten to emphasize citizenship in the new entity, Kurdistan—geographically based and ethnically Kurdish. In their emphasis on human rights and more democratic values, they are also different from those in Saddam's former Iraq.

These identity issues are reflected in responses to the attitudinal questions I asked Kurdish leaders. Kurds strongly support cooperation with the U.S. and the West, to whom they look for future protection. Although religious affiliation has been increasing in recent years, most Kurds, especially the younger generation of women, are strongly secular, and even the religious parties, like the Kurdish Islamic Union, are very moderate.

Kurds support democracy. The Kurdish area is more open to outside influence. But the two nationalist parties (the KDP and the PUK) keep a firm control on their areas, although other parties—especially religious parties—are present and participate in the Kurdish Regional Government. These may be gaining strength. A younger, often unemployed, generation is restive under the current leadership. On the ground and in their current negotiations at the central government level, Kurdish leaders give the impression that they are seeking the framework for a future independent state. However, they realize this is a distant possibility. Federalism is a way of bridging this gap and reintegrating Kurds into the central government in Baghdad.

Although Kurds are not likely to get independence, their strong desire for it, especially among the youth, could hamper Iraq's future development—as well as that of the Kurds—if it is not handled well. Frictions, even violence in areas like Kirkuk, could slow development. The need to accommodate other ethnic identities (Turkman, Christian, and Arab) is another difficulty. Frictions, meddling, and even military intervention by neighbors such as Turkey or Iran are also possible. Moreover, in the past, Kurds have been unable to protect their borders. The PKK (Partiya Karkeran Kurdistan: Kurdistan Workers' Party, a radical Turkish Kurdish group) is still nested all along the Turkish border in the north. In the east, failure of the PUK to control the border around Halabja resulted in a no-man's land on the Iraqi-Iranian border into which radical Islamic elements (for example, Ansar al-Islam) were able to take control.

At present, the Kurds are in a strong position in the Iraqi political system, and their sense of Kurdish identity is at a peak. Where they will go—and take Iraq—is one of the chief uncertainties of the future. Kurdish experience in governing; their attitudes toward democracy and the West; their secularism—all could provide benefits and balance in the central government and influence the direction Iraq takes in the future. Independence is not on the cards for the short term. The older generation of Kurdish leaders is aware of this difficulty; the younger is not. Their attitudes will be shaped by how attractive the rest of Iraq becomes in the next few years and how well they compromise. Kurdish progress in the North may also exert some attraction for the rest of Iraq, providing a model for development and cooperation with the West.

Sunnis

The Sunni community is harder to categorize in terms of identity. Like the rest of Iraq's ethnic and sectarian groups, it is not homogeneous. Most Sunnis have not thought of themselves as sectarian or even religious. In some senses they may be compared to WASPs [White Anglo Saxon Protestants] in the American experience. Since Iraq's founding, Sunnis have been the dominant political and social elite. Increasingly, in the last decades of Saddam's rule, they saw themselves as such. They perpetuated their status and their hold over the political system, not through sectarian identity, but rather through nationalist ideologies—mainly Arab, but also Iraqi, especially in the last decade of Saddam's rule. They are the community that has always identified themselves most strongly with the state because they ran it.

Two major groups can be differentiated in the Arab Sunni population. First, the Sunni population living in the smaller, provincial towns of the Tigris and Euphrates north and west of Baghdad has strongly developed tribal and clan loyalties. These Sunnis in the provinces also have ties across the border in Syria and Jordan with other Arab Sunnis giving them a strong sense of Arab Sunni support and hence a stronger affinity for Arab nationalist ideologies. Among this group, there has been a distrust of Shiism and Iran. Under Saddam, Sunnis from this area were Baathized, given rapid upward mobility, and became a privileged, entitled class. While mainly secular, in the last two decades, and particularly under Saddam's "Faith Campaign" in the 1990s, religiosity made considerable headway in the Sunni community, especially among youth, and in cities like Fallujah and Ramadi. Both Muslim Brotherhood influence and Salafi teachings have gained in strength.

A second part of the Arab Sunni community is urban—mainly in large cities and towns such as Baghdad and Mosul. Generally educated, and at the upper levels well traveled, these urbanites worked and often intermarried with Shiites and even Kurds. Ethnic, sectarian, and tribal identities faded among middle-class professionals. Political identities, such as Baathism, replaced them. This Arab Sunni community today is largely fragmented, although it is beginning to develop leaders and a public voice as it rejoins the political process.

Both communities—the provincial and the urban—have been abruptly displaced by the occupation and the emergence of the Shiite and Kurdish leaders. Marginalized and alienated, their dissatisfaction has fed the insurgency, which is the chief threat to the establishment of a new Iraqi political order. While insurgent groups comprise a variety of factions (such as jihadists, ex-Baathists and Saddam supporters, unemployed youth, and angry nationalists) two themes emerge: dislike of foreign forces and resentment at marginalization and displacement from power.

Some Arab Sunnis are participating in government and the political process, after having boycotted the January 2005 elections with disastrous results. Sunnis participated in the December 2005 election for a permanent Council of Representatives, running on several tickets. The Iraqi Concord Front, which included the Iraqi Islamic Party (IIP) and several more secular groups, won 44 seats in the Council of

Representatives and is included in the national unity government formed in 2006. The leader of the IIP is a vice president of the republic. A more secular Sunni ticket won seats in the assembly but not in the government. But many Sunnis, such as those represented by the Muslim Scholars Association, are not yet willing to join the political process, although they are part of the open debate on Sunni aims and objectives. Still others remain underground passively or actively supporting the insurgency and must be won over if the new political order is to succeed.

Based on their public statements, as well as individual interviews with Sunni leaders who have joined the process, the following general picture of Sunni thinking about the future of Iraq emerges:

- They generally claim to be nonsectarian. While a strong sense of Arabism lingers, most want to be identified as Iraqi—or in the case of those with more religiosity—Muslim. Most oppose sectarianism and want to dissolve sectarianism in a larger identity. Their newly acquired "Sunni" identification is imposed in their view by others and generally reflects their perception of their changed status, from dominance to an aggrieved, even persecuted minority.

- Their view of governance is different from Shiites (who favor elections which put them in power) and Kurds (who want federalism). These Sunnis emphasize: a rule of law and a strong court system (i.e., a secure, stable environment); a nonsectarian political system (they disapprove of the current slide into Lebanization); a meritocracy (appointments based on competence and education); and delayed, carefully prepared elections to level the playing field. While these are favorable aspects of democracy, they would give Arab Sunnis an advantage—or at least reduce their disadvantages in the political struggle.

- Their attitudes to the role of religion in the state are not clear—probably indicating divisions over the issue. Some Arab Sunnis, especially former Baathists, are decidedly secular and want a separation of mosque and state. Others are more religious. Religion has increased among the Sunni population in recent decades. IIP support appears strong in Anbar. Salafist sentiment appears strong in the insurgency.

- They are profoundly opposed to the occupation and foreign control, although this has recently been tempered by a greater fear of Iran and its potential domination of a Shiite-led Iraq.

Common Ground?

Is there any common ground among these communities? If we do not treat communities as monolithic, there are areas of overlap in which groups could find commonality. The secular-religious divide appears in all communities. Secularism is strongest among the Kurds, but exists in all communities. Nonetheless, religious sentiment and sectarian identity are increasing. Religious groups range from moderate to extreme; only the latter are likely to be excluded from debate. This issue may be cross-cutting, if it is treated correctly.

Attitudes towards foreigners will divide Kurds from Sunnis and some Shiites, such as the Sadrists, where the divergence is sharpest. But many Shiites are ambivalent about Western influence. Those in power now will want some Western support for the future to stay in power. Attitudes to neighbors will be divisive: with Shiites oriented to Iran, Kurds to Turkey, and Arab Sunnis to the Arab world.

The greatest commonality may be found in economic development and social mobility. This is neutral ground. All agree on wanting more of both (though they may disagree on how). Economic development could help mitigate tensions, provide alternative visions for Iraq, and reduce ethnic and sectarian strife. But political leaders will have to focus more attention on economics rather than political goals. Oil is a critical factor: its distribution and benefits could keep Iraq together. If we are looking at ways in which we can strengthen the unity of Iraq, we should be thinking of ways to support economic development and to advance the middle class. This would give all of these groups a different vision of the future and tend to reduce the sharpness of ethnic and sectional divisions.

The power equation—and the desire to control it—will also be important, along with definitions of democracy including federalism, elections, and rule of law. Sharing power—and how it is done—will be critical, including integration of more of the Sunni community. Here the question of elections should be considered. The national list and the proportional representation systems seem to have encouraged huge blocks to vote on an ethnic and sectarian basis when, in fact, Iraqi is a more diverse and complex society. More emphasis on district and local elections might help balance that. Ways need to be found to diffuse power, increase diversity, and encourage political alliances on the basis of interests, rather than on ethnic and sectarian lines.

Notes

1. Editors' note: This paper was created from Dr. Marr's informal talk given on April 23, 2005. She has kindly provided some updates. The research which she mentions within it is undertaken for the United States Institute of Peace. Part of an ongoing study, it has most recently been reported in Phebe Marr's "Who are Iraq's New Leaders? What Do They Want?," USIP Special Report 130, (Washington, D.C.: United States Institute of Peace, March 2006) accessible online at http://www.usip.org/pubs/specialreports/sr160.pdf.

Summary of Iraq Discussion

The situation in Iraq is complex and multifaceted in ways not often understood outside Iraq. The popular press refers to the Sunnis, Shiites, and Kurds as though they are monolithic groups. In the case of the Shiites, there are three main political blocs: the Sadr, Dawa, and SCIRI (Supreme Council for the Islamic Revolution in Iraq) movements. Within each of them there are splits. More complexity is added at the provincial and district levels where there are different ideologies and interests.

Three important elements must be kept in mind: 1) foreign connections; 2) representation of the broader public; and 3) the role of militias. Regarding the first, groups within Iraq have different attitudes toward foreign neighbors, even within the same religious tradition. Within the Shiites, for example, the SCIRI is pro-Iran but the Sadrines are anti-Iran. Regarding representation of the general public, if Iraq is to develop a more pluralist, secular politics the country needs to move from a proportional-representational list system to a constituency-based system in which people vote for individuals.[1] Unfortunately, the U.S. does not support such a change because it appears too complex, nor do the Syrians or Iranians who support particular movements. As for militias, they present a threat to the rule of law. If the governors of provincial councils are unable to implement their policies through legal methods, they may decide to use their militias to implement them.

The militias are not well-organized military groups but they are well armed. They have demonstrated that they have the power to take over substantial areas of the country. Essentially the coalition lost control of two out of the four provinces in southern Iraq over a period of about six months. Neither the alternative of absorbing these militias into a national army or confronting them is very good.

While the militias are important politically, from the standpoint of public welfare the Dawa Party plays a more important role than the Sadr or Badr Brigades. In Karbala, for example, the Dawa run a variety of social programs, including teaching computer skills and the English language.

Since the U.S. invasion, power has shifted from institutions to individual religious leadership, especially to the Shiite *marja* (the religious leadership within Shiism). Since the fall of Hussein, at every crucial point the *marja* has intervened to shape events. It was the *marja* who said that any election held had to be one person/one vote. It was the *marja* who realized that if all the major Shiite parties ran as a single list they could have a majority in parliament. It was disappointing that the Grand Ayatollah Ali al-Sistani and the *marja* generally did not include more Sunni Arabs in their list. Here was an opportunity for the *marja* to act as a pan-Iraqi institution, a role to which it aspires.

Among the Shiites in southern Iraq, the Grand Ayatollah Sistani dominates. He is able to issue a *fatwa* (a ruling in Islamic law), which reassures the people and persuades them to follow his broad policies. Once he is gone, who will replace him? In Karbala and Najaf there is no one his equal.

In Shiism when the Grand Ayatollah dies, another leader emerges. In addition to Sistani there are four other important senior clerics. There will be a period of consolidation of power, but there will be a successor. Whoever steps in will need to project the *marja* as a focal point for the Shiite community. The two most likely successors to the Grand Ayatollah Sistani will be Muhammad Fayad, an Afghan who came to Iraq with his family when he was a child, and Bashir Najafi, a Pakistani. Fayad is more pro-American than Sistani and is opposed to the clerical theocracy in Iran. He believes that clerics should intervene to uphold the social order but should not meddle in politics. Najafi, on the other hand, has expressed bitterness towards the United States for allowing the 1991 uprising to be crushed. Also the difficult relationship between Shiites and Sunnis in Pakistan might influence how he acts in Iraq. Whether Fayad or Najafi succeeds Sistani will have important policy implications for Iraq because of the centrality of the institution of the *marja*. Given what is happening on the ground in Iraq today, it is critical that the U.S. not look at the political situation in conventional, secular terms but respect the *marja* as a necessary and powerful institution. Even after Sistani the *marja* as a tradition will continue its central role.

Washington in the short term is working with SCIRI and Dawa to promote democracy and elections. However, if a more liberal leadership were to emerge with an Iraqi identity distinct from the Iranian model centered at Najaf (the holiest of Shiite cities), a different democratic model might emerge that would recognize commonalities with other communities such as the Kurds and the Sunnis.

How should we think about Iraq now? What are the primary goals of the United States? The U.S. obviously wants to prevent a civil war. Is the goal now to create a sufficiently stable situation in order to withdraw but at the expense of democracy and civil rights? Does the U.S. want to prevent the creation of a sectarian religious government contrary to a pluralistic democratic system?

We must avoid thinking about nationalism and Iraq in simplistic, dichotomous terms such as religious or secular. In Iraq, as in the case of Palestine and Israel, the secular and religious cannot be neatly separated. At the rhetorical level, Iraq seems to have become an Islamic cause and is conflated with Palestine.

At the core of the problem in thinking about Iraq is the extent of our collective ignorance about the situation, in particular at the local level. The coalition approach to Iraq has been full of hubris. The intervention was not thought through, and the results are unpredictable. We see a continually shifting range of justifications and explanations about the goals of the intervention as the coalition attempts to adjust to the impossibility of the notion of foreigners creating a useful society, without sufficient knowledge. The coalition began by talking about a liberal, democratic, state that would live peacefully with its neighbors. Policy makers began the invasion of Iraq with a clear set of views on how the politics, economics, and security of the country should be transformed. They wanted to move from a centralized to a more decentralized government; they wanted to avoid a theocratic state. Many were worried about not giving too much of a role to minorities or tribes. The aim was to go from a centrally planned market to a free market, and on the security side from a Saddam-style police state to a gentler, human-rights-respecting infrastructure based on civil society. Almost all of these aspirations have now fallen away. In the context of chaos and insurgency, people are happy if they have a modicum of stability. Therefore, there is now a greater tolerance for the possibility of theocracy, for a police-state-style administration, for central planning economics.

In the light of the current situation, U.S. policy seems very reactive. While American policy may be more realistic today than two years ago, there appears to be no grand strategy. There also seems to be no clear-cut policy debates within the U.S. administration. Some neoconservatives may still harbor the hope of establishing military bases in Iraq after the U.S. pulls out. The situation on the ground is extraordinarily difficult: the military is stretched very thin. Building a national army and creating an acceptable level of security is going slowly at best. How can the diverse constituents of Iraq be brought together without returning to a Sunnized Baathist situation? Can a sufficiently stable situation be created within the next two years to expedite an influx of resources to be used to rebuild the Iraqi infrastructure and develop the economy? The escalating insurgency has enhanced separation within Iraq. The center—Baghdad and the Sunni areas—is cut off and unsafe. The Kurds, for obvious reasons, are staying in the North, and the same is largely true of the Shiites in the South. So, instead of normal exchanges through trade, education, and tourism that would bring people together and start to overcome differences, the insurgency perpetuates separation. The insurgency and increasing American casualties are also having a marked impact on American public opinion. It would appear, however, that for the next five years the U.S. will be deeply engaged in Iraq.

For many, the intervention into Iraq was going to solve the Arab-

Israeli conflict; create a beacon of light in the Middle East; establish a new order and a spring board for overthrowing Syria and Iran; secularize the Middle East; and introduce the delights of consumer capitalism. These ideas and ideals have disintegrated in the face of realities in Iraq. The bulk of the success there since the invasion should be attributed to the actions and ideas of Iraqis, especially the Shiite community.

Notes

1. Editors' note: The December 2005 elections did include some reforms and resulted in continued sectarian voting. However, we believe the point still stands.

CASE STUDY: SRI LANKA

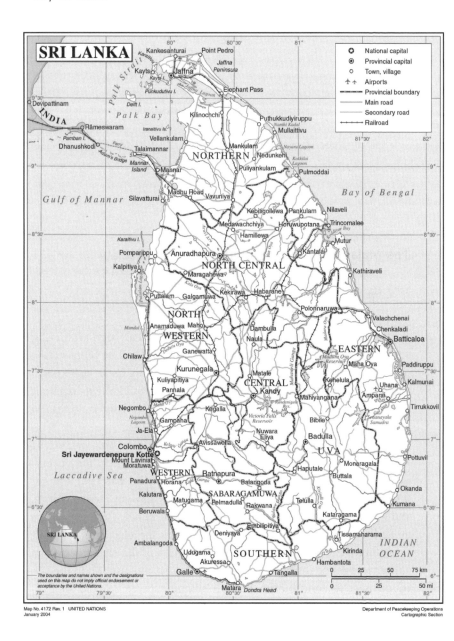

Sri Lanka Map No.4172 Revision 1, January 2004
Courtesy of United Nations Cartographic Section

The Malaise of Contemporary Sri Lankan Society

H. L. Seneviratne

Sri Lanka's ethnic conflict in its armed form has been around for some time, and it has been written about a great deal by scholars and other commentators. Rather than repeating what is quite well known about the history and sociology of the conflict, I would like to focus my comments more broadly and impressionistically on contemporary Sri Lankan society as a whole.

In my view the deep and pervasive source of the ethnic conflict, as well as the present deadlock in the negotiations between the government of Sri Lanka and the Tamil rebels, is part and parcel of a larger social and moral crisis going back to the early days of independence, and which has asserted itself with increasing force since the resurgence of Sinhala Buddhist nationalism signified by the electoral victory of these forces in 1956. The gradual politicization of the civil service that culminated in the introduction of a presidential constitution in the late 1970s made its contribution to this fundamental crisis. So did the free-market economy of the same period and under the same government.

The opening up of the country to free-market capitalism did have the effect of stimulating business enterprises to some degree, but on a much wider scale it also has led to an unleashing of the kind of economic activity that Max Weber described as piracy and adventure capitalism and the resulting social disruptions and discontents. These have contributed to an unprecedented collapse of the moral foundations of the social order.

British colonial imperialism has also played a role in the current crisis. On the positive side the British introduced conceptions and institutions of political civility and administrative rationality that kept ethnic, religious, and other primordial divisions in abeyance. During the first ten years after independence there were hopeful signs of a prosperous, peaceful secular state. However, the developments in Sri Lanka within the last half century have systematically demolished the edifice of values and rational institutions built during the period of British colonial rule. The departure of the British left open the logical possibility and promise of replacing the rational order derived from Western civilization with a rational order derived from Buddhist civilization. But that possibility and promise failed to become a reality. Instead, the grand parliamentary institutions, the rational bureaucracy bound by a code of professional ethics, the independent judiciary, and enlightened ideas regarding individual rights and the rule of law (all of which the British had in place when they left) were compromised one by one, leading to a state of social breakdown that we can rightly call anomie. This should not be construed as saying that everything was perfect during all of British rule. These enlightened ideas and structures were gradual introductions, and even during their heyday serious violations of the principles underlying them did take place. Nevertheless, it is hard to deny a qualitative change as these ideas and structures were diluted or abandoned altogether, eventually replacing more or less modern rational ideas and structures with those based on parochial, personalistic, patrimonial, and "feudal" ones.

It is this general breakdown of a more or less modern rational order that constitutes the broadest underlying factor in the continuing failure to achieve a resolution to the ethnic conflict. This social and moral crisis is well recognized and acknowledged. It is being talked about by many ordinary people as reflected in discussions and correspondence in the press and other popular media.

At the heart of this breakdown is a crisis in leadership and political culture. Sri Lanka is burdened with an entrenched and bankrupt leadership lacking in both the vision and the integrity to comprehend and articulate the need of the hour, which is to place the national interest above partisan interest.

Evidence of what I have just described as a general breakdown of social order is everywhere: in the high crime and suicide rates; in widespread corruption in high, middle and low places; in a bitter and antagonist political culture devoid of any accountability or ethical basis; in a judiciary President Kumaratunga herself described during her term in office as corrupt; and most dramatically in the frequency of highway death and injury caused by indiscipline on the highways. The ethnic conflict itself and the obstacles to its resolution are expressions of this underlying malaise. So is the unappeased nationalist extremism of both the Sinhalas and the Tamils. And the Muslims are in the process of crafting an extremism of their own, fueled by pan-Islamic religious fundamentalism and a local environment hospitable to it.

This crisis is also bringing about the eclipse of the one bright spot in the Sri Lankan sociopolitical scene, namely, the absence of religious conflict. The brewing religious confrontation is not between Tamil Hindus and Sinhala Buddhists. It is a movement marked by organized violence directed against Christian churches, led by certain Sinhala Buddhist elements against what are considered "unethical conversions."

This violence is not directed at the established churches but at the aggressive new evangelical groups, of whom a staggering figure of over 500 are active in Sri Lanka. While they have a right to proselytize, it should be said that their techniques and approaches are insensitive to say the least, and should be repugnant to conscientious Christians. This also puts certain segments of Sri Lankan society who believe in modernity, human rights, equality, and so forth in the difficult position of appearing to take sides with the Sinhala Buddhist right.

This new wave of attacks gives us insight into how economic factors underlie ethnic and religious conflict. These attacks and the attempt to bring about legislation to outlaw "unethical conversions" are directly related to the life and death of a popular Buddhist monk, Gangodavila Soma, who became the champion of an urban petite bourgeoisie riddled with anxieties about openly competing with other ethnic and religious groups in their economic activities. I contend that the sight of the vast emotional crowds, faithfully broadcast by television and other media for the ten days between the death and the cremation of this monk, led to the present state of religious tension, the dissolution of parliament by the president four years ahead of time, and the solidification of nationalist forces that led to the political alliance behind the present government, which is trying to enact anti-conversion legislation.

The nationalist extreme that coordinates the anti-conversion movement and the general assertion of Sinhala Buddhist hegemony consists of a number of groups. These are supported ideologically by what might be termed a conservative "think tank" and financially by middle-level traders, a petite bourgeoisie primarily located in Colombo and its suburbs. The nationalist extreme can be described as the political expression of the sense of insecurity of this petite bourgeoisie, arising from its competition with Tamils and Muslims engaged in the same businesses. This sense of insecurity is packaged and spread far and wide by a conservative, nationalist media complex, consisting of the national radio and television and some powerful news establishments. This takes the general form of depicting the Sinhala Buddhists as a beleaguered majority, constantly subject to conspiracies and attacks by imperialists, separatists, terrorists, and fundamentalists.

The worldview of the nationalist extremists includes:

1. A division of the universe into two spheres, "indigenous" (*deshiya*) and "foreign" (*videshiya*), surprisingly failing to see the miniscule nature of the former when compared to the latter, and asserting the superiority of the former over the latter in all respects, including power and success, contrary to common sense;

2. While defining itself in opposition to "foreign" in general, most of that opposition is expressed in the form of a fierce anti-Western sentiment and rhetoric, so that "foreign" in fact becomes a euphemism for "Western";

3. This anti-Western sentiment and rhetoric is extended to cover Christianity, in particular in its manifestation as the

agent of "unethical conversions," regarding which there is a confounding of the established Christian church with the aggressive new evangelical groups;

4. A romantic conception of an ideal society of the precolonial past, centered on the Buddhist temple, the irrigation reservoir, and the rice cultivation based on that system. This ideal society or utopia is imagined to be indigenous, but in fact, it is a trickle down from the romanticizations of British colonial writers reacting to the ravages of the industrial revolution in their own country;

5. Related to the above, a conception of an indigenous economy based on agriculture and the idea of self-sufficiency, which implies a rejection and condemnation of the principle of market economy and economic globalization;

6. A preoccupation with the idea of "unitary" (ekeeya) as the basis for the organization of the state, in which is embedded an emphatic denial of federalism and devolution of power to the minorities, which leaves militarism as the sole remedy to the violence-ridden ethnic conflict that has plagued the country for the last 21 years;

7. An insistence on the union of the state with Buddhism, along with the condemnation of secularism as a Western import.

If the conflict in Sri Lanka is part of a general malaise as I have argued, then its solution should be a remedy for that malaise, as a whole. A superficial and piecemeal solution will only treat the symptoms, not the disease. An overall and holistic approach would include the following considerations:

1. Sri Lanka, a comparatively rich country at the time of independence in 1948 when the indicators of the physical quality of life were impressive, has deteriorated socially, politically, and economically, and is on the brink of serious disruption;

2. This is the result of an unappeased nationalism that emerges every now and then, and which has been fed by irresponsible politicians in their ruthless pursuit of power, preventing the formation of a national consensus;

3. Such a consensus, which alone would lead to good gover-

nance and economic prosperity, should consist of:

a. ensuring the independence of the civil service, the judiciary, the electoral process, the media, and the police force;

b. a national economic policy that includes an immediate welfare package to ease the day-to-day burdens of the masses of the people as an interim measure, so that social unrest is minimized during the economic recovery;

c. a national education policy consistent with economic development, and designed to instill a civic sense and a cosmopolitan patriotism in the young;

d. effective legal safeguards of minority and individual rights;

e. commitment to the principle of secularism;

f. constitutional reform so that the well-known weaknesses of the present Constitution are remedied.

Without such a consensual understanding, the country will rapidly deteriorate further, ensuring the enthronement of the radical nationalist leftist youth party, the People's Liberation Front (known as the JVP), which is the most effective political expression of the nationalist project, with disastrous results to the nation. It will lead Sri Lanka away from its traditional democratic and free-market base, and contribute to regional destabilization.

It is therefore of the utmost urgency, in the interest of Sri Lanka's prosperity and happiness as well as regional stability, that the two major Sri Lankan national parties, the United National Party (UNP) and the Sri Lanka Freedom Party (SLFP), engage themselves in a creative dialogue and agree on the politically responsible course of joining hands in the pursuit of such a national consensus, which alone will avert the certain path of ruin on which the country treads today. It is within such a broad framework of social reconstruction alone that we can ensure religious and ethnic harmony and the rebuilding of a viable nation.

Religion and Nationalism in Recent Peace Initiatives in Sri Lanka

Rohan Edrisinha

As H. L. Seneviratne pointed out in his presentation, there is a crisis with respect to Sri Lanka's political culture and its institutions. Sri Lankans today have very little confidence in most of the democratic institutions in place in Sri Lanka. This is particularly tragic given the fact that Sri Lanka had a fairly vibrant and healthy constitutional democracy in the 1950s and 1960s. H. L. Seneviratne also referred to the apathy and cynicism that has developed in Sri Lanka, with respect to its political leadership. My remarks will focus on the issues of religion and nationalism in the context of the recent initiatives for peace during the period 2002 to 2004. As many of you know, there is a stalemate in the peace process at present. There have been no further talks between the government of Sri Lanka and the main separatist group, the Liberation Tigers of Tamil Eelam (LTTE), since 2003. In a sense, there is a stalemate of competing nationalisms.

I shall briefly describe the two competing nationalisms. On the one hand, you find a Sinhala nationalism, deeply intertwined with Buddhism, the religion of the majority in the country (hence references to Sri Lanka being a Sinhala Buddhist nation). There is, therefore, a feeling that people who are not Sinhala Buddhists (an ethnic and religious identity) somehow have a lesser claim to the island in terms of legitimacy. You also have a mind set of majority and minority. It is often said—and I heard it recently when I was in Sri Lanka—"It's all right for the minorities to have rights, so long as those rights do not infringe on the rights of the majority." Then, of course, you have a complicating factor: the Sinhala Buddhists are a majority with a minority complex. The peace process of 2002-2003 and the spread of evangelical Christian groups in recent years have contributed to the resurfacing of this complex. There is a feeling of vulnerability among Sinhala Buddhists, an apprehension that Sinhala is a minority language, used only in Sri Lanka, and that Theravada Buddhism in its pristine form is practiced only in the island of its homeland, Sri Lanka. Special measures are therefore necessary to protect and preserve both the Sinhala language and Theravada Buddhism. In contrast, the Tamil language and culture can be found in India, Malaysia, Singapore, and South Africa. Hinduism is the dominant religion in India. Furthermore, Sinhala Buddhism is a nationalism with a tremendous sense of grievance. Many Sinhala Buddhists feel that during the 443 years of colonial rule (first by the Portuguese, then the Dutch, and then the British) minorities were privileged and favored. There was, therefore, the need after independence in 1948 to redress the imbalances caused by that long period of colonial rule. The Sinhala Buddhist nationalism has a minority mentality that is, in part, a legacy of the colonial period.

On the other hand, the competing Tamil nationalism is less intertwined with religion. It is a more secular nationalism, with emphasis on language, on a geographically based homeland. It is a nationalism that has evolved over the years. Some Tamils would describe it as a type of defensive nationalism. It began by focusing on issues of political representation and language. It has evolved over the years to issues of discrimination and equality, and then to a struggle for autonomy and self-determination.

The challenge for the Sri Lankan peace process is then to try to evolve or work out a compromise to reconcile these two nationalisms within a united country. What are the options in constitutional/political terms? The Sinhala Buddhist nationalist position wants a unitary, centralized, majoritarian nation-state with constitutional and legal protection of the Sinhala language and Buddhist religion, while offering protection to the rights and freedoms of minorities. The Tamil nationalist position was articulated in 1985 in a set of principles, which are key to understanding what the Tamil political leadership, the LTTE, and democratic Tamil political parties are seeking. These are known as the Thimpu Principles of 1985. They were formulated at a conference held in Thimpu, Bhutan, which was hosted by the Indian government. The Thimpu Principles are:

1. The Tamil people constitute a nation.
2. The Tamil people have a traditional homeland.
3. The Tamil nation has the right to self-determination.
4. Complete equality in terms of citizenship, language, and religion.

The problem with these concepts—nation, traditional homeland, self-determination, and equality—is that they are vague, ambiguous, and have no clear legal definition in law.

Let me turn to the peace talks of 2002-2003. You may be aware that due primarily to the facilitation of the Norwegian government, six rounds of talks between the Government of Sri Lanka and the separatist LTTE took place during this period. They were and remain controversial. I would like to suggest that some significant progress was made during those rounds of talks. It started off with a Cessation of Hostilities Agreement in February 2002, which stopped the fighting between the Sri Lankan armed forces and the LTTE. It basically introduced a no-war situation. There was skepticism soon after the ceasefire agreement was signed, that it was an agreement of convenience entered into by the government and the LTTE, and that nothing would flow from it. But much to everyone's surprise, in September 2002, negotiations commenced.

Between September 2002 and March 2003, there were six rounds of talks that took place in various countries around the world. If you look at the starting positions of the two sides, you will see the government of Sri Lanka basically started off with the existing constitutional framework: a unitary majoritarian constitution, where the language and the religion of the majority were given privileged status. The

Constitution included some devolution arrangements introduced due to Indian pressure, not due to any commitment to devolution on the part of the Sri Lankan government that introduced the constitutional reforms in 1987. On the other side were the Tamil Tigers (the LTTE), committed to a separate state, but willing to subscribe to the Thimpu Principles, sufficiently ambiguous and vague to support either independence and a separate nation-state or something short of that.

In my view, the most significant development of the six rounds of talks was an agreement or an understanding that was reached in the Oslo meetings in December 2002. The Government of Sri Lanka and the LTTE agreed to explore a federal solution based on the principle of internal self-determination in areas of historic habitation of the Tamil people within a united Sri Lanka. They also resolved that a solution should be acceptable to all communities, which meant that the solution should be acceptable not only to the two major communities but also to the third largest community in Sri Lanka, the Muslim community. As the negotiations commenced, there was concern that the Sinhalas and the Tamils would come together, strike some sort of deal, and shortchange the Muslim community.

As you can imagine, federalists welcomed the Oslo compromise because this helped to clarify the position. Federalism is a dirty word in the politics of Sri Lanka, though perhaps less now than it was five years ago. There is a widespread belief, certainly within the majority community, that federalism is a steppingstone to secession. There are numerous reasons for this belief. One relates to language and terminology. In the Sinhala language, the words for united (*eksath*) and unitary (*ekeeya*) are often used interchangeably. This linguistic convention has contributed to the perception that if the country is to be united it has to be unitary. The fundamental fear is that federalism will lead to secession. When the LTTE and the government agreed to explore federalism within a united Sri Lanka, and when the adjective, "internal," was used to qualify self-determination, this was a significant breakthrough.

Unfortunately, the negotiations broke down in March 2003. From a cynical perspective, the talks broke down just when the parties were due to meet to discuss the roadmap to realizing the so-called Oslo Declaration of Internal Self-Determination. Furthermore, the LTTE began to distance itself from this agreement in several ways. First, they rejected the phrase, "Oslo Declaration," claiming it was not really a declaration but merely an understanding that was reached. Second, they emphasized the fact that they agreed to explore federalism, not that they had actually agreed to it.

This distancing on the part of the LTTE has given rise to speculation that there is division within the LTTE between the thin nationalists and the strong nationalists. The thin nationalists might be willing to contemplate some federal arrangement. That will need to be a Quebec-style, asymmetrical, federal arrangement if it is to encompass the principle of internal self-determination in the north and east of the country. It cannot be an orthodox, conventional federal arrangement. The strong nationalists, however, are still committed to a separate state or something very close to it. The strong nationalists have actually published some proposals in which they talk of a two-nation confederation, consisting of a Sinhala nation and a Tamil nation, each with their prime ministers, parliaments, judiciaries, and armed forces, coming together in a very loose confederal alliance, with the possibility of a referendum in each nation to decide whether the "marriage" should continue or not. This is an example of a strong nationalist option. Indeed, one of the LTTE's chief constitutional advisors, a distinguished academic from the University of Singapore, has written an article in which he has suggested that the Tamil community should push for a two-nation confederation, because two-nation confederations never work and after a while, it would inevitably collapse and lead to the creation of an independent Tamil nation-state. The article, unfortunately, is widely known in Sri Lanka and often cited by groups opposed to federalism.

Moving to more recent developments, the peace talks collapsed in March 2003. There were then frantic attempts to get the Government of Sri Lanka and the LTTE to resume negotiations. The LTTE decided to insist on the establishment of interim arrangements for the duration of the talks, which they said could last for years. This demand proved to be a sticking point. Constitutional parameters existed within which an interim arrangement could be formulated. The LTTE rejected these on the grounds that it had never accepted the legitimacy of the Constitution, which was drafted without the active participation of the

Tamil people. Constitutional obstacles were therefore not its problem, but that of the Sri Lankan government.

In October 2003, the LTTE published a set of proposals called, "Proposals for an Interim Self-Governing Authority, ISGA." These proposals were welcomed in certain quarters because it was the first time that the LTTE had proposed something concrete in a constitutional/legal form. Hitherto, the LTTE had confined itself to vague and emotive concepts, such as nationhood and self-determination. The LTTE invited a number of distinguished scholars from the Tamil diaspora from all over the world to a meeting in Dublin to help formulate the proposals.

Apart from the fact that the proposals could not be accommodated within Sri Lanka's existing constitutional framework, there were serious flaws in the proposals themselves. First, they went far beyond the Oslo Compromise. They were confederal in terms of their substance. Second, there were serious deficiencies in the ISGA proposals when viewed from a constitutionalist and federalist perspective. For example, federalism seeks to combine self-rule and shared rule. There was not one element of shared rule in the ISGA proposals. It was a maximalist document drafted by the strong nationalists or the confederalists within the LTTE's constitutional advisory team. Third, there was an irony in the proposals that resonates with some of the other situations that we are discussing at this seminar. The Tamil political leadership and the LTTE for years have campaigned against a unitarian, majoritarian constitution for Sri Lanka. But the LTTE proposals for the north and the east of the island, which it claims as the Tamil homeland, were absolutely unitarian and majoritarian in character. There were serious deficiencies with respect to the protection of the Muslim and Sinhala minorities. The proposals envisaged a highly centralized political structure. Traditional constitutional safeguards for the rule of law, an independent judiciary, and separation of powers were completely absent.

The issue of how one deals with the Muslims in the peace process raises important and difficult challenges. The Muslims constitute only about 8 percent of the population of Sri Lanka. But in the eastern part of Sri Lanka, which is part of the area claimed by the Tamils as their traditional homeland, they constitute between 30 and 35 percent of the population. Their concerns and fears are obviously very important. They need to be addressed if Sri Lanka moves toward an asymmetrical federalism, with imaginative constitutional mechanisms to protect the interests of the Muslims. There was reference in the introduction to this seminar to sub-state nationalism. The situation of Muslims of Tamil ethnicity in eastern Sri Lanka illustrates the need to focus also on sub-sub-state nationalism, sub-regional autonomy arrangements, and sub-regional minority rights protection, certainly in eastern Sri Lanka.

One feature of the LTTE's ISGA proposals was that they stated that the north and east would be secular. The LTTE has consistently stood for a secular state. Its nationalism is based on homeland and territory. However this proposal has been misunderstand by some Sinhala Buddhist nationalists. Let me relate a story to illustrate the complexity of the situation. There was a prominent People's Alliance (the ruling coalition) member of parliament, a lawyer, who appeared on television in early 2005. He stated that the Sinhala Buddhists constituted a majority in Sri Lanka and, for that reason, Buddhism was given the foremost place in the Constitution. He claimed that privileging Buddhism was eminently reasonable and understandable. He then referred to the proposal for a secular north and east in the LTTE's ISGA proposals. He questioned why the LTTE was reluctant to give Hinduism, the religion of a majority of the Tamils, a special status in its proposed homeland, a reasonable and logical demand in the view of the Sinhala MP. The MP then argued that the LTTE chose not to privilege Hinduism because of the support the LTTE received from the Christian church. One sees in this example how religion and nationalism become intertwined, and also the complexities involved in the Sri Lankan ethnic conflict.

I have sounded positive about the LTTE's commitment to a secular state. However, lest I be misunderstood, let me add some grave concerns, too. The LTTE is committed to a strong nationalism, not only in terms of what they have advocated, but also in terms of their actions. Their obsession with their "homeland" and self-determination is so great that they even argue that they are not interested in the Tamil people who live outside the homeland. As you know, there are a large number of Tamils who live in the south of the country, in Colombo. I was in

Jaffna, in the north, about a year back, and I spoke to a middle-level LTTE political leader. I asked him about the LTTE's position on Tamils who lived outside the north and east. He stated dispassionately that the LTTE was not interested in anything that happened outside the Tamil homeland. It was one of the most depressing encounters that I had in northern Sri Lanka. This sole focus on the creation of the Tamil homeland justifies almost anything. Tamils who undermine or weaken, even unintentionally, the struggle for national liberation are traitors. The LTTE and its supporters often justify child recruitment, the killing of political opponents, and other violations of human rights in the name of national liberation. Recently, some Tamil journalists close to the LTTE have started articulating the theory that collective rights are more important than individual rights as part of their justification for the killing of people who disagree with the LTTE.

Two recent disturbing trends in Sri Lanka deserve comment. Throughout the postindependence period and the ethnic conflict, Sri Lanka had a good record on religious tolerance and interreligious harmony. Unfortunately, due largely to the activities of American-sponsored Christian evangelical groups, tensions have emerged in the past couple of years which have resulted in violence and a campaign for legislation to prohibit so-called "unethical" religious conversion. It is interesting that the campaign for the legislation was led by Buddhist and Hindu organizations working together. (Most Buddhists are Sinhala; most Hindus are Tamil.) They worked together to prepare the first draft of this legislation, which was modeled on the controversial legislation that was introduced in the state of Tamil Nadu in India. This campaign for legislation raised a number of difficult issues. The older Christian churches—Roman Catholic, Anglican, and Protestant—have responded by acknowledging the existence of a problem, condemning conversion by coercion but opposing the anti-unethical conversion legislation. Human rights groups and religious groups challenged the legislation on the basis of incompatibility with the Constitution. The challenge was partially successful, but the sponsors of the bill seem determined to pursue the matter.

Another disturbing trend is that in the last couple of months, a group called the Patriotic National Movement, led by a junior partner in the ruling coalition, the People's Liberation Front (JVP), has launched a vicious campaign against nongovernmental organizations (NGOs) and other civil society groups. This group has called for the appointment of a select committee of Parliament to investigate whether NGOs have engaged in unpatriotic acts and undermined the sovereignty of the country. Their criticism of NGOs is as follows:

Most NGOs in Sri Lanka are funded by the West. They are, in fact, funded by Western governments. Therefore, they are not really NGOs. They are agents of foreign governments. These foreign governments are Western and they are Christian. These governments are using these NGOs to further the interests of Western colonialism. It is a type of neocolonialism.

This group has called upon all the patriotic forces to unite to fight against the growing influence of the NGOs. The movement has won the support of some famous sports and film personalities. NGOs at the forefront of the campaign for peace and a negotiated political solution to the ethnic conflict and their leaders have been singled out for attack. This development is very worrying. The campaign links ethnicity with religion and is based on a type of majoritarian nationalism and patriotism. An extract from one of the leaflets that was distributed at a meeting of the Patriotic National Movement that was held in Sri Lanka, in Colombo in early April reads as follows: NGOs "export various concepts to Sri Lanka, such as asking us to elevate the rights of minorities and place them above the rights of the Sri Lankan nation as a whole." This group suggests that the rights of minorities, the secular state, federalism, are all concepts that are promoted by the West to further its interests.

In conclusion, we have a situation of paralysis with regard to the peace process. Significant developments will probably not occur in Sri Lanka until after the presidential elections in 2006. There is a rise of strong nationalism within both the Sinhala and Tamil communities. The rise of strong nationalism among the Sinhalas may be due to insecurity on the part of the Sinhala majority about the peace talks and the military success of the LTTE. The increase of Christian evangelical groups has made the situation worse. There is, fortunately, also an increase in the number of moderates of all communities who acknowledge the need for fundamental changes in the constitutional architecture of the country. At present, however, prospects do not look very good for the peace process in Sri Lanka.

Summary of Sri Lanka Discussion

As with Iraq, it is important to be aware of the diversity and complexity of the situation in Sri Lanka. A conventional approach often views conflict resolution through the lens of two opposing sides: hence, in the case of Sri Lanka the conflict is often couched in terms of the government versus the LTTE. This view tends to simplify the situation on the ground—differences within the government and the LTTE, the ethnic and ideological complexity among the Sinhalas and Tamils—and largely ignores the interests of Muslims, Christians, and the tea estate or hill Tamils who are among the most marginalized of Sri Lanka's labor force. Comparatively, Iraq, like Sri Lanka, is much more complex and diverse than the broad designations of Sunnis, Shiites, and Kurds.

The peace process must certainly engage the LTTE. The reality is that the LTTE controls territory. However, human, civil, and minority rights cannot be ignored in trying to negotiate a peace settlement with complex, diverse populations. Several NGOs in Sri Lanka argue that these issues should be conditions of the process itself and not simply assumed that they will be worked out after a peace settlement is reached. After the Cessation of Hostilities Agreement in 1995, civil society groups issued a Memorandum of Understanding arguing that the next step should be to address issues of human rights.

Unfortunately, the memorandum was supported only by the Muslim representative. The LTTE did not want to touch it, and the Norwegians pressured the Sri Lankan government not to include the issue of human rights, raising a number of concerns.

Human rights represent both constitutional and judicial issues. Tamils believe that the Sri Lankan Supreme Court has failed to use even the very limited constitutional protection of minorities guaranteed in past and present constitutions. As well as greater protection in the Constitution and in Sri Lankan law, a new constitutional court arrangement is needed that is more representative and with members who are more sympathetic to the rights of minorities.

The political situation in Sri Lanka became increasingly bitter and fragmented after the 1956 election of S. W. R. D. Bandaranaike, who ran on a platform that privileged Buddhism and the Sinhala language. The outbreak of violence in 1983 inaugurated the beginning of bloody hostilities between the government and the LTTE that continued until a Norwegian-brokered peace agreement in 2002.

In recent months, however, the situation in Sri Lanka has become increasingly polarized, extreme, and nationalistic. The maximalists on the LTTE side advocate an independent Tamil homeland. They are being encouraged and supported by elements among the over 150,000 Tamils in diaspora, especially among the more recent asylum seekers who have a greater sympathy with the LTTE. A meeting of LTTE representatives and members of the Tamil diaspora in spring 2003 in Dublin supported a maximalist position. In Sri Lanka itself, the LTTE in the north and east see the Tamils in the south as not being true Tamils. They encourage Tamils in the south to sell their property and move to the Tamil "homeland" in the north. The Sinhala nationalists, on the other hand, see Colombo Tamils as participants in an integrated nation-state over against northern and eastern Tamils who are themselves now splintered. Splits also exist on the government side. President Kumaratunga has forged a coalition with the People's Liberation Front (JVP) that advocates an extremist position of Sinhala nationalism and Buddhist supremacy. The JVP has taken a strong stand against any devolution plan that would give the Tamils self-governing authority. As Rohan Edrisinha indicated, the Sinhala ultra nationalists can be seen as a majority with a minority complex. While Sinhalas constitute 70 percent of the island's population, globally they are vastly outnumbered by Tamils and, specifically within the South Asian context, the shadow of Tamil Nadu looms over the island. Furthermore, comparatively speaking, Tamil language and literature also have a greater international prominence.

The issue of religion and ethnicity in Sri Lanka is complex. Should religion be seen as a function of the political process, or do religious beliefs drive political strategies? Buddhism has figured prominently in the rhetoric of Sinhala nationalism and has been central to the construction of Sinhala identity. School textbooks, for example, depict Sri Lanka as a Buddhist country, reflecting an identification made in the mythologized legends of the founding of the island and more aggressively in the early stirrings of Sinhala nationalism in the late nineteenth and early twentieth centuries. In contrast to the Sinhala nationalists, the LTTE has not invoked Hinduism in their fight for a Tamil homeland. Land and language have figured more prominently in their rhetoric. Although over 80 percent of the Tamils in Sri Lanka are Hindu, Christians are an influential minority, and Christians of other ethnicities have often joined forces with the Tamils in Tamil-dominated territory.

Buddhist supremacy has also expressed itself in a recent upsurge of anti-Christian sentiment brought about in part by an increase in aggressive, evangelical missionary activity. A right-wing group, the Pure Sinhala National Heritage (JHU) established by the Sinhala Urumaya (SU), and an associated organization of Buddhist monks (Jathika Sangha Sammelanaya, or JSS) has engaged in an anti-Christian campaign and is advocating legislation that would outlaw "unethical conversions." They have also agitated for greater control over Western NGOs who command greater financial resources and who support pluralism and democracy. Older, established churches and secular human rights groups have opposed anticonversion legislation for fear that it will be used as an excuse to harass Christian churches. They have made an alternative proposal, an interreligious council consisting of leaders of all the religious traditions in Sri Lanka that would investigate allegations of unethical conduct by Christian missionaries.

The tumult of forces competing with each other in Sri Lanka bears some similarity to Iraq—internal ethnic and religious conflict, an influential diaspora, interference of international actors. In both cases there is the prospect of good or bad political and constitutional solutions. The process by which an agreement is reached is crucial to the substance of the solution. Any solution must be workable, should have consent, should affirm pluralism and democracy, and must protect minority and human rights. The best solution for Sri Lanka appears to be an asymmetrical federalism similar to Quebec, but it must be more than a two-unit federal system and may entail reducing the number of provinces in the country from nine to three or five. The JVP's insistence that the LTTE disarm before there can be any talk of federalism is unrealistic, in part, because of the history of the government going back on its promises.

CASE STUDY: SUDAN

Sudan Map No. 3707 Revision 7, May 2004
Courtesy of United Nations Cartographic Section

Sudan's 1998 Draft Constitution: Should It Be Required Reading for the Leaders of the New Iraq?[1]

Ann Elizabeth Mayer

Given the context in which Iraqi leaders are working to lay a sound foundation for a stable polity and a peaceful future, the answer to the rhetorical question in the title should be "yes." As they wrestle with the difficult tasks of addressing the relationship between religion and state, deciding on the terms of power and wealth sharing, defining policies on religious and ethnic diversity, and dealing with Kurdish demands for self-determination, Iraqi leaders must be cognizant of the calamities that befell Sudan after a hasty Islamization program was launched, calamities that subsequently provoked a dramatic rethinking of the premises of this program. This rethinking is embodied in the text of Sudan's 1998 Draft Constitution. In the wake of the escalating inter-communal violence in Iraq in 2006, lessons from Sudan should be taken seriously in Iraq.

As they work to unite Iraq under the rule of law, members of Iraq's Shiite-dominated government should review the previous Sudanese experience to grasp how closely their task resembles the one that faced Sudan in 1998 and to appreciate how fateful this moment could be. Informed by their study of the Sudanese record, they should grasp why they should not let ideological enthusiasms sway them with the result that they leave crucial problems unaddressed and allow other problems to fester to the point that civil war ignites.

Setting forth the foundational principles of the Iraqi and Sudanese states involves grappling with similar issues. Both Iraq and Sudan are fragile states that encompass diverse populations. Their governments must deal with problems that include state building in countries whose frontiers, set by colonial governments, do not correspond to natural ethnic or religious groupings or the logic of geography. Leaders in both Baghdad and Khartoum have to struggle with acutely disaffected minorities, who would either like to exit the country or to maximize their autonomy if they remain.

In response, leaders in both countries have tended to try to impose a single unifying ideology with the aim of countering centrifugal tendencies. However, in such societies resorting to any particular religion or ethnic nationalism as a central component of a national ideology will engender a backlash. Any government that does not take this dynamic into account will be prone to exacerbate the alienation of crucial groups and further destabilize states that are already wracked by intense inter-communal rivalries.

In the past, Arab nationalism has played a major political role in both Iraq and Sudan, despite the obvious problem that neither country possesses a uniform Arab identity—unlike Syria and Saudi Arabia, for example. Espousing Arab nationalism has proved divisive in both Iraq and Sudan and has offended crucial minorities. More recently, as the luster of Arab nationalism has become tarnished, Islamism has emerged as a potent political force in both countries. This trend, which started earlier in Sudan than in Iraq, has been one of the government deciding to embrace elements of Islamist ideology. However, government-endorsed Islams may be as problematic in Iraq and Sudan as Arab nationalism once was. Governmental Islams prove divisive, because there is no national consensus that supports the officially sanctioned versions of Islam. Moreover, within the context of ethnically diverse countries such as Sudan and Iraq, Islamism runs the risk of becoming a version of Arab nationalism dressed in Muslim garb.

Not only is Islamization divisive in countries like Iraq and Sudan, but also it is associated with a mentality that impedes the recognition that it is divisive. Adopting an Islamist ideology is problematic because by its very nature it sweeps critical problems under the rug. Like communism in the former USSR, Islamization is oblivious to the ethnic, cultural, linguistic, and ideological fractures that afflict polities like the ones in Iraq and Sudan. Since these categories do not exist in Islamic law, which assumes that everyone should convert to Islam and that all believers should be united in one religiously based community, Islamists imagine that under their utopian schemes these divisions will cease to be relevant. This attitude exacerbates the existing tendency among rulers to downplay the need to address minority grievances. For example, the Islamists' tendency to brush aside minority issues is one reason why the Berber minority in Algeria became so hostile to Islamist forces. The Islamists simply could not reckon with a central problem—the Berbers' distinctive ethnic and linguistic identity and their deep resentment of Arabization-Islamization projects. According to the Islamists' ideology, because Berbers were Muslims, they should not or could not have a separate Berber identity from the majority.

As the task of building a working state looms, Iraqi Shiites, victorious in the January 2005 elections that at last brought them to power, are in danger of falling into the trap of triumphalism—an excessive celebration of their victory at the expense of their former Sunni oppressors. Iraq's Shiites have seen their world turned upside down, from one where a vicious Sunni ruling clique was on top to a new world where at last Shiites hold the reins of power.

In this new situation, Shiite clerics wield great influence, and there are already hints that Shiite leaders may decide to resort to Shiite jurisprudence as a central plank in their plans for reconstructing Iraq as a way of memorializing the triumph of Shiism. Iraq's newly powerful Shiite leaders should be mindful of the grave perils of celebrating their ascendancy by emulating Iran's 1979 Constitution and accentuating the Shiite character of the new Iraqi constitution.

Iran's postrevolutionary constitution was written in an era of exuberant Shiite triumphalism after clerics succeeded in establishing their domination of the government. The Iranian constitution equates Shiism with Iranian nationalism, giving the nation a distinctly Shiite identity and enshrining Shiite jurisprudence as the basis of public institutions and laws. This has caused bitter disaffection on the part of Iran's large Sunni minority, whose members suffer from religiously based discrimination and persecutions. Iraq's Shiite leaders should resist following Iran's example and avoid measures that define the national identity in such sectarian terms. They should keep the door open by conciliating disaffected Iraqi Sunnis and suspicious Kurds, convincing them that they have a secure and respected place in the new Iraq.

Exalting Islamic jurisprudence (in this context, Shiite jurisprudence), as though by doing so they could bypass or overcome Iraq's intercommunal tensions, will set Iraq on precisely the wrong course. This will alarm the Sunni minority and lead them to fear that their interests are about to be trampled on, much in the same way as Saddam's regime formerly ran roughshod over the interests of the majority Shiite community. Sunnis would be anxious in any case after the overthrow of the Sunni ruling elite, but they will be doubly so given the example of neighboring Iran. The record of misrule by Iran's Shiite clerics and their active persecution of Sunnis give Sunnis in Iraq strong reason to fear Shiite domination and the ascendancy of a clerical elite insensitive to minority concerns.

Pressing a Shiite identity will also sound alarm bells for the Kurds, because it will indicate that Iraq's leaders will be inclined to downplay the significance of Kurdish nationalism, an essentially secular force. Consulting Islamic jurisprudence will not help Shiite leaders to appreciate the nature of Kurdish claims and the urgent need to address them. Instead, it will distract them from facing vital issues such as how to deal with Kurdish demands for autonomy and the Kurdish determination to benefit from a large share of the revenue derived from the oil concentrated in the Kurdish region.

If the new Iraqi leaders want to learn about the factors on which they should focus, they should study the provisions of Sudan's 1998 Draft Constitution, which embodies attempts to calm the desperate crisis that imprudent Islamization measures and indifference to the welfare of the South had previously engendered. This document shows that Sudan's leaders, although still wanting to carry out the

Islamization agenda that they had been pursuing since 1983 (with one brief democratic interlude), were obliged to back down from their earlier ambitions. Their program had foundered on the reality of the deep hostility and tensions that it engendered, igniting a protracted and devastating civil war and causing deep wounds that may take decades to heal.

The 1998 Draft Constitution embodies the compromises that the northern proponents of Islamization were obliged to offer at a time when they were feeling an urgent need to conciliate the South, which insisted on a political system respectful of diversity and on economic policies that allotted southerners a fair share of oil revenue as the price for agreeing to stay linked to the North—at least for an interim period.

The pattern of making concessions to conciliate the restive South has continued in the Sudan. As has been reported, in order to have the South agree to stop fighting, the 2005 Sudanese peace accords offered southerners the option of breaking free in six years, giving them the right to establish an independent state if they were dissatisfied. By making this bargain with the South, the North has now been compelled to contemplate the possible destruction of this fragile and artificial state. If the North had made timely accommodations of southern grievances, then southern hostility might never have reached such a near-fatal level.

Sudan's Islamization was supposed to serve—at least in the minds of certain backers—the ends of Sudanese nationalism. In this connection, I should mention a conversation that I had with the prominent Islamist, Hassan al-Turabi, in 1985 in Khartoum when Nimeiri was still in power. Turabi's views deserve consideration, since, although he has suffered frequent reverses, he has been lurking in the corridors of power since the 1980s and has greatly influenced Sudan's Islamist ideology. From surprisingly candid remarks during our conversation, I learned that Islamization was for him a means to an end: the goal of his religious ideology was to serve the cause of nation building.

According to Turabi, Sudan was in need of a dynamic ideology in order to move forward, and Islamization was the only resource with the potency to mobilize the Sudanese population. In other words, for him Sudanese Islamism would promote Sudan's development and success as a nation. Although he did not intentionally underline this aspect, from his various deprecatory references to "Africans" and "African culture" (bemoaned as obstacles to his project), I could tell that his philosophy comprised elements of Arab ethnic and linguistic chauvinism. The Islamization project was associated with a barely concealed racism and contempt for Sudan's African minority. As events showed, under Islamist rule this minority was to be subjected to forcible Arabization at the same time that its members were being pressured to convert to Islam. As is often the case, an ambitious nationalism turned out to be tied to a mentality that despised diversity and imagined that the nation could grow strong only by crushing diversity and adopting a common culture and religion.

The policies of Islamization-cum-Arabization combined with the North's selfish exploitation of the resources of the South for the benefit of the North provoked an explosion of counternationalism and revolt. Far from bringing the different communities together under one encompassing ideological umbrella, official Islamization exacerbated Sudan's fissiparous tendencies, making southerners more acutely conscious that they were not Arabs and not Muslims—and that unless they were willing to forfeit their identity, they had to fight the North. Increasingly, southerners decided that they would be better off by breaking away.

The North was slow to grasp that their Islamization policy was deepening fissures, dramatically weakening Sudan's cohesion and exacerbating southerners' hatred for the North. By the 1990s the more perceptive members of the leadership finally came to appreciate that they needed to send signals that they were ready to compromise.

Well before the 2005 peace accords, the 1998 Sudan Draft Constitution had shown that Sudan's rulers had had to come to terms with the reality that to avoid destroying the country, ethnic and religious differences had to be accommodated, at least on paper. Of course, in this connection, Sudan's international isolation also played a role in prompting the concessions tendered by the North.

Iraq's Shiite leaders may protest, asserting that any predictions that Iraq may be on the verge of recapitulating the history of Sudanese Islamization are unwarranted. After all, Shiites came to power through elections (even if the Sunnis complained about them), whereas Sudan's Islamists were able to win the power to implement their Islamization project only by forging coalitions with military dictators. However, the relatively more democratic basis for Shiite authority in Iraq does not alter the fact that constitutions and governments in both countries must try to resolve similar problems in the interests of keeping the countries from disintegrating.

Iraq shares important similarities with Sudan, ones that make the Sudanese experience relevant. If the lessons of the Sudanese experiment with pursuing an imprudent and ultimately counterproductive Islamization campaign are ignored, the new Iraqi constitution could turn out to be a factor aggravating an already explosive situation.

Some Iraqi Shiites seem disposed to exploit their newly dominant position to insist that the state should espouse the Shiite cause. In this they resemble the proponents of Islamic ideology in Sudan, who formerly labored under the delusion that their Islamic ideology could serve as a vehicle for nation building. Islamists in both Iraq and Sudan have often seemed oblivious to the fact that they must contend with opposing camps, including sizeable groups that favor either a minimal public role for Islam or a secular state. Islamists thereby overlook how misguided it is to rely on Islamization as the mortar for their political projects in societies riven by intercommunal antagonisms. In such a situation, Islamization will tend to fracture the polity rather than reinforce it.

Among the important principles in the 1998 draft are those outlined in Article 1,[2] which establishes that the Sudan is to be a multicultural and multireligious state. Constitutions in the Arab world normally stress an Arab identity and usually establish Islam as the state religion. Thus, it is noteworthy that this draft does not follow this pattern. Article 1 provides:

> 1. The State of Sudan is an embracing homeland wherein races and cultures coalesce and religions conciliate. Islam is the religion of the majority of the population. Christianity and customary creeds have considerable followers.

Thus, the state is deliberately redefined in an inclusive way.[3] Islamic culture is not treated as normative. Racial, religious, and cultural diversity is acknowledged. This amounts to an implicit repudiation of the formerly aggressive pursuit of a unitary Islamic identity.

Along related lines, the draft also indicates at various points, such as in Article 18, that Islamic law applies only to Muslims. Moreover, in stipulating the sources of law, Article 65 mentions both Islamic law and factors such as the "consensus of the nation" and "public opinion." In addition, Article 65 refers to custom, leaving space for respecting African traditions. That Islamic law is not stipulated as the sole source or even the main source of legislation constitutes a significant retreat from earlier attitudes.

In Article 27 the draft expressly accommodates pluralism and promises respect for diversity in cultures and religions. It also tacitly concedes that previously the North had sought to obliterate African culture and coerce conversions to Islam. This emerges from the promises that it makes to the effect that the Sudan will forebear from doing this in the future. Article 27 reads:

> 27. There shall be guaranteed for every community or group of citizens the right to preserve their particular culture, language or religion, and rear children freely within the framework of their particularity, and the same shall not by coercion be effaced.

The beginning of Article 24 makes similar points:

> 24. Every human being shall have the right of freedom of conscience and religious creed and he shall have the right to declare his religion or creed, and manifest the same by way of worship, education, practice or performance of rites or ceremonies; and no one shall be coerced to adopt such faith, as he does not believe in, nor to practice rites or services he does not voluntarily consent to...

Article 6 renounces both sectarian fanaticism and racism. It amounts to an indirect admission that southern complaints claiming that the Islamization program comprised racist elements were well grounded. Of course, the racist elements could not be blamed on

Islam, because Islamic law does not discriminate on the basis of race. The racism had been injected into Islamization as a result of Sudan's peculiar society and culture and the Arab chauvinism of the northern ruling elite. The article provides:

> 6. The country is united by the spirit of allegiance, in conciliation between all the people, and co-operation for the distribution of national power and wealth in justice and without grievance. The State and the society shall strive to entrench the spirit of conciliation and national unity between all the Sudanese for aversion of religious partisan, and sectarian fanaticism, and eradication of racism.

Article 16 declares that it is necessary to consider what serves the unity of the country in promoting morality. It thereby indirectly acknowledges the need to abandon dimensions of the Islamization project that included enforcing Islamic morality in a variety of spheres on Muslims and non-Muslims alike, heedless of the antagonism that this created. (Among other things, non-Muslim Africans had resented the ban on alcohol, as beer is an important element in their customary diets.) Article 16 states:

> 16. The State shall endeavour by law and directive policies to purge society from corruption, crime, delinquency, liquor among Muslims, and to promote the society as a whole towards good norms, noble customs and virtuous morals, and towards such as may encourage the individual to actively and effectively participate in the life of society and guide the same towards rallying those around him for good collective gain, solidarity and fraternity by the firm divine cord in a way that preserves unity of the country, stability of governance and progress towards civilized renaissance and higher ideals.

Moreover, like the previously cited Article 6, Articles 2, 8, and 11 all indirectly acknowledge that in the past the oil-rich South had been plundered for the economic benefit of the North. These articles do so by asserting that Sudan will in the future adhere to the principle of justice in the treatment of different regions and that revenues from natural resources will be equitably shared. The repetition of the point in these articles highlights how important the issue of equitable distribution of wealth among regions has become:

> 2. The Sudan is a federal republic, the supreme authority thereof is based on the federal system drawn by the Constitution as a national centre and States, and administered at the base by local government in accordance with the law, to ensure popular participation, consultation and mobilization, and to provide justice in the distribution of power and wealth...
>
> 8. The State shall promote the development of national economy and guide it by planning on the basis of work, production and free market, in a manner fending off monopoly, usury and fraud, and strive for national self-sufficiency for the achievement of affluence and bounty and endeavour towards justice among states and regions...
>
> 11. The State shall give due regard to social justice and mutual aid in order to build the basic components of the society, to provide the highest standard of good living for every citizen, and to distribute national income in a just manner to prevent serious disparity in incomes, civil strife, exploitation of the enfeebled and to care for the aged and disabled.

Significantly, the concessions in the 1998 draft were offered only reluctantly, made at a time when members of the ruling elite in the North still remained wedded to their Islamist agenda, even though practicality required sacrificing many of its features. Indeed, the draft offered numerous signs that, despite recognizing that they had to backtrack on the issues most crucial for conciliating the South, Islamists among the drafters had been unwilling to scuttle all aspects of their agenda. For example, references to *jihad* as a duty in Articles 7 and 35 reveal that the mentality of members of the northern ruling clique still was imbued with Islamist ideas. But, in the main, the language of the constitution showed that they had realized that to avoid losing the South, they had to promise to retreat. Specific Islamic references are minimal in comparison with the constant stress on Islamic values and law that characterizes Iran's 1979 Constitution.

Could the conciliatory attitude on these various crucial points amount to nothing more than a public relations move? This is a distinct possibility, particularly since after making the 2005 peace accords, members of the northern military elite did not show themselves to be dedicated to carrying them out in good faith. However, the possible and perhaps even probable insincerity of the northern leadership in putting forward the conciliatory ideas in the 1998 draft does not alter the fact that that draft recognized the unworkability of the previous policy on Islamization in Sudan and the vital need to conciliate the disaffected South. Members of the northern ruling elite may be antidemocratic in their basic philosophy and may have perpetrated a kind of misrule that has opened them to the severest criticism on many counts, but eventually they did have the capacity to grasp what had to be done to prevent the destruction of the country. That is, they took their painful political lessons seriously enough to offer a document that, despite their continued sympathies for the ideals of Islamization, essentially repudiated their own previous policies.

Conclusion

What should the Shiite leaders of Iraq derive from reading the 1998 Sudan Draft Constitution and pondering the context in which it was issued? Of course, the 1998 draft is far from offering an ideal model with provisions that deserve to be emulated in all aspects. Indeed, it includes a number of troubling and problematic features: in particular, the failure to include any endorsement of international human rights law. If ever there was a country that needed to guarantee to protect human rights according to international standards, it was Sudan. However, despite its manifest deficiencies, the 1998 draft did offer an object lesson for Iraqis who were prone to overlook the perils of indulging in factional triumphalism.

Iraqi leaders need to recognize how similar Iraq and Sudan are in crucial respects. After seeing the compromises that Sudan's military rulers have been forced to make, they should appreciate the vital need to pull back from any temptation to pursue an ambitious Islamization program, in this case, Islamization in Shiite style. In states like Iraq that are afflicted by deep intercommunal tensions, groups eager to pursue Islamization should shelve their plans lest they jeopardize national survival. Instead, they should direct their efforts towards addressing the real grievances of the communities that might seek to break away from the Iraqi polity.

Iraqi leaders need to start at the point that Sudanese Islamists had finally reached by 1998. By 2006, bitter antagonisms between the newly powerful Shiites and the Sunni and Kurdish communities, aggravated by pervasive incidents of violence and counterviolence, have brought the country to the verge of civil war, and talk of the country splitting into three separate entities is commonly heard. Devising a national compact that would appease disaffected minorities and pull the nation back from the brink of civil war has become a matter of the greatest urgency. Iraq still has a chance to avoid following the disastrous course that Sudan formerly took. It is to be hoped that Iraq's leaders have the wisdom to avoid repeating the mistakes that have made Sudan a land of death and destruction and left it a fractured polity that will be very hard to reconstruct as a united country.

Notes

1. Editors' note: Professor Mayer's presentation on April 23, 2005 focused on the relevance of Sudan's 1998 Draft Constitution for those drafting the Iraq Constitution. Iraqi voters ratified a constitution in the fall of 2005 which included both a reference to Islam as the official religion of the state and a guarantee of religious freedom in Article 2. (See the Washington Post website for an English translation of the Iraqi Constitution by the United Nations, courtesy of Associated Press, http://www.washingtonpost.com/ wp-dyn/content/article/2005/10/12/AR2005101201450.html). Much still remains to be resolved, both in the evolution of that constitution and its implementation, as well as how the rule of law will be maintained in Iraq. Thus, we still find Professor Mayer's argument very salient to the situation in Iraq. We have slightly updated some of the text in the paper to reflect the situation in 2006.

2. All quotes are from the text of the draft 1998 constitution, downloaded from the website of the Sudan Embassy to the U.S.:http://www.sudanembassy.org/ default.asp?page=documentsreports_constitution in April 2005. Editors' note: In May 2006, the site does not refer to it as a draft, nor provide a date. It may be replaced by a new constitution drafted pursuant to the 2005 peace accords. In July 2005 an Interim National Constitution was ratified. It declares that Sudan is a "democratic, decentralized multi-cultural, multi-ethnic, multi-religious, and multi-lingual State," according to the U.S. Department of State's Bureau of African Affairs, Sudan Background Notes, January 2006, available at http://www.state.gov/r/pa/ei/bgn/5424.htm. See

also the State Department's Human Rights Reports which are available yearly. The 2005 report states that *sharia* law still applies except for the 10 southern states. The report is available at http://www.state.gov/g/drl/rls/hrrpt/2005/61594.htm.

3. Editors' note: The Iraqi Constitution tries to have it both ways, relying on Islam as a base and allowing for religious freedom. For example see Article 2:

> First: Islam is the official religion of the State and it is a fundamental source of legislation:
>
> A. No law that contradicts the established provisions of Islam may be established.
>
> B. No law that contradicts the principles of democracy may be established.
>
> C. No law that contradicts the rights and basic freedoms stipulated in this constitution may be established.
>
> Second: This Constitution guarantees the Islamic identity of the majority of the Iraqi people and guarantees the full religious rights of all individuals to freedom of religious belief and practice such as Christians, Yazedis, and Mandi Sabeans.
>
> (The source for the text is the Washington Post website previously cited.)

Darfur, Sudan: Ethnicity, Islam, and Citizenship[1]

Alex de Waal

Introduction

The conflict in the Darfur region of Sudan arises in part from unresolved issues of ethnicity, religion, and citizenship. This paper locates Darfur within competing projects for political Islam in Sudan and the central Sahara, and the counterideology of political Africanism in both Chad and Sudan, as refracted through local political-ethnic dynamics.

At the center of the analysis is the Sudanese Islamists' strategy for western Sudan, originating in two decisions made about thirty years ago. One of these was an attempt to bridge the traditional Arab orientation of political Islam in the Nile Valley and the "African" Islam of Sahelian West Africa.[2] The second was the development of military and security organs within the Muslim Brothers. While the embrace of non-Arab Islam turned out to be superficial, the intrusion of security officers into the heart of the movement proved long lasting. The Islamists' exile in Libya in the early 1970s created links with the Saharan "Arab Gathering," adherents of the Qoreishi Arab supremacist ideology who in turn were utilizing militarized ethnicities in central Chad and northern Darfur for political mobilization, specifically the Baggara Salamat and the Abbala Rizeigat. Localized disputes over tribal authority in Darfur had left the Abbala Rizeigat as an unmanageable element in provincial administration and ready recruits to militarized tribal irrendentism. This is the origin of the Janjaweed. The ideology of political Africanism, manifest in Chad from the 1960s, was later nurtured by the Sudanese People's Liberation Army (SPLA) in Sudan, in its attempts to build a grand alliance of marginalized peoples. From southern Sudan, political Africanism spread to Darfur, completing the absorption of Darfur into a polarized framework of ideologically racialized ethnicity.

The convergence of all these factors subsequent to the fragmentation of the Sudanese Islamist movement in 1999 opened the way for the Sudan government to utilize the Janjaweed as its principal political-military client in Darfur, unleashing destruction on non-Arab Muslim communities across central and western Darfur.

Sudan at the Cusp of Two Islamisms

Sudan's Islamist movement came of age in the 1960s. It faced the challenge of building a constituency in competition with well-entrenched sectarian parties that had powerful claims on the loyalties of most of the Muslim population. In addition, most of the educated elite of that generation was increasingly secularized and scornful of the idea that Islam could provide a political program. Hassan al-Turabi, leader of the Muslim Brothers in Sudan, studied the precedent set by "al-Mahdi," (the Islamic messiah, leader of a revolt against colonial forces) in the 1880s. The Mahdi, rebuffed by the riverine communities from where he hailed, had moved to western Sudan and drew most of his following from the less politically sophisticated rural people of Kordofan and Darfur. Sudan's westerners offered several advantages to the Mahdi: they were numerous, devout, and many of them were influenced by itinerant preachers from west Africa who were spreading Mahdist doctrines.[3] While the Mahdi's primary goal was to conquer the Nile and the Fertile Crescent, he also engaged in active diplomacy with the Muslim states of the Sahel, and contemplated military and ideological campaigns along that axis, too.

The lesson that Turabi drew from this experience was that the

Muslim Brothers also needed a "western strategy." Turabi carefully investigated the possibilities of building a powerful Islamist constituency in western Sudan. This would, however, involve a significant shift in the cultural orientation of the Islamist movement.[4] Following in the footsteps of their Egyptian parent organization, the Sudanese Islamists closely aligned their political-religious project with the adoption of the civilizational values of the Arab world. Arabism and Islamism were closely linked.

This formula would have to be changed for western Sudan, where the majority of the population was non-Arab, and where the indigenous Arab Bedouins were mostly illiterate and racially indistinguishable from their non-Arab neighbors. The dominant form of Islam in the region was the Tijaniyya sect, which differs from the dominant Sufi sects along the Nile in two major respects. First, Tijani clerics (*fakis*) are mostly poor, running small Quranic schools, and exercising no political power. The sect's organization is highly decentralized.[5] The principal sect of the Nile and eastern Sudan, the Khatmiyya, is centralized, politically powerful, and wealthy.[6] Second, the Tijanis taught that an individual could achieve closeness to Allah without needing to be literate. Intuition, intense prayer, and adherence to the basic precepts of Islam were sufficient. Preachers from the Nile who insisted on Islamic orthodoxies and learning before an individual could be fully recognized as a true Muslim made only slow headway outside urban centers.

The Muslim Brothers had no intention of abandoning their learned elitism and their adapted orthodoxies. However, Turabi realized that the movement would need to be open to "African" manifestations of Islam and—equally importantly—to be color blind. The strategy was to provide a political home for the new class of educated Sudanese westerners who arrived in Khartoum as students. This group was unsympathetic to the sectarian parties but were intimidated and repelled by the decadence of urban life, and excluded by the racism of the secular elites.

The exemplar of both the capacity and the limitations of the western strategy was Daud Yahya Bolad. An ethnic Fur, Bolad became president of the Khartoum University Students Union (KUSU), the first KUSU president not from the riverine elite. He was elected on the

Islamic Trend ticket, promoting Islam as a route to emancipation for marginalized peoples. All previous KUSU presidents had left university and followed an accelerated track to national political prominence. But Bolad did not do so. The racism of the political establishment and his own lack of family connections worked against him. Thwarted, he turned towards regional political mobilization, and ended up two decades later joining the SPLA. As senior Islamists subsequently noted, the Islamist movement's acceptance of non-Arab Islamists was only tactical. The cultural change was less than skin-deep.

The Islamists also saw the western Sudanese as much as an opening to west Africa as a constituency in themselves. Subsequent analyses of the Islamist potential of the tribes of Darfur described the Fur and Masalit as "introverted," and the Fellata (Sudanese of west African origin[7]) as a more strategically useful group, given their links to Chad, Nigeria, and Niger.[8]

The western strategy took on greater significance after March 1970. In that month the recently installed leftist government of Jaafar Nimeiri attacked the Islamists, who had joined the Ansar (followers of the Mahdi) at the latter's stronghold of Abba Island on the Nile. After that bloody assault, both the Ansar and Muslim Brother leadership fled into exile, eventually finding their way to Libya, where they became partners in Colonel Gaddafi's schemes for spreading his somewhat heterodox forms of Islamism in Africa. The bases provided for the National Front, as the opposition alliance became known, were adjacent to Chad and Darfur, and developing a constituency in those regions became essential.[9] The Islamists' sojourn in Libya lasted only until 1976, when their invasion attempt failed and instead they sought to return to Sudan under Nimeiri's "National Reconciliation" initiative. But the alliances forged in the Libyan desert camps were significant. In 1972, Gaddafi created two separate but parallel organizations, the Islamic Legion and the Arab Gathering (see below).

The Security Strategy of the Islamic Movement

The founders of the Sudanese Islamic movement were determined not to repeat a critical error made by Hassan al-Banna, founder and

leader of the Egyptian Muslim Brothers. Although the Egyptian movement started as a civilian organization, it developed an armed wing, the
Special Branch. In the 1940s, armed Islamist cadres carried out assassinations targeting officials of the Egyptian government and its British
patron. This in turn brought down the wrath of the government and al-
Banna himself was killed. Thereafter the Special Branch hijacked the
Muslim Brotherhood itself, sidelining the remaining civilian leadership. Fought to a standstill, the new security leaders then sought peace
with their adversaries. Having studied this history, Turabi and his lieu-
tenants were determined to keep civilian control over the movement
and concentrate on building up a civilian base.

The Islamists also distrusted the armed forces. They disliked the
hard-drinking, womanizing ethos of the staff club with its undisguised
admiration for Gamal Abdel Nasser and other secularists, and were
suspicious of the bonds of loyalty formed among classmates graduat-
ing from the military academy. The tight-knit camaraderie of the officer corps, in which interpersonal loyalty surpassed principle, was
anathema to a movement founded on Islamic ideals.

The 1969 Nimeiri coup and its bloody aftermath at Abba Island
changed the calculus. The Islamists had frequently veered into violent
confrontation at Khartoum University, utilizing physical and moral
intimidation against their adversaries. Now, from exile in Libya, they
developed an armed wing and internal security services. At this stage in
their development, the Islamists were still a small minority of the
National Front opposition. The Ansar were much more numerous and
powerful. Nonetheless, the Muslim Brothers provided an intellectual
leadership and strategic capacity that surpassed their sectarian allies. In
the Libyan desert camps, the first Islamist security officers received
military training. Subsequently, after National Reconciliation, Turabi
began to insert Islamist cadres into the national army and police, as
well as trying to win an older generation of sectarian officers around to
sympathizing with the Muslim Brotherhood.

The Islamists' penetration of the army and security forces proved
its short-term salvation after the 1985 popular uprising. General Abdel
Rahman Suwar al-Dahab, who led the military takeover, was an
Islamist sympathizer who softened the backlash against Turabi and

other Islamists seen to be associated with Nimeiri's most egregious abuses. The old alliances with the Ansar and the Libyans proved a mechanism for mobilizing parallel forces, notably militia among the Baggara of Kordofan and Darfur, which could potentially be used as a counterweight to the army. The old relationship with Gaddafi helped ensure a supply of fuel and arms to Sudan. Meanwhile, the Islamist army cells held in reserve the possibility of an Islamist coup should they be shut out of power. In June 1989, Brigadier Omar Hassan al-Bashir (President and chief of the armed forces since that time) took power on behalf of his mentor, Hassan al-Turabi. The securitization strategy had brought the Islamists to power.

In that triumph lay the seeds of the Islamists' crisis. Bashir and the other army officers who formed the Revolutionary Command Council were loyal to the Islamist movement, but they were even more loyal to the army and to themselves. As they had garnered influence before the coup, a number of opportunist security officers had attached themselves to the Islamist group. After the coup, the number of old-time security operators in government grew, and a powerful group of officers consolidated at the very center of government. Outside Khartoum and especially in the war zones, military intelligence became the government itself. A range of specialist security agencies sprang up, several of them clandestine and off-budget. The Islamist movement was an uneasy coalition between this security wing and the old civilian leadership. Just as Turabi had feared in the 1960s, the security officers ended up by hijacking the movement itself, and at the end of the decade Turabi himself was the principal casualty.

The western strategy and the Islamist engagement with Africa became still more significant in 1990–91. In August 1990, Turabi made an immense strategic gamble when he backed Saddam Hussein in the Gulf War. This cost Sudan almost all its friends in the Arab world: it was blocked from all but Libya, Iraq, Palestine, and Yemen. The problem was compounded by Saddam's disastrous defeat. In response, the Sudan government turned its focus towards its African neighbors, where events were turning dramatically in its favor. In December 1990, Khartoum provided extensive military assistance to Idris Deby's grab for power in Chad. In January 1991, Siad Barre was removed from power in Somalia, creating a vacuum which the Islamists were able to exploit. A few months later they won the biggest prize of all, when the Eritrean and Tigrayan liberation fronts overthrew Mengistu Haile Mariam and installed new regimes, very friendly to Khartoum, on Sudan's eastern border. In just a few months, Africa seemed to offer a vast hinterland for Islamist influence, and the strategy of toppling governments by guerrilla insurrection seemed to be the way of the future.[10] Sudan's Islamic government learned the wrong lessons both from its humbling and from its vicarious victories, and it overreached domestically and internationally.

Unresolved Identities among the Darfurian and Chadian Arabs and the Origin of the Janjaweed

In the Libyan camps in the early 1970s, the Islamists' western strategy developed its military element alongside its political. Because of the alliance with the Ansar, which had its constituency overwhelmingly among the Arab Bedouin, and because the seminomadic groups (Arabs, Zaghawa, and Meidob) were the best fighters, the Islamists' military alliance pursued a parallel track to its political mobilization, which was still focused on the Fur and Fellata. As the fortunes of the security officers within the movement rose, so did the military power of their favored allies in Darfur.

The Bedouin Arabs of Darfur and Chad had their own agenda. They have a distinct genealogy from the riverine Arab tribes such as the Shaigiyya and Jaaliyyin. The Juhayna Arabs have been part of the ethnic and political landscape of Darfur and Chad for at least half a millennium, arriving across the Libyan desert at various times between the fourteenth and seventeenth centuries.[11] In the middle of the eighteenth century, the Fur Sultan provided extensive land grants (*hawakir*, sing.: *hakura*) to the four main Baggara (cattle herding) tribes, Rizeigat, Habbaniya, Beni Halba, and Taaisha along the southern frontiers of the Sultanate. No comparable grants were provided to their Abbala (camel herding) cousins in northern Darfur. The nature of camel herding precluded occupying a bounded territory, and the lands of northern Darfur had been closely administered for several centuries so there was no free land to allocate. Instead, the Abbala Arabs, who hailed from the same lineages as the Baggara, were incorporated under the multiethnic administrative systems already in place. Two hundred and fifty years later, many Abbala attribute their land hunger to the inequities of the Sultanate's land allocation system, and explain that their nonpossession of a *hakura* is why they are involved in the war while most of the Baggara are not.

The Fur state was bilingual between Arab and Fur[12] and provided political status to the indigenous Bedouin Arabs as well as to the Arabs from the Nile. Both these entities were Muslim "African" kingdoms for which "Arab" and "African" were complementary rather than polarizing identities.[13] This tradition survived in vestigial form into the colonial era, but was doomed by the state-building ideologies of Chad, Libya, and Sudan, which provided no space for such multiple identities.

In Sudan, the main contradiction was between North and South, giving rise to a continual and as-yet-unresolved national discourse on whether the country has an "Arab" or an "African" identity or is rather a bridge between the two.[14] Darfur was marginalized in this discourse, and never found an authentic political or intellectual voice in the debate over Sudanese national identity. Arabism has dominated in Sudan, modulated in the early 1970s by an inclusive secularist ideology and in the early 1990s by a flawed attempt to build an inclusive Islamism. Although the Arabism of the riverine elite is distinct from the Arabism of the Juhayna Bedouin, the fact that the two use the same identity label and speak the same language brought them into an alliance.

In Libya, "Arabism" was used in an expansive manner to refer to all people of Bedouin stock. Gaddafi's Islamic Legion included not only Sahelian Arabs but also Tuareg from Mali and Niger, various Chadian nomadic groups such as the Toubou and Goraan (until the latter turned against him), and the Zaghawa and Bedeyat of Darfur and northeast Chad. In parallel, Gaddafi also formed the Arab Gathering, an exclusively Arab grouping, which with characteristic ambiguity was both a parochial Chadian-Darfurian alliance but also possessed broader ambitions and included Syrians and others. As political mobilization in Chad and Darfur took an increasingly ethnic turn in the 1980s, the "Arab" identification of Libyan policies became more pronounced. At the end of the 1990s, Gaddafi abruptly reversed course, expressing his frustration at the ineffectiveness of Arab governments, and began placing his faith in African leaders instead. By that time, the damage had been done.

In Chad, political Africanism was dominant from 1960 until the late 1970s. The discourse of "authenticity," borrowing strongly from Zaire, antagonized the Muslim northerners, who turned to Khartoum, Cairo, and Tripoli for ideological solidarity and political and military assistance. The ethnic polarization of the Chadian Muslims occurred in a series of political twists throughout the 1980s and early 1990s in the context of the civil war.[15] In Darfur there was no such protracted conflict or polarizing state agenda. Rather, a set of problems specific to the Abbala Rizeigat tribes of northern Darfur led them to become an unmanageable factor in provincial politics, drawing them into alliance with their Chadian brethren. This has been almost wholly undocumented in the published literature, because of the nearly total absence of the Abbala Rizeigat and its leadership from secondary sources. For example they remain unmentioned in the otherwise detailed account of the Chadian wars by Burr and Collins[16] and are wholly absent from the deplorably superficial sketch of the Darfur conflict by Prunier.[17] The core problem of the Abbala Rizeigat is the absence of a unified tribal authority. This was not unique to them: under the Sultanate this was the common situation of several northern Darfurian Arab groups. But while the British colonial authorities succeeded in creating unitary authorities for others during the 1920s tribal reorganization that accompanied the establishment of the Native Administration system, this did not happen for the Rizeigat. Despite tribal conferences in 1925 and several times thereafter, the leading families of the Mahamid and Mahariya sections could not agree on a single candidate.[18] The rivalry intensified in the last years of British rule and the postcolonial period, with the Hilal Abdalla (Mahamid) and Adud Hasaballa (Mahariya) competing to attract followers to build a political base in order to lay claim to the chieftaincy.[19] Up to their deaths in 1990 and 1991 respectively, none succeeded, and the rivalry continues with their sons, Musa Hilal and Mohamedein Adud.

This rivalry had three major implications. The first was that with-

out a paramount chief, the Abbala Rizeigat could obtain no land jurisdiction (*hakura*). The British had created a *hakura* for other Arab tribes
in northern Darfur, and some Abbala Rizeigat claim that a vast area
north of Kutum was set aside for them, but never demarcated. With a
hakura, the government would have been able to construct reservoirs
and drill wells, thus providing the herders with their own migration
route and year-round pastures. A second consequence was that no single individual had authority over all sections and clans. Internal dis-
agreements resulted in one disaffected section simply moving else-
where. The dispersal of the Abbala Rizeigat clans, especially during
drought years, created many instances of strife which were difficult to
resolve because of the incomplete hierarchy of tribal administration.
But the third consequence was the most significant. In order to build
their respective constituencies, the rival sheikhs began encouraging
Chadian sections to join them in Darfur. Both Mahamid and Mahariya
are well represented in Chad, and these Chadian sections were by the
mid-1970s becoming well armed.

In 1973, when the Libyan government was looking for an interme-
diary to smuggle weapons to its client Salamat militia in Chad under
the command of Ahmat Acyl Aghbash, it was logical to look to the
Abbala Rizeigat. The Mahamid of Hilal Abdalla began transporting
weapons clandestinely along their migration route from the edge of the
Libyan desert to the Chadian border town of Foro Baranga, where they
had long been engaged in selling camels to the Salamat. Thus was born
the political-military alliance that became the Janjaweed. The struggle
in Chad spread conflict to western and northern Darfur in 1987–89.[20]

The Arab Gathering, the Janjaweed, and Qoreishi Ideology

The Salamat-Abbala alliance began as a marriage of convenience.
But it had wider repercussions. Ahmat Acyl was more than a militia
commander. He was also an officer in Gaddafi's Islamic Legion, and he
was an adherent of the Qoreishi ideology. For a long time regarded as
a marginal aberrant credo of little significance, Qoreishi beliefs have
been thrust to the fore as the organizing doctrine of the Arab Gathering
and its militia, the Janjaweed.

The Qoreishi ideology holds that lineal descendants of the prophet Muhammad are entitled to rule Muslim lands. In the context of the central Sahara, this means that the Juhayna Arabs, who trace Qoreishi ancestry, should govern the territories between the Nile and Lake Chad. According to the second Qoreishi manifesto, which is dated to approximately 1999, the Arabs of the river Nile are in fact "Arabized Nubians" and should not claim Arab descent. It is racism, pure and simple. Its lack of sophistication belies a power that derives from its convergence with the patrilineal kinship organizing principle of Arab Bedouin life.

The Qoreishi movement is shrouded in ambiguity. Some Darfurians report that its antecedents were apparent as early as the late 1960s when the Chadian Arab opposition began organizing. But its first notable intrusion into Darfur was observed in 1987, when a group of Darfur Arab politicians demanded recognition of Arab solidarity in the so-called "Arab letter" to Sadiq el Mahdi, Sudanese Prime Minister at the time. At one level, simply an attempt to build a united electoral constituency across the Arabs of the region, the Arab Gathering was the standard fare of competitive politics. At another level, it displayed an emerging agenda for regional domination. The following year, after the appointment of Tijani Sese Ateem, an ethnic Fur, as governor of Darfur, members of the Arab Gathering wrote a secret letter laying out their plans for destabilizing his government. Subsequent documents make it clear that the Qoreishi agenda includes controlling not only Darfur—seen as the heartland of the eastern Sahel as it is the source of the main watercourses—but also Kordofan, Chad, and the Central African Republic. An ideology of pastoral nomadism also emerges.

The Qoreishi agenda is power and domination. The aim is not to annihilate the non-Arab groups or to seize all their land, but to control the territory. Given the *hakura* system, this is best done by possession of the offices that control the granting of *hakura*.

The power of the Qoreishi belief system lies in the fact that it converges neatly with the lineage organization of the Arab Bedouins, underwriting their social order and tribal aristocracy, and justifying their claims to provincial power and land. It is a parochial vision but it also lays claim to solidarities across the Arab world, from Mauritania to Libya to Syria. The Arab Gathering has its international dimension, too.

Political Africanism and Darfur

The kingdom of Dar Fur was an "African" kingdom that embraced both Arabs and non-Arabs.[21] Run by a Fur aristocracy, it gave deference to Arabs and the Arab language because Islam was the religion. Arab holy men, scribes, and scholars were brought to court, and seen as different from the indigenous Arab Bedouins. It was an African state that incorporated two different kinds of Arabs as equals. Arab and African were not seen as polarized or even necessarily physically distinguishable. The Fur were politically crushed in 1916, stripped of state power and their landed estates, and their currency declared worthless. The inclusive Sudanese tradition of the Fur Sultanate was consigned to history; in Darfur inclusive Africanism was dead. Darfur was incorporated into Sudan on unfavorable cultural and political terms. In the last generation, just as an Arab supremacist ideology encroached upon the region from the north and west, an ideology of indigenous political Africanism also came to have an impact.

Political Africanism first showed its face in Chad. The Sudanese variant originated in southern Sudan but under John Garang (leader of the SPLA until his death in 2005) generated national ambitions. Unlike most southern Sudanese, Garang was always a convinced unionist, believing that southern Sudan was best served by demanding its fair share of power and wealth in Khartoum, rather than seeking separation. In riposte to the Islamist argument that because Sudan's population was majority Muslim, it should therefore be an Islamic state, Garang argued that because most were non-Arab Africans, the country should be ruled by that demographic majority. Garang's strategy for the North included incorporating members of the riverine elite (for example the former minister, Mansour Khalid) and building up constituencies among the marginalized. The strongest allies were the Nuba of southern Kordofan and the people of Blue Nile, substantial numbers of whom joined the SPLA. Garang also made openings to others including the Beja and Darfur. The SPLA's biggest success was its recruitment of Daud Bolad, but this card was squandered in a reckless military incursion into Darfur in December 1991. This ill-planned expedition sparked repression in Darfur, left a generation of radical leadership imprisoned or silenced, and sowed distrust between

Darfurian radicals and the SPLA. Failing to make inroads into the Fur and Zaghawa communities, the SPLA was however able to recruit among the Masalit, briefly and belatedly. Several hundred Masalit joined the SPLA's New Sudan Brigade in Eritrea in the late 1990s. Some of these fighters were relocated to southern Sudan in 2001, reportedly with the aim of making a second SPLA incursion into Darfur. That did not materialize and many made their way home, ultimately joining the Masalit wing of the Sudanese Liberation Army (SLA), the largest rebel group in Darfur.

The SPLA and the emergent Darfur resistance reconnected again only in January 2003, by which time the guerrillas based in Jebel Marra in Darfur were already staging attacks on police posts and army vehicles. Garang seized his chance, arguing that the name of the movement be changed from the Darfur Liberation Front to the Sudan Liberation Army. He assisted in writing their manifesto. When the SLA announced its existence the following month, the SPLA helped in giving it publicity. There can be little doubt that Garang saw the SLA as part of a grand alliance of Sudan's "African" peoples, one that might justify his longstanding belief in national unity, and might even propel him to the national presidency in due course.

The political discourse of "Africans" and "Arabs," adopted by the SPLA and then the government, and in due course by the leaders of both SLA and Janjaweed when dealing with international interlocutors, provided a convenient shorthand for the world to picture the unexpected crisis in Darfur. The lens of southern Sudan was readily at hand, as was the lens of Rwanda a year later when the massacres multiplied to reach genocidal proportions. Dealing with one another, Darfurians still negotiate their multiple identities. But the simplified and polarized labels are not only useful for soliciting international solidarity—with the Western world on the part of the SLA and with the Arab world on the side of government and Janjaweed—they also come to have a powerful purchase of their own in a situation of profound fear. And the labels "Muslim" and "Islamist" were losing their traction.

The Fragmentation of the Islamist Movement and the Darfur War

By the late 1990s, Sudan's Islamists were in deep trouble. The zenith of their overreach was marked in June 1995 when a terrorist cell affiliated with Sudan in Addis Ababa, Ethiopia, tried to assassinate Egyptian President Husni Mubarak as he attended the Organization of African Unity summit. As this news broke, Khartoum's ruling elites were plunged into turmoil, with bitter recriminations directed at the security officers who had backed the plan without the knowledge of others including the President. Conflicting agendas among the Islamists were thrown into sharp relief.

Meanwhile, the complaints of Egypt, Eritrea, Ethiopia, and Uganda that Sudan had been secretly destabilizing their countries, seeking to impose new Islamist governments, were dramatically vindicated. Three of those four neighbors had already begun military backing for the Sudanese opposition, and thereafter their efforts were substantially stepped up. The Sudanese civil war became an undeclared regional conflict with entire battalions of foreign troops operating on Sudanese territory.[22] Sudan's opening to Africa was over. Coordinated external military pressure brought the Khartoum government back to the negotiating table at the Inter-Governmental Authority on Development (IGAD) and forced it to make major concessions to win over southern armed groups, such as agreeing to the right of self-determination for southern Sudan. Meanwhile, pressure from Egypt, Saudi Arabia, and particularly the United States intensified, leading to the expulsion of Osama bin Laden and other actions to suppress militants in the country.

By the mid-1990s, the energetic ambitions for transforming Sudan into an Islamic state were foundering. Projects such as the *Daawa al-Shamla* (Comprehensive Call to God) had failed in their vanguard regions such as Blue Nile and southern Kordofan, and had only succeeded in sparking intensified local resistance. Western Darfur was in flames following a botched administrative reorganization. Even devout conservative rural Muslims in eastern Sudan were turning to armed resistance. A chorus of allegations of corruption and favoritism grew louder in Khartoum, focusing on how Islamic charities had abused their tax-free status and how the sons of the elite had evaded conscription or front-line service in the war. Some leading Islamists began to argue in public that the Islamist agenda had been too ambitious and too crudely implemented, and that the government had no option but a negotiated peace. Others, particularly from Darfur and Kordofan, began documenting the continued domination of the state apparatus by a small elite from the three riverine tribes, the Shaygiyya, Jaaliyyin, and Danagla. This led in due course to the release of the "Black Book" in June 2000, which stated openly for the first time what Sudanese had known for so long—that the ruling elite was drawn from this very narrow ethnic base and regarded state and country as its own personal property.

The Islamist movement was fragmenting. The most dramatic manifestation of this was the split between President Omar al-Bashir and his mentor, Hassan al-Turabi, which culminated in December 1999 in Bashir stripping Turabi of his position as speaker of parliament, declaring a state of emergency, and later placing Turabi under arrest. Most of Turabi's supporters left the government and ruling party at this time, but not all joined Turabi's opposition Popular Congress Party. Others left later. Although many commentators have attributed all opposition activism after 1999 to Turabi's cadres, in fact it is better to see the Islamist movement as fragmenting, with multiple new organizations springing up. Few of these organizations are formalized and many are informal networks, and all are in communication with each other. Each has a slightly different critique of where Sudan's Islamist experiment went wrong. Many blame the decision to develop an Islamist security organ. Those from Darfur criticize the movement's inability to move beyond its original riverine constituency and promote westerners to senior positions. Darfurian Islamists took the lead in establishing the Justice and Equality Movement (JEM) which announced itself two weeks after the SLA, and established a good working military alliance with the more numerous forces of the latter.

From the viewpoint of Darfur, the precise causes and dimensions of the fragmentation of the Islamist movement are of less import than its consequences. Most Darfurian Islamists abandoned the government and party, partly because the victors in the struggle—Bashir and Vice President Ali Osman Taha—relied increasingly on their own kin, and partly because one of the points of dissension had been whether state governors should be elected or appointed. Bashir favored presidential appointment. In 2000, Darfur was governed by presidential nominees whose major brief was regime security. The governor of North Darfur was a particularly significant appointment: the position went to air force general, Abdalla Safi el Nur, a friend of Bashir who is from the Ereigat, a lineage closely allied with the Abbala Rizeigat. Safi el Nur began putting Ereigat and Abbala Rizeigat men into key security positions including the Popular Defence Forces. Up to this point, the Janjaweed had operated with tacit government approval. Now they had a formal military alliance.

The remainder of the story is one of political miscalculation and military escalation, with the logic of military confrontation and political survival taking first place over any ideological projects. The manipulation and militarization of ethnicity has been a staple of Sudan's civil wars,[23] and Darfur in 2003 was merely one of the most extreme exemplars. As the conflict intensified, ethnic identity markers became, unsurprisingly, more salient. Speculation mounted about links between the JEM and Turabi, and whether the master manipulator had a strategy for taking power in Khartoum using JEM as his flanking forces. Given the distrust between the Darfurian Islamists and those, including Turabi, who hail from the center, and the overall disarray and fragmentation among the Islamists, the idea of a coordinated takeover in this way seems improbable. On the government side, the military alliance with the Janjaweed gave greater political muscle to the Arab Gathering, some of whose members were already serving in government positions. Politically, each needs the other for survival. On an ideological level, the two share a reflex Arabism, but their agendas are not identical.

Conclusion

Sudan as a whole and Darfur in particular are now in a "post-Islamist" phase which is dominated by the politics of survival and a regression to ethnicity and kinship-based mobilization. This is true in the caucuses of power in Khartoum, the lines of military command in Darfur, and the mobilization of resistance. Ideologies that are best adapted to this security imperative fare best, and the Qoreishi Arab supremacism, refracted through the lineage structure of Abbala Bedouin, is one of those. Political Africanism is proving its value as a means of mobilizing solidarity with the SPLA and, equally important-ly, the international advocates and relief agencies that have become such powerful agents in Sudan's crisis. The war in Darfur is fought over the ruins of Sudan's Islamist project.

President Bashir and his ministers have not described their count-er insurgency in Darfur as *jihad*, although some of their Janjaweed lieu-tenants, for example Musa Hilal, have done so. Theirs has been a war solely for power and control. And, with the utmost brutality, it has suc-ceeded. The offensives of late 2003 and 2004, spearheaded by the Janjaweed and the air force, killed tens of thousands and drove millions from their homes. The rebels were stopped in their tracks. By 2005, organized violence continued at a lower level, much of it removed to new areas of eastern and southern Darfur where the rebels tried to open new fronts. In these areas the government responded by recruit-ing new militia, generically labeled "Janjaweed." The phenomenon of government-sponsored militarized ethnicity was spreading to other areas.

An African Union force dispatched to Darfur in 2004 has been able, at best, to contain the violence, and not to halt it. All agree that a more robust international force is needed to protect civilians and espe-cially to enable them to return safely to their homes and rebuild their lives. The most important mechanism for restoring peace and stability in Darfur is a negotiated political agreement, involving not just the Sudan government and the armed movements, but also the numerous community-based militia that have not succumbed to official entreaties to go on the offensive against any groups suspected of supporting the insurgency. The "Darfur Peace Agreement" signed on May 5, 2006, is a beginning. The key next step is what is called the "Darfur-Darfur Dialogue and Consultation," a series of conferences to rebuild local trust and bring all Darfurians together to discuss their common future.

For most Darfurians, a brutalizing day-to-day reality is still miser-ably and terrifyingly dominant. On all sides, fear for basic survival is reshaping identity and allegiance. "Conflict reveals origins" is a

Darfurian proverb,[24] and the current war is compelling Darfurians to fall back upon reconstructed versions of primordial loyalties. The challenge of peacemaking is to enable Darfurians to re-examine their common heritage of an inclusive political order that once made it possible to be both African and Arab, and see if they can find a means to rebuild that.

Notes

1. Editors' note: The detailed, historical description of this paper will be particularly appreciated by knowledgeable students of Sudan. For those unfamiliar with the history, de Waal's comprehensive analysis demonstrates the intricate complexity, not only of Sudan, but of each country considered in this volume. Because each of these difficult situations involve a complex of tightly interwoven factors, significant local knowledge is required to understand them and to make effective recommendations.

2. Editors' note: the Sahel is the transition area between the Sahara Desert and the more fertile south, stretching east-west across all of Africa.

3. See Ahmed Mohammed Kani, *The Intellectual Origin of Islamic Jihad in Nigeria* (London: Al Hoda Press, 1988).

4. Abdelwahab El-Affendi, "Discovering the South: Sudanese Dilemmas for Islam in Africa," *African Affairs* 89 (1990): 371-89; and *Turabi's Revolution: Islam and Power in Sudan* (London: Grey Seal, 1991).

5. Awad Al-Sid Al-Karsani, "Beyond Sufism: The Case of Millennial Islam in the Sudan" in *Muslim Identity and Social Change in Sub-Saharan Africa*, ed. Louis Brenner (Bloomington: Indiana University Press, 1993); and Muhammed Mahmoud, "Sufism and Islamism in the Sudan," in *African Islam and Islam in Africa: Encounters Between Sufis and Islamists*, eds. David Westerlund and Eva Evers Rosander (London: C. Hurst & Co., 1997).

6. Ali Salih Karrar, *The Sufi Brotherhoods in the Sudan* (London: C. Hurst & Co., 1992).

7. C. Bawa Yamba, *Permanent Pilgrims: The Role of Pilgrimage in the Lives of West African Muslims in Sudan* (Washington D.C.: Smithsonian Press, 1995).

8. "The Islamic Movement and the Fur Tribe," unpublished ms, Khartoum, n.d. (in Arabic).

9. Millard Burr and Robert Collins, *Africa's Thirty Years' War: Chad-Libya-The Sudan, 1963–1993* (Boulder, Colo.: Westview Press, 1999).

10. See chapter 6 of Alex de Waal, *Islamism and Its Enemies in the Horn of Africa* (London: C. Hurst & Co., 2004).

11. H. A. MacMichael, *A History of the Arabs in the Sudan* (Cambridge: Cambridge University Press, 1922).

12. R. S. O'Fahey, *State and Society in Dar Fur* (London: C. Hurst & Co., 1980).

13. Alex de Waal, "Who are the Darfurians? Arab and African Identities, Violence and External Engagement," *African Affairs* 104 (2005): 181-205.

14. Abd al-Rahim Muddathir, "Arabism, Africanism and Self-Identification in the Sudan," in *Sudan in Africa*, ed. Y. F. Hasan (Khartoum: Khartoum University Press, 1971); Francis Deng, *War of Visions* (Washington D.C.: Brookings, 1994); and Deng A. Ruay, *The Politics of Two Sudans* (Uppsala: Nordiska Afrikainstitutet, 1994).

15. Sam Nolutshungu, *Limits of Anarchy: Intervention and State Formation in Chad* (Charlottesville: University Press of Virginia, 1996).

16. Burr and Collins, *Africa's Thirty Years' War*.

17. Gerard Prunier, *Darfur: The Ambiguous Genocide* (London: C. Hurst & Co., 2005).

18. Sudan National Archives, Khartoum, Civsec (1) 66-12-107, Rizeigat (1917–41).

19. Julie Flint and Alex de Waal, *Darfur: A Short History of a Long War* (London: Zed Books, 2005) chapter 3.

20. Sharif Harir, " 'Arab Belt' versus 'African Belt': Ethnic and Political Strife in Darfur and Cultural and Regional Factors," in *Sudan: Short Cut to Decay*, ed. Sharif Harir and Terje Tvedt (Uppsala: Nordiska Afrikainstitutet, 1997).

21. R. S. O'Fahey, *State and Society in Dar Fur*.

22. See chapter 6 of Alex de Waal, *Islamism and Its Enemies*.

23. Sharif Harir, "Militarization of Conflict, Displacement and the Legitimacy of the State: A Case from Dar Fur, Western Sudan," in *Conflicts in the Horn of Africa: Human and Ecological Consequences of Warfare*, ed. Terje Tvedt, (Uppsala: Uppsala University Research Programme on Environmental Policy and Society, 1993).

24. Musa Abdul-Jalil, "The Dynamics of Ethnic Identification in Northern Darfur, Sudan: A Situational Approach," in *The Sudan: Ethnicity and National Cohesion* (Bayreuth: Bayreuth African Studies Series, 1984).

Summary of Sudan Discussion

The Comprehensive Peace Agreement (CPA), signed in January 2005, brokering peace between the North and the South, can be seen as a continuation of the more liberal view of the 1998 Draft Constitution, but the more liberal elements were forced on the Sudan government in both instances. The Draft has to be seen in the specific context of 1998 when the Sudan government was under very serious military threat: not only was it fighting the Sudanese People's Liberation Army (SPLA), it was also fighting Ethiopia, Eritrea, and Uganda. The government urgently needed to stop fighting on the home front so that it could fight its external enemies. It, therefore, made concessions on several internal issues to different groups, including the right of self-determination for the South. The Sudan government soon regretted those concessions because the Eritreans and Ethiopians, who were on their way to capture Khartoum, withdrew their troops due to their own war. The Sudanese government then backed away from the concessions it had made. The negotiators convening the first discussions in Kenya that led to the CPA had a dossier of all the agreements signed by the two parties, not only with each other but with the different factions, including the 1998 constitution and the 1997 agreements. When the Khartoum negotiators rejected self-determination, the conveners invoked the precedents of those earlier agreements and made them part of the negotiation.

In Darfur, where the warring parties are all Muslims, religion is not the issue, but in the North and the South it is. As the wars continue, the religious issue has polarized people. Twenty years ago, the majority of southerners were followers of what the 1973 constitution called "noble spiritual beliefs," the theism of the indigenous people. Christianity has been growing since then, particularly evangelical Christianity in South Sudan.

In the North the civilization project of Turabi and the Muslim Brothers was about a particular vision of Islam tied to Arab ethnicity. Arabization and Islamization went hand in hand. In the North, as it is evolving under the new arrangements, the ethnoreligious connection will continue to be salient. There is also a strong backlash against the imposition of religion, whether Christianity or a particular Islam. When the SPLA opened its office in Khartoum, an impressive number of ordinary nonpolitical, northern Sudanese joined. Support for the SPLA is seen by some as support for traditional forms of indigenous peoples' worship in the mountains. But it is complex: the former leader of the SPLA in the mountains was Muslim, one of his wives is Christian.

It is important to note also that the Muslim Brotherhood has never had a monopoly on Islam in Sudan. Because the Sudanese state and its politics were never entirely secularized, there were other sectarian parties, the Umma Party and the Unionist Party, with irreproachable Islamic credentials. Because of their constituencies, their ambitions, and the coalitions they needed to form, the leaders of those parties have been ready to be creative with their interpretations, so Islam in Sudan has had more flexibility than much of the Arab world.

In Sudan, as in many other places, Islamism comes out of the universities. Khartoum University has had a strong liberal social science faculty forcing the Islamists to reflect more deeply. Because if the Islamists can not intimidate their fellow faculty (and despite many attempts they have not been successful), they have to deal with the discourse that comes out of the faculties of law, social anthropology, and other disciplines.

There is a difference between Islam and Islamists. The tradition of Islam can be used to legitimate a program or to criticize it. One example, not particularly linked to Sudan, is Islamic feminism. Anchored in Islam, Islamic feminism has an excellent technique for delegitimizing measures that oppress women. Islamic feminism looks at the "original" Islam: the Islamic community, the example of the Prophet, the text of the Quran. It uses these to argue against Islamic legal rulings against women. Its proponents return to what they claim (others would dispute this) is the true Islam, free of sexist bias. Islam provides enormous resources that can be used for many different and conflicting political acts.

There is both a North-South and an East-West dimension to Sudan. The focus has most often been on a North-South polarity, with an elite group in Khartoum identifying with Egypt and the Arab world, and the South identifying with East Africa. That obscures the East-West axis. Throughout the entire twentieth century, the Sudanese state balanced on this North-South polarity, with a stereotypical racial distinction which did not originally exist in western Sudan, where the ruling Furs had a kingdom that was both Arab and African.

In his book on Sudan, *War of Visions*, Francis Deng makes a point of what he calls a Northern inferiority complex with respect to race. He uses the term race, although the term as such is not found in Arabic. His contention is that the northern Sudanese feel inferior to the lighter skinned Syrians, Lebanese, and Egyptians. Feeling beleaguered and oppressed themselves, they take those feelings out on black Africans. In Khartoum, there has been a very clear racial consciousness, but expressed in different categories still related to skin color: green, blue, yellow. Intermarriage has been seen as offensive by some. The northern Sudanese, for example, have very offensive terms for the very dark people and the very light people. There is, however, a malleability to views of race in Sudan that there has not historically been in the United States. In Darfur, the Janjaweed and the Fur look alike. It is possible to switch groups. For example, if someone decides to walk cattle and become a nomad instead of farming, that person would become an Arab as well. The dichotomy of Arab versus African is extremely misleading of the social complexity of this differentiation. Moreover, if one of the Janjaweed were to settle in a Darfur-speaking village and their children ended up not knowing Arabic, they would be Fur.

This is not our Western concept of race. In thinking about the situation, it is important not to impose Western conceptions, particularly of race onto Sudan. The U.S. press talks about the Arabs in Sudan oppressing the African population. That can be heard in a particular way in Detroit, for example, because Detroit has Arabs and African-Americans. The American conception of what is going on is completely different from how the Sudanese think. However, external and elite discourses create a reality. In Darfur twenty years ago, no one would have used the word, African. Everyone was African—Arabs were African. Arab meant Bedouin, essentially. The designation would be used for all sorts of groups that actually did not speak Arabic. With the intrusion of the Qoreshi ideology, the Africanism of John Garang, and the way that this conflict has been constructed in Western discourse, these terms have taken on a reality of their own. It is no longer possible to describe the situation without referring to them. Race is ideologically constructed after interaction with many sources, but it has an impact in Sudan now.

The color blindness of the "western strategy" of the Islamists' early years was unfortunately fleeting, a project that did not work. Some of the Islamist leadership said race does not matter because we are all Muslims. They chose this stance partly for tactical reasons, but also because they believed it. The antidiscrimination measures needed did not come or came too late to become an institutionalized part of the political culture and political apparatus of the Islamist movement and government. When the movement split and the government reverted to type, the security cabal, which had risen partly from the securitization of the Islamic movement itself in the 1970s and partly because Sudan was at war and backed by generals, turned away from the antiracist stance. The long-ruling cabal is highly racist and from just a handful of families.

Will the peace negotiated through the Comprehensive Peace Agreement last? Does it contain the conflict? What happens over the next few years depends crucially on the political decisions that the Sudanese People's Liberation Movement (SPLM, the political arm of the SPLA) makes. Until very recently the most logical outcome was that the country would be one country, two systems, but that each of them would basically be an oil-based, quasi-despotic kleptocracy. The price of peace is that the SPLA/M of the South and the governing cabal of the North each get a big share of the pie. The plan has been that each of them would get complete immunity, and the democracy provisions would be watered down. That has been upset by the war in Darfur and by the International Criminal Court refusing immunity in that conflict. This suits the SPLA because it is not involved in Darfur. None of its commanders will be on any list generated by the International Criminal Court coming out of Darfur. However, some of the very senior government people will be.

The SPLM has two other options. It could return to the alliance Garang formed during most of the 1990s with the old sectarian parties (the Umma Party, for example). These parties probably still command the electoral majority. The SPLM could insist on elections going ahead in four years' time and become part of a grand alliance, which would be now North-South. The third option would be a grand alliance of the marginalized including Darfur, the East, the Blue Nile, and all the displaced, combined with many of those in the center. [Editors' note: The following discussion took place before the untimely death of Garang in July 2005. Whether that would have happened is impossible to know now.] The Bashir government is so unpopular that Garang stands quite a good chance, particularly since the demographic majority is not Arab in Sudan.

The SPLM's main constituency is the South. Most of the southerners are so distrustful of the North that they will vote for separation. Garang is a unionist, and he might be able to broker a unity vote for the South on the condition that he be made president.

The CPA provides for a countrywide presidential election in four years, but in such a way that if both the main parties to the agreement object, they can find reasons to get around it. The SPLM could decide to hold the line and insist that in four years there be parliamentary and presidential elections. Then racial identification might well be the main issue at stake in those elections.

There is a poignant turn of the politics of race and identity in Sudan. In the 1920s, when Sudanese nationalism began, its leader was a black Southern Dinka Muslim. When arrested, he refused to identify himself tribally. Under the British administration of that time, everybody had to have a tribal identity. They said they could not release him because there was no tribe into whose custody he could be released, so he spent the rest of his life in custody. All the Sudanese intellectuals and nationalists disagreed with the British policy, which divided Sudanese into major races and tribes. Now, with the failure of the secular nationalist project and the Islamic nationalist project, the irony is that most Sudanese are identifying with precisely those categories that the British invented 75 years ago.

This war has gone on for so many years and has many complicated issues. The peace of the CPA may work simply because so many people are exhausted by the war. Five years ago if asked to bet on whether there would be a comprehensive peace agreement between the North and the South in Sudan, most observers would have put the odds at 100 to 1. But extraordinary events can happen. The 2005 Dali exhibit reminds us of that in the context of Spain. In the center of the exhibit are his paintings from the period of the Spanish Civil War. These convey dramatically the polarization of Spanish society and the brutality of the conflict then. After Franco's triumph there was a long period of conservative Catholic rule, with indoctrination in the schools and repression. But now Spain has been transformed into a country that is multicultural and tolerant. A candidate for Basque separatism ran openly and was defeated. Early in 2005 gay marriage was legalized in Spain. In the 1930s, Spain was literally torn apart with terrible suppression. From the 1930s to 2005, the country has healed. Sometimes there is hope even in the gloomiest scenario. It is worth remembering Spain when we despair about Sudan.

CASE STUDY: BOSNIA AND HERZEGOVINA

Bosnia and Herzegovina Map No.3729 Revision 5, June 2004
Courtesy of United Nations Cartographic Section

Pilgrimage and "Ethnic Cleansing" in Herzegovina

Michael Sells[1]

This paper considers symbolic violence within the Herzegovina region of Bosnia and Herzegovina (hereafter B&H). The paper focuses on the marshalling of religious symbols as a way to create, define, deny, and eliminate a religious other. It concludes with comments on different approaches to resisting and overcoming the process of radicalization that occurred from 1992 to 1995 during the wars in B&H. Such use of religious symbols is not necessarily a function of religious observance or commitment; many militant religious nationalists had been lifelong communist secularists who became deeply effective at manipulating religious symbols. At some point the manipulator of the symbol becomes manipulated by the symbol. Those who start out using religious symbols instrumentally to gain power or other benefits end up becoming servants of those symbols psychologically. In many cases these former communist officials became very attached to their new religion:

- Socially, in the sense that they have now become leaders of communities that they helped form by splitting them out from other groups, with violent consequences to all sides. They are invested in keeping that conflict alive.

- Economically, in the sense that they have now become leaders of economic units dependent on religiously constructed ethnic cleansing.
- Legally, in the sense that they must now marshal all the symbols available to them to defend against the legal consequences of major war crimes, the most glaring of which is Srebrenica (a place where thousands of unarmed Boshniak[2] boys and men were separated from their families and led away for torture, execution, and burial in mass graves). These leaders use the institutions and leadership of religion to deny that the atrocities occurred, thereby preventing any recognition of the atrocities, a necessary precondition for true reconciliation.

The two major militant religious ideologies in B&H have been Orthodox Serb nationalism and Catholic Croat nationalism. Islamic militancy existed but it lacked the kind of theological structure that I am examining in this paper. I will use a few aspects of the symbolic dimension of the Serb religious ideology as a comparison to something very different that happened under the control of Croat militant nationalists.

This militant religious ideology did not generate itself. It took several years of instrumentalization by people like Franjo Tudjman in Croatia, Slobodan Milosevic in Serbia, and militants within B&H. These leaders instigated violence, used the media to create an atmosphere of fear, recalled past atrocities, and made blanket accusations about their imminent reoccurrence in order to generate the symbolic paradigms of conflict-identity. In some sense I am entering the narrative in mid-story, describing the paradigms at the high point of the violence.

Serb militants drew on an ideology of "Christoslavism" that reaches back to the nineteenth-century Serb revolutionary discourse against the Ottomans. That discourse portrays Slavs as Christian by nature and any conversion as a betrayal of the Slavic people and Slavic race. It further claims that Slavs who converted to Islam have "Turkified" and their descendants no longer belong in Europe, but have transmogrified racially or ethnically into Turks and belong in Turkey.

Serb Christoslavism centers upon the story of the death and martyrdom of Prince Lazar, the Serb prince who died fighting the Ottoman Turks at the battle of Kosovo in 1389 CE. During the nineteenth-century Serb struggle for independence from Ottoman rule, the battle of Kosovo came to be known as the "Serb Golgotha." Lazar was explicitly portrayed as a Christ figure in the art and literature, often surrounded by twelve knight disciples (one of whom gave the battle plans to the Turks), ministered by a Mary Magdalene figure. In the 1980s as Yugoslavia began to disintegrate, these figures were revived in a particularly virulent fashion, in connection with the momentous six hundredth anniversary of the death of Prince Lazar and the annual liturgical events associated with Lazar's commemoration day. (The day is officially known as Vidovdan, i.e., St. Vitus Day, but for a century and a half Lazar has replaced St. Vitus as the main focus of commemoration). The sesquicentennial passion play of 1989 drew over one million people to the battleground in Kosovo. Militant bishop-politicians and others took it over and used the passion play to affect a collapse of time. The audience—on site and around the Serb Orthodox world—were drawn through the power of the passion play into seeing themselves, not as spectators at a representation of a past event, but as living that event as original participants in the drama unfolding in an eternally present now. At the same time, media campaigns on television, radio, newspaper specials, historical novels, and publications of the Serb Orthodox worked to militarize the 1989 commemoration by portraying the Slavic Muslims of contemporary Yugoslavia as bearing on their hands the blood of Lazar and other medieval Serb martyrs.

World War II memories that had been repressed deliberately under the Tito regime resurfaced during this period and powerfully combined with the Lazar story. After Tito died, clergy and intellectuals organized ceremonial disinterments of Serb victims of the Ustasha (Croatian fascist) and Nazi genocide of World War II. Religious nationalists used these occasions to portray Croats, Albanians, and Slavic Muslims as peoples of collaborating with the Nazis and to exalt Serbs as heroic victims and resisters to fascism. The reality was more complicated: Serbia had its own Nazi-collaborationist government during the war, and the antifascist partisans came from all Yugoslavia's ethnic and religious groups, including large numbers of Slavic Muslims, Albanians, and

Croats. Serb nationalists also accused Croats, Albanians, and Slavic Muslims of being genocidal by nature, ready to resume attempts to destroy the Serb people, nation, and religion.

The bitter dispute over the Serbian province of Kosovo—known to many Serbs as the "Serb Jerusalem" for its magnificent medieval Serb monasteries—added a third element to the already combustible preparations for the 1989 Vidovdan commemoration. During the 1980s, tension between the majority ethnic Albanian population and the minority Serb population led to a flight of the minority Serbs from Kosovo, with a subsequent increase of the Albanian-to-Serb population ratio. Serb nationalists orchestrated a propaganda campaign accusing ethnic Albanians in Kosovo of organized annihilation of Serb monuments from the golden age of medieval Serbia, organized rapes of Serb women, and mass killings. (The propaganda was refuted decisively by Serb dissidents, but the refutations could not gain any kind of attention in a nation controlled by Yugoslav President Slobodan Milosevic and his allies.) A 1986 letter from the Serbian bishops charged that ethnic Albanians were carrying out genocide against Serbs in Kosovo. The genocide charge was taken up in the notorious 1987 memorandum of Serb intellectuals that signaled the beginning of the end of the nation of Yugoslavia. That same year, Milosevic capitalized on the fear of Serbs in Kosovo by ordering his agents to organize a riot there.[3] He then showed up, in a prestaged and highly effective televised intervention, to assure a frightened crowd of elderly Serbs that he would never allow "them" to attack Serbs again. The event helped launch Milosevic's rise to absolute power, the revocation of Kosovo's constitutionally granted autonomy, and the dissolution of Yugoslavia.

Various elements then flowed together at the 1989 Vidovdan commemoration. Primordial time (the Serb Golgotha), sacred place (the Serb Jerusalem), historical memory (the horrors of World War II), and contemporary fear (the alleged Albanian genocide against Serbs in Kosovo) merged to create a discourse of fear and anger more powerful than any of its parts. Through that period and after it, the Serb Orthodox Church has been united in supporting the religious national project. In 1992 the Holy Synod of the Serb Orthodox Church issued a unanimous statement saying that the camps in Bosnia allegedly run by

Bosnian Serbs never existed and never could have existed in the face of overwhelming evidence to the contrary. In 1994 three Serb bishops assisted at the spectacular wedding of Arkan, a self-confessed leader of an ethnic-cleansing militia, at which the groom dressed as a knight of Lazar and the bride appeared as the Maiden of Kosovo. At Vidovdan 1995, just a few weeks before the massacre of Srebrenica, the major Serb Orthodox bishops of the region appeared with accused genocide architects, Radovan Karadzic and Ratko Mladic.

The Catholic Church has presented a less uniform stand vis-à-vis the Bosnian tragedy. The Bishop of Sarajevo, Vinko Cardinal Puljic, resisted calls by Croatian nationalists for an all-Catholic territory to be carved out of B&H and annexed to Croatia, as did Bishop Komarica who was nominated for a Nobel Prize for his refusal in the face of persecution by Orthodox Serb militants to give up on the ideal of a pluralist nation in which religions could live together in peace. Many Franciscans, especially in Sarajevo, also worked throughout the war to resist religious militancy. On the other hand, Catholic leaders in the Mostar area of Herzegovina fully supported militant Catholic nationalism in the region. These leaders included the Bishop of Mostar, Ratko Peric, and local Franciscans associated with the nearby monastery complex called Siroki-Brijeg and the Medjugorje pilgrimage site. Medjugorje gained worldwide popularity during the 1980s which continues up to the present day. It is the largest Catholic pilgrimage site in the world.

According to an indictment from the International Criminal Tribunal, the "ethnic cleansing" that destroyed the non-Catholic communities in large parts of Herzegovina emerged from a criminal conspiracy organized by Tudjman, the president of Croatia; Gojko Susak, his defense minister, a rich Canadian émigré who helped mobilize the diaspora community to support the hard line position on Croatian nationalism in the Balkans; and Mate Boban, leader of the self-declared state of Herceg-Bosna in the Herzegovina area of what is now B&H. Croat nationalist militias in B&H, backed by the Croatian national army, sought to cleanse Herceg-Bosna of its Muslim and Orthodox Serb populations in preparation for eventual annexation to Croatia. Although the International Criminal Tribunal does not take account of the role of religious leaders and the role of religious symbols, they also played key roles in promoting ethnoreligious conflict. The first goal was to separate society into three religiously homogenous groups viewed as enemies. The second goal was the annihilation of designated others through killing, internment, and expulsion of the designated others followed by the annihilation of their religious and cultural heritage. In this case all Orthodox Serb churches and all mosques were targeted as well as all other aspects of religious life, including Sufi shrines, monasteries, art works, collections of folk art, collections of manuscripts, anything with Arabic writing, and copies of the Quran. This endeavor was systematic and scholarly: art historians, archeologists, and other members of the intellectual elite helped designate and find all the valuable private collections that were to be destroyed. Between them, Croat or Serb nationalists destroyed some 2,000 mosques and other Islamic sacred sites, many dating back to the fifteenth and sixteenth centuries.

In the Mostar region, after the destruction of religious heritage there came the destruction of common heritage. Common civic architecture that might be associated with the Ottomans or the Austrians was viewed as evidence of pollution, out of line with the ethnic religious homogeneity that was being sought. The Great Bridge of Mostar, the Clock Tower, and almost all the Ottoman structures around the country were systematically demolished. After that came the imposition of the conquerors' religious and national symbols. Throughout the area of Mostar, Holy Family crèches or large crosses were erected on the sites of destroyed mosques. Crosses were also placed on hilltops and on the roads entering ethnically cleansed villages. Crosses also adorned public buildings, schools, civic institutions, and city halls, both inside and outside, often along with images of the Blessed Virgin Mary and symbols of Croatia, (the checkerboard coat of arms or the actual Croatian flag).

Religious symbols were used not only to define and deny the religious other but also to homogenize the religious self. Croat Catholics who refused to participate in the militia were persecuted or marginalized. Croat Catholic identity was purified by the myth of stable Catholic identity over the centuries (as opposed to the historical reality of continual conversions back and forth throughout the history of B&H), by the construction and purification of a Croatian language (as opposed to the common language in the area that had been known as Serbo-Croatian), and by the destruction of evidence of Catholic Croat participation with Islam, Judaism, and Serb Orthodox in the construction of a common civilization.

Internal politics within a particular group is often crucial to understanding violent militancy. Catholic Croatian nationalism emerged in the late twentieth century around several concentric tensions. The Catholic Church's struggle against communism provided the first tension. That struggle took its most militant form in the declarations of Our Lady of Fatima in 1917 and in the early messages of Our Lady of Medjugorje (known also simply as Gospa, the Croatian word for lady), the apparition of the Virgin Mary who allegedly first spoke to a group of Croat schoolchildren in a small town near Mostar in 1981. A second conflict emerged as internecine warfare among Croat clan groups over the Medjugorje pilgrimage which constituted a lucrative tourist site in an otherwise impoverished area. By 1995 up to 20 million people from around the world visited Medjugorje; in 2006 pilgrimage packages can cost from $1,000 to $2,000, not including airfare.

The third conflict broke out between the Franciscans in the area of Mostar and the Bishop of Mostar over the control of parishes. The Franciscans came in the thirteenth century and therefore had claims to certain parishes. The bishop wanted to regain control of those parishes for his diocese. An early message attributed to the Virgin was the statement that the bishop was wrong in criticizing the Franciscans, enraging the bishop who denounced the entire Medjugorje phenomenon as a fraud and appealed to the Vatican to reject it. (The Vatican to this day has neither affirmed nor refuted the alleged apparitions, auditions, and other miracles attributed to the Gospa). Militias associated with the bishop battled those associated with the Franciscans. With the help of their militias, Franciscans and diocesan clergy seized one another's churches, took them over, and barricaded them. In 1994 a pro-Franciscan mob captured Bishop Ratko Peric of Mostar, took him to a Franciscan monastery, roughed him up, and stripped him of his pectoral cross, a symbol of his ecclesiastical authority.

The return of repressed traumas from World War II served as the axis for the fourth center of conflict. In 1982 the Serb Orthodox Church asked the Catholic bishops for a dialogue on the role of the Croatian Catholic Church during World War II. They wished to discuss the public silence of Bishop Aloysius Stepinac, the leader of the Croatian church during the genocide conducted under the Fascist government of Ante Pavelic by the Nazis and the Ustasha (Croatian fascists). The Serbian Orthodox Church also wanted to discuss Stepinac's prewar, vocal support for Pavelic's Catholic nationalism and the complicity of Catholic clerics, including the WWII Archbishop of Sarajevo, in the fascist movement and, in some cases, in the mass killings, concentration-camp brutalities, and forced conversion of Orthodox Serbs to Catholicism. The Croatian bishops, who viewed Stepinac as a courageous resister to the post-WWII communist government, rejected any discussion. As Franjo Tudjman converted from his lifelong stance of atheistic communism to Catholic nationalism in the 1980s and began to push for an independent Croatia, proposals to canonize Stepinac as a saint and to promote the pilgrimage site of Medjugorje took center stage within the resurgence of Croatian nationalism sentiment. In 1994 as war was raging through the Balkans, Pope John Paul II visited Croatia to support the process of canonization for Stepinac; in 1998 John Paul returned to Croatia to celebrate Stepinac's beatification. When Tudjman announced Croatia's independence in 1991, he chose the tenth anniversary of the alleged appearance of the Gospa as the country's independence day. Medjugorje was a stronghold for neo-Nazi militias and sentiment. The nearby Franciscan monastery of Siroki-Brijeg held three large portraits in its entryway: WWII Fascist leader, Ante Pavelic; Croatian President, Franjo Tudjman; and Tudjman's Defense Minister, Gojko Susak.

The final center of conflict was that between Catholicism and the non-Catholic communities in the region. From 1992 through 1995, Medjugorje and Mostar were staging points for Croat nationalist ethnic-cleansing operations. Much of the money pouring into the Medjugorje site found its way into the coffers of the militant militia groups. The Medjugorje Franciscans and the Diocese of Mostar rivaled each other as defenders of Catholicism, each proposing a version of absolute conflict, and each struggling to be the lead knights and defenders in that conflict. The violence perpetrated against the Serbs and Muslims emerged in part through that rivalry among subgroups of Catholics vying for strategic position.

In Medjugorje a place called Cross Hill (Krizevac) plays a major part in the pilgrimage. After the non-Catholic shrines were destroyed in the town of Stolac near Mostar (including a Serb Orthodox church, a nearby Orthodox monastery, and 11 mosques—four of them major historical monuments from the sixteenth and seventeenth centuries), supporters of the Bishop of Mostar and the Stolac diocesan parish priest took over the old pre-Roman fortress and erected 14 crosses along the pathway leading to the fortress. At its center, they placed another large stone cross in an effort to make their own Cross Hill/Krizevac. The largest cross was created from the stones of the national monument of the fortress in violation of Bosnian law and of the Dayton Peace Accords. Bishop Peric, who had made no objection to the destruction of non-Catholic heritage in Mostar during the war, became incensed at requests to remove the illegally placed crosses, crosses that turned the symbol of a religiously diverse Stolac into a Catholic devotional site. When an unknown vandal tipped over some of the crosses, the Diocese of Mostar issued a blistering condemnation of the act, citing the pain it caused, and condemning what Peric viewed as aggression against a sacred Catholic site. The statement's naming of the site as Krizevac was a clue to the intention of the Mostar diocese: to support groups that had ethnically cleansed the town; its vehement opposition to the reconstruction of the great Bazaar Mosque, the town's major monument destroyed in 1993 by the Catholic militia; and its boy-cotting of efforts at interreligious dialogue in the area. In reaction to financial, social, and religious power flowing to the bishop's bitter Franciscan rivals at Medjugorje and to their Krizevac, the bishop clearly wished a diocesan Krizevac of his own.

Religious buildings have served as a focal point for organizing eth-noreligious communities. Three large institutions have mobilized militancy in B&H. From the 1980s through today, Serbs around the world rallied to continue building St. Sava in Belgrade, a massive cathedral on the scale of St. Peter's in Rome. During the preparations for the sesquicentennial Vidovdan commemoration in 1989, the St. Sava project raised large amounts of money and mobilized the diaspora into a powerfully organized group, laying the groundwork for them to support the larger militant nationalist project both ideologically and financially.

Sts. Peter and Paul in Mostar is the priory church built by the enormously wealthy Franciscans of Medjugorje. The massive structure towered over the ruins of the town in 1995, out of scale with the surviving buildings and stylistically incompatible with the local traditions of architecture. Its campanile dominates every vista from the town and throughout the area, earning it the nickname, "the finger," from local residents.

Sarajevo's new King Fahd Mosque anchors the Dawa program of Saudi Salafism (or Wahhabism as it is known to critics) in the region. Saudi groups were also actively engaged in encouraging the destruction of whatever classic Islamic monuments remained after the destruction caused by Croat and Serb nationalists. The Saudis view these ancient mosques and monuments with suspicion as part of the Ottoman heritage, which grew out of contact with Europe and Christians and Jews, rather than with Arabs.

These hyperscale architectural visions contrast with the efforts of Bosnians and Herzegovinians to reconstruct their traditional structures, structures that reveal close civilizational intertwining among Jewish, Catholic, Muslim, and Orthodox Serb architecture and a consideration for the siting and scale of religious buildings in relation to one another.

In the summer of 2004, the keystone of the reconstructed Mostar Bridge was set in a ceremony attended by major local and international figures. That same summer saw the reconstruction of the ancient Zitomislici Orthodox monastery and the Stolac Bazaar Mosque. At the same time, the number of refugees returning to their prewar homes reversed in some part the ethnic cleansing and defied the hopes of local warlords and the skeptical expectations of many in the international community. Yet social reconstruction remains hauntingly slow and much of the Mostar area remains in a state of enforced religious segregation.

The International Forum Bosna has organized an attempt by Bosnians of all religious backgrounds and nonreligious Bosnians and

Herzegovinians to begin reconstructing Catholic, Orthodox, and Islamic monuments. The goal of the project is not to have specific communities reconstruct their "specific religious centers" but as Bosnians to reconstruct together their common heritage. Through that process they resist the effort to annihilate the cultural memory of B&H, enlisting people of all different groups in the common project to reconstruct a pluralist past.

Others have been encouraging diasporic interactions with the homeland by finding international Bosnian refugees before they are too alienated from their homeland both culturally and linguistically. Constructive diasporic involvement may be the key to the success of a religiously diverse B&H, just as diasporic radicalism helped promote the effort to destroy it in the period from 1986 to 1995.

Medjugorje pilgrims could play a role in creating a positive future for the region. Many of the pilgrims from wealthy Western countries have expressed idealistic sentiments. They make deeply moving statements about the peace they have experienced there. They refer to the feeling of hearing the Ave Maria and Alleluia sung in different languages, the hush of humans and even birds when the Virgin appears, the gentle and humble smiles of the devotees, the rapturous countenance of the visionaries, and the maternal compassion of the Blessed Virgin.[4] These pilgrims are shielded from the evidence of destruction and war by the Franciscans who give them the tours.

Criticism of Medjugorje has concentrated on challenges to the validity of the Virgin's appearances. There is no doubt that pilgrims experience something that for them is profound, even life changing. If Medjugorje pilgrims were exposed to the story of the conflict, could such knowledge galvanize their energy and experiences of peace at the site in a way that connects their ideals to the realities of the Herzegovina area? Or does the pilgrimage itself engender a desire by the pilgrims to screen out the brutal reality around them? Medjugorje confronts us with a paradox concerning religious experience; apparently genuine and deeply felt expressions of love for humankind and desire for peace occur as one side of an experiential coin, the other side of which is militant religious exclusivism.

The structural flaws in the Dayton Peace Agreement are widely known.[5] Much of the progress that has been made has been by consular fiat from the UN and European Union High Representative there from 2002 to 2006, Paddy Ashdown. However, despite frustration with those flaws, much has improved in the last decade. In 1994 most people would have considered it very optimistic to believe that there would be a country such as B&H in 2005 or that refugees would be returning at a dramatic rate.

For Ivan Lovrenovic, "Bosnia" is not simply the sum of its various cultures nor should it become a monolithic nation that would subsume and drown out its cultures. Rather, the name Bosnia should designate a process of civilization that has existed for centuries and is "practiced in everyday life with equal vitality by all." In this process of interaction, he continues, "national cultures participate as variables, retaining their special identities and exposing themselves to continuously culture-creating relations of giving and receiving."[6] This paper has focused on the use of religious symbols to create monolithic, eternally warring identities. The bad news is how powerful such symbols can be in such a project. The good news, which would need a full treatment on its own, lies in the nonviolent work of those who, despite the violence unleashed upon them, refuse the essentializing and totalizing programs of ethnoreligious exclusivism in the region.

Notes

1. Editors' note: This paper was created from a transcript of Professor Sells's talk on April 23, 2005.
2. Editors' note: Boshniak is used here to describe someone from Bosnia of Muslim heritage. See also note 5 of Mojzes's paper in this volume.
3. See the interview with Miroslav Solevic who helped stage the incident and who speaks about his role in it with pride in the video, *Yugoslavia: Death of a Nation Part 3* BBC/Discovery, 1995. See also Laura Silber and Allan Little, *Yugoslavia: Death of a Nation* (New York: TV Books, 1995), 37-38.
4. I have paraphrased here the eloquent statement of Elleta Nolte, "Medjugorje in Reflection," from her personal website on Medjugorje, http://www.ourmedjugorje.com/Medjugorje%20in%20reflection.htm {accessed August 19, 2006}.
5. Editors' note: see the Appendix on Bosnia and Herzegovina for discussion of these flaws.
6. Both quotations in this paragraph are from Ivan Lovrenovic, *Bosnia: a Cultural History* (New York: New York University Press, 2001), 228.

Is Religion Disengaging Itself from Ethnic Conflict in Bosnia and Herzegovina?

Paul Mojzes

The question raised by David Little in the preconference paper as to whether Iraq and Bosnia as part of the former Yugoslavia may share some parallels in having experienced a similar colonial existence (Iraq as a British colony and Bosnia/Yugoslavia as one of the former Soviet Union) needs to be answered in the negative. The parallels are too insignificant to matter. For only about three years was Yugoslavia directly in the Soviet camp after which it became a nonaligned country, although generally anti-Soviet in its behavior. The fact that it remained a communist/socialist country should not be viewed in colonial terms, even though some nationalists currently aim to characterize its history in this way. It should be pointed out that of all Eastern European social- ist countries, Yugoslavia's communism was highly indigenized, theo- retically and practically independent of the Soviet model, and broadly accepted by its population. The implosion of communism in Yugoslavia needs to be explained by different paradigms other than that of liberation from colonialism. If anything, what transpired in Yugoslavia in the 1980s and 1990s had more to do with the colonial experiences under the Ottomans and the Hapsburgs than under communism. That analysis exceeds the parameters of this paper. I will proceed to deal with the question of how postwar religious issues relate to the nationalisms of Bosnia and Herzegovina.

Pope John Paul II called Sarajevo "the European Jerusalem" during his visit to the war-ravaged city in April of 1997.[1] Undoubtedly he meant it as a compliment, yet the analogy has a disturbing side because we know how turbulent the history of Jerusalem has been. The late pope was aware of the difficulties when he warned that "the process of renewal of interethnic coexistence in Bosnia will be long and difficulties will persist."[2]

Most informed people are aware that the question as to whether the wars of the 1990s in the former Yugoslavia were wars of religion has received different answers. Leaders of all three major religious communities—Orthodox Christian, Catholic, Muslim—have given emphatic negatives. Some people who tend to see religion as the major cause of wars and mayhem worldwide conclude that this was also the case in Bosnia and Herzegovina (hereafter referred to as B&H). A third category of people claimed that other groups waged a religious war but their own group did not. Thomas Bremer, a thoughtful and perceptive German Catholic theologian and close observer of diplomatic developments in the former Yugoslavia, concluded in 2003 that, even when taking into consideration the turbulent historical legacy that complicated the ability of a free response by the religious communities in B&H, they did not do as much for peace and reconciliation as they could and should have done.[3] When I looked at these issues during the 1990s in *The Yugoslavian Inferno: Ethnoreligious Warfare in the Balkans* as well as in "The Camouflaged Role of Religion in the War in B&H," my answer was that, indeed, religion played a significant, although not a determining role, in the outbreak and conduct of the war.[4] I have seen no evidence to dissuade me from that assessment.

I continue to view B&H's religion to be of the traditional, collectivist, folkish, customary type. Under the influence of communist atheization, religion became increasingly implicit while most of the republic's citizens considered themselves simply as Bosnians or Boshniaks,[5] thereby diminishing the visibility of their ethnic and religious identification. In the period between World War II and the war of

1992–1995 in terms of explicit religious activity, the Croat Catholics seem most active, followed by the Boshniak Muslims (who were in the process of their ethnic formation as a nation and thereby accentuated their Muslim identity especially in the 1970s and 1980s), and finally by the Serb Orthodox whose religiosity seemed minimal.

Tito's policies, including *bratstvo-jedinstvo* (brotherhood and unity), failed. This became particularly apparent after his death in 1980. The winds of democratization played a disintegrating role in Yugoslavia and led to policies of ethnification and religionization of the population. Those who had considered ethnicity and religiosity to be a marginalized phenomenon were surprised by the rapid return of ethnic politics, fanned by politicians who feverishly created political parties that almost invariably identified themselves ethnoreligiously. The clergy maintained that because they, more than anyone else, had been the guardians of the identity of their people over the centuries (especially since the nineteenth century), they deserved again to assist their people to find themselves after the atheist/socialist hiatus. I have deep suspicions about the efficacy and genuineness of the transition from a one-party system to democracy. It seems to me that the proverbial jump from the frying pan into the fire took place in Yugoslavia. Most people reading this paper are aware of the course of events in the former Yugoslavia in the 1990s; many may disagree with my apportioning of responsibility. I do not regard the Serbs or even Milosevic as the sole culprits for the genocidal warfare that took place in Croatia and B&H (and later in Kosovo). In early April 2005 I visited the city of Vukovar in Croatia, fourteen years after its near destruction. I can testify that it suffered a horrendous devastation for which neither the official Croat nor Serb interpretation provides an adequate answer.

But leaving details aside, one should stress that *fear*, fear of each other (different from the earlier fear of Tito's secret service), became the dynamo that drove people to seek refuge with those allegedly most similar to them. Those that did not have a clear ethnic identity soon came to embrace one, if for no other reason than that it was forced upon them, sometimes artificially. For instance, a young Christian woman, Svjetlana Subotic, quickly disguised herself by using the name, "Senada," whenever she found herself in a predominantly

Muslim area. In this atmosphere, Faruk became Franjo or Savo in a Christian area. Another instance was that of an atheist Serb confront-ed by a drunk Serb *chetnik*[6] who insisted that the man prove himself to be a real Serb by reciting the Serbian version of the Lord's Prayer or else he would be killed. Since he was an atheist, he did not know any version of the Lord's Prayer and nearly lost his life. While these are not the most gruesome stories from those wars, I use them to illustrate how fear homogenizes people. There being no leaders such as Vaclav Havel or Lech Walesa but rather ones like Franjo Tudjman, Slobodan Milosevic, and Alija Izetbegovic (not to mention the more bloodthirsty executioners at these politicians' bidding), such fear was manipulated and encouraged not only by politicians but also by the religious leaders at all levels.[7] The flight to the religious communities began: people were baptized and circumcised. They learned prayers, genuflected, kissed icons, prostrated themselves, changed their diets, lit candles, and so on. Religion was IN; Marxism was OUT. Some clergy explicitly promoted intolerance and even hatred; others, such as Pope John Paul II, Catholic Bishop Franjo Komarica, Orthodox Bishop Lavrentije, Orthodox priest Father Jovan Nikolic, as well as a number of Bosnian Franciscans promoted peace, dialogue, forgiveness, and reconciliation.

So, what happened after the Dayton Peace Agreement? Did interna-tional intervention change the process of separation, exclusion, and an unwillingness to live together in tolerance? Is there any good news for Iraq from the Bosnian model? Have the religious communities become peacemakers?

The results are not too encouraging. The greatest positive impact of Dayton is undoubtedly that the bloodshed has stopped. For that we must be thankful. I recall a comment by Monsignor Dr. Mato Zovkic, auxiliary bishop of Sarajevo in charge of ecumenical and interreligious relations for the Sarajevo archdiocese, opining that there is a need for continued international military presence for another twenty years because otherwise the war could easily break out again. In a telephone interview in April 2005, Friar Marko Orsolic stated that slowly there is a readiness on the part of people to live together more peacefully, but there seems to be a lack of political will.[8] A literary round-table discus-sion organized in Sarajevo stated rather bluntly that those who are in favor of multiethnic cooperation are now opposed to the Dayton agreement and the constitution of B&H based on that agreement, whereas those who have an ethnic orientation favor it. In the words of Srdjan Dizdarevic, the president of the Helsinki Committee of B&H, "...the ethnic principle is becoming the absolute criterion of living. We here do not live as people, but as Serbs, Croats, and Boshniaks. If this trend continues we will become the black hole of Europe."[9]

Both ethnonationalism and the religion of Bosnians has been fed not only from within but also from without, namely by Serbia, Croatia, and Islamic countries. The paradox of the Bosnian people is that simultaneously they can be friendly and cooperative as well as vicious and confrontational. The bright side is their endearing aspect while the second is the dark side of the Bosnian/Herzegovinian soul. It all depends upon what they are being fed. Regretfully, their co-religionists from abroad usually encourage them to become confrontational. For instance, in Croatia the radical right wing is making a bid for power now that the HDZ (Hrvatska Demokratska Zajednica or Croatian Democratic Union) is no longer an all-Croat movement but simply a political party. Among the Croatian Catholic hierarchy, very nationalistic bishops are rejecting entry into the European Union. Fortunately, Josip Cardinal Bozanic, the archbishop of Zagreb, delivered a very pro-European Easter message in 2005, thereby keeping the focus of both the church and the state on the Vatican-supported European option.[10] Marko Orsolic, unsurprisingly, charged that the Catholic bishops did not understand Vatican II and accused them of being medieval in not having separated church and state, saying, "They divide people by religion whereas we differ in our religions but shouldn't be divided by them."[11]

One would like to believe Orthodox Bishop Lavrentije of Sabac-Valjevo[12] when he said that many people expected that conflicts to break out based on religion in the recent war but that this did not happen due to previous ecumenical meetings which had softened the Balkan religious antagonisms. Lavrentije represents the pro-ecumenical trend in the Serbian Orthodox Church (hereafter SOC), of which the Orthodox churches of B&H are a part. However, there is a huge conflict within the SOC. Bishops Artemije (Radosavljevic) of Raska-Prizren,[13]

Bishop Amfilohije (Radovic) of Montenegro-Adriatic Coast, and Bishop Atanasije (Jeftic) formerly of Trebinje-Herzegovina, represent the antidialogical hardliners and a bitterly anti-ecumenical strand in the church.[14] Patriarch Pavle and Bishop Irinej (Bulovic) of Backa vacillate but could be said to be more moderate with regard to ecumenical contacts. Each of these competing wings has their impact in B&H. There is a clear faction among the Serbian Orthodox faithful who wish to clericalize society and for higher clergy to play a distinct political role. Many believers who are waiting for cues on civic issues from church authorities have been inspired by this group.[15] Clearly there are those who are happy with the reaffirmation of the saying, "All Serbs are Orthodox; those who are not Orthodox are not true Serbs." It is fair to say that Serbian Orthodox clergy, quite naturally, wish to gather all Serbs into the embrace of the Orthodox Church. They also feel that the clergy ought to have a say as to what is genuinely important for church members not only in regard to the "heavenly kingdom" but also here on earth.

What is true of the SOC clergy is also true for the Croat Roman Catholic and Boshniak Muslim clergy. Jelena Lovric, a Croat journalist, correctly identifies this kind of religion as militant and combative.[16] She describes a significant number of Croat Catholic leaders as being resistant to papal ecumenical initiatives to reconcile the Catholic Church with the Orthodox and to establish dialogue with Muslims. These leaders remain rigidly nationalistic, xenophobic, and right wing. Cardinal Bozanic created quite a stir with his previously mentioned Easter message that was distinctly pro-European and implicitly critical of such Croat Catholic separatists.[17] Not only is it true that Catholic clerics wish to include all Croats into the arms of the Catholic Church, but many of them, including Vinko Cardinal Puljic, archbishop of Sarajevo, have a knee-jerk reaction to "defend" all things Croat. Cardinal Puljic joined the chorus of those who are alarmed by what they see as a decrease in Croat population.[18] They opportunistically warn that B&H is on the way to becoming (because of a widespread conspiracy) a nation of only two ethnicities, Boshniaks and Serbs, while the Croats are on the way of becoming a mere minority in B&H. Ivan Lovrenovic wrote in the *Feral Tribune*, "What democratic principles can we talk about when a cardinal [Vinko Puljic], who should be the vertical moral axis, defends the greatest mafioso and criminal [meaning Dragan Covic, former member of the presidency of B&H] among the people. It is impossible to avoid the question, why does the cardinal do it?"[19] He provided no answer to his rhetorical question. Fortunately, Stipe Mesic, Croatia's president, urged B&H Croats not to look to Zagreb (capital of Croatia) but to Sarajevo (capital of B&H) for solutions to their problems, which a number of Croat politicians promptly declared as a betrayal of B&H Croats.

Bosnian Muslims are in a similar dilemma as to which direction to turn but their leaders are directing them to greater ethnoreligious nationalism. One example is that Spahic, the deputy of Mustafa Ceric (Reis-ul-Ulema and spiritual leader of Boshniak Muslims), called on all Boshniaks to support Hasan Cengic, member of SDA (Party of Democratic Action, consisting almost entirely of Boshniaks), the same way as Croats supported Covic.[20] It was already rumored during the war that Mustafa Ceric harbored political ambitions. Similarly to Puljic, Ceric tends to be defensive when problems arise among Bosnian Muslims. For instance, when a Muslim man killed an entire Croat family in Kostajnica, Ceric correctly regarded the man as one of many mentally deranged people rather than a religiously motivated murderer, but very quickly went on the counterattack by blaming Milosevic and Tudjman for poisoning the minds of people. He further stated that this crime tended to increase mutual recriminations between Croats and Muslims. All members of the Interreligious Council of B&H (Reis Ceric, Metropolitan Nikolaj, Cardinal Puljic, and Jacob Finci) issued a joint declaration about this murder explaining it as an aberrance of mental illness, trying thereby to prevent revenge killings. Nevertheless, Ceric took aim at Puljic for having claimed that while this murderer was captured, the true murderers—those who taught the man to hate and kill—were still free. Ceric wondered whether Puljic himself was blameless. He pointed out the role of the Serbian Orthodox Church in the war, impugning the Catholic clergy who distributed prayer beads to Croat soldiers prior to their carrying out brutal crimes.[21] Not one word was spoken of any Muslim misdeeds.

At a celebration for the defenders of Sarajevo, Reis Ceric

Islamicized those who were killed, claiming that they were *shahids* (martyrs) giving their lives for Allah. He stated that Bosnian Muslims had only two options during the war of the 1990s, namely *hijra* (withdrawal) or *jihad*.[22] In an interview in London given to Nadeem Azam, Reis Ceric answered the question "Will Bosnia remain a secular state or develop into a theocracy?" by providing a lengthy answer about Islamic concepts of state:

> In the third, intermediate category, *Sulh*, the situation is such that Islam or the sharia cannot be implemented fully, but the government should endeavour to put it into practice as much as possible.
>
> Bosnia is not in the first category, but the third.[23]

Sarajevo has been transformed from a multiethnic, multireligious city into a Muslim city in which Bosnians of the other two ethnicities feel awkward or even threatened.[24] Financial support received from Islamist circles in Saudi Arabia, Iran, and Libya has strings attached. This seems to be leading to the radicalization of Islam, which the West, according to Cardinal Puljic, has failed to curb.[25] There is still a lingering influence of the foreign *mujahedeens* who came to the assistance of the B&H Muslims during the war of 1992–95. U.S. intelligence sources have claimed that among them are al-Qaeda operatives, some of whom were extradited to the U.S. Bosnian Muslim crowds protested the extradition, saying that it proved that B&H was not a state of law but an American colony.

During the period of the international protectorate, the political division of the country into the Republika Srpska and the Federation of Bosnia and Herzegovina (in turn separated into Muslim and Croat enclaves in ethnoreligiously determined cantons) has frozen or even deepened the ethnoreligious divides. The population has become passive and dependent on foreign aid.[26] There seems to be a near consensus among journalists that the foreign High Commissioners de facto confirmed the ethnoreligious division of the country created by the war and strengthened the political domination of the political powers that supported the war. Politically, the three ethnoreligious groups are at a stalemate that has paralyzed the country. Donald Hays, the American deputy to Paddy Ashdown, the High Commissioner at that time, declared upon returning to the U.S. that B&H is only a "façade of a country" according to the *Feral Tribune*.[27] Wolfgang Petritsch, Ashdown's predecessor, picturesquely stated that while Dayton was intended to be a "life jacket," it now has become a "straightjacket," prompting Cardinal Puljic to respond that he was insulted by this remark (though Puljic himself has said he does not like Dayton).

I will illustrate the depth of this separation by an example from the sports' world because sport is a barometer of nationalism in Europe. When a soccer match was being played between the Serbia and Montenegro national all-star team against B&H, the most vocal and boisterous fans for the Serbia and Montenegro team were the B&H Serbs. Similarly, when the junior team of Croatia played in 2005 against B&H, the B&H Croats brought Croatian flags and signs which said, "Croatia—My Homeland."[28]

Pointing to fear as a cause of interethnic and interreligious mayhem may not be surprising, but my thesis that democracy and Western intervention are co-responsible may come as a surprise. I do not mean to suggest that democracy is bad, but only that it needs to grow organically and gradually. The Western push for democracy as an anti-communist strategy found many nations unprepared for democracy yet willing to adopt a multiparty system which should not be equated with democracy. This method was used for the transition from controlled communist nationalism to a poisonous competitive multiparty orgy in which each party competed in the spread of militancy and chauvinism. Sociologist Nenad Kecmanovic correctly points out that, "the same political institutions and procedures in countries with different traditions and culture produce entirely different political practice."[29] Kecmanovic is correct in saying that nationalism is not merely a childhood disease of post-communism, but that its persistence is a testimony to the vitality of the nationalist phenomenon. National questions were not created by the advent of democracy in this part of the world but only brought to the surface by it. Nor did dictatorships create nationalism but only suppressed certain expressions of it.[30] I myself underestimated the power of ethnoreligious nationalism.

Ten years after the Dayton Agreement, Bosnia is still politically divided along ethnic lines with religious hierarchies playing a pronounced political role. Ethnic divisions are deepening. Non-Bosnians continue to dominate military, economic, and governmental structures. If there are parallels between Bosnia and Iraq, then ethnoreligious nationalism and foreign involvement in Iraq will be long term and will cripple Iraq's ability to recover.

In the period between 2000 and 2002 non-nationalist parties received only 1 or 2 percent of the votes. Democracy brought to the surface undesirable nationalistic politicians who were then removed from office by the foreign power brokers (about 200 elected officials have been removed from their posts). This resulted in anger and resentment by those who voted for them. Religious leaders see themselves as protectors of their discontented flock and remain defenders of narrow ethnonational interests.

One insider described B&H and the entire population of the Balkans sarcastically as devious, unruly children whose teachers lost patience in Dayton and are now forcing them to do their homework in a pedagogical experiment that has now lasted for ten years, employing thousands of efficient teachers of democracy without any obvious progress by the pupils. The characterization of Bosnians as devious and unruly children is simplistic and demeaning; the point is that the changes are painstakingly slow.

As I see it, there continues in B&H, in the words of the Bulgarian sociologist of religion, Ina Merdjanova, "the reciprocal instrumentalization of the political and religious."[31] By way of conclusion Merdjanova states that after the collapse of communism, "the discourses of religion and nationalism became and are politically relevant,"[32] but she questions whether those discourses can continue effectively in a secularized—and I would add multiethnic and multireligious—society without a clear-cut separation of church and state and without being "subsumed into the operative discourse of civil society."[33] However, if a clearer separation between church and state were to take place in B&H, both nationalists and religious leaders would lose some of their importance. In that case, religious leaders could remain in the public eye constructively if they were to involve themselves wholeheartedly in the nascent interreligious dialogue for the purpose of interethnic reconciliation. Regretfully, that remains a prospect rather than a reality.

Notes

1. Silvije Tomasevic, "U Sarajevu, 'europskom Jeruzalemu,'" *Slobodna Dalmacija* (Split, Croatia), 78, April 9, 2005.
2. Quoted in Tomasevic. All translations from Croatian, Bosnian, or Serbian in this paper were made by Paul Mojzes.
3. Thomas Bremer, *Kleine Geschichte der Religionen in Jugoslawien: Koenigreich—Kommunismus—Krieg* (Freiburg: Verlag Herder, 2003), 119-22.
4. See Paul Mojzes, *The Yugoslavian Inferno: Ethnoreligious Warfare in the Balkans* (New York: Continuum, 1995), 125-51; and his essay in Paul Mojzes, ed., *Religion and the War in Bosnia* (Atlanta, Ga: American Academy of Religion Books, 1998), 74-98. The book contains essays by nineteen diverse authors. For additional thoughtful reflections, see Mitja Velikonja, "The Role of Religion and Religious Communities in the Wars in Ex-Yugoslavia, 1991–1999" [Interviews with Zeljko Mardesic, Paul Mojzes, Radmila Radic, and Esad Zgodic] in *Religion in Eastern Europe*, 23, no. 4 (August 2003): 1-42.
5. A term for Bosnians of Muslim heritage. A great deal of complex and confusing discussion has taken place on what to call the inhabitants of the area known as Bosnia. A partial agreement was reached to call all inhabitants, regardless of ethnicity, Bosnians. Since many of the so-called Muslims were secularized and nonreligious, the term Boshniak was accepted for them, although from time to time Bosnian Croats and Serbs also claim that name insisting that the two are simply synonyms. In this chapter we will use Bosnian for all inhabitants and Boshniak for those of Muslim heritage.
6. *Chetnik* is the name given to traditional Serb paramilitary units who were reconstituted in the recent wars. It also denotes a negative name for all nationalist Serbs by Croats and Bosnian Muslims. An equivalent practice by Serbs was to call nationalist Croats *ustashe*; both Serbs and Croats called Bosnian Muslims *balije*. On a positive note, the use of these derogatory names shows that the population did not consider the entire other nation as culpable for belligerence and war crimes.
7. Editors' note: This essay demonstrates another finding of the conference: the importance of the attitudes and roles of specific religious and political leaders in regard to the outcome of conflicts, not only in B&H, but in our other case studies.
8. Marko Orsolic, telephone conversation with author on April 8, 2005.
9. Quoted by Senita Sehercehajic, "Okrugli sto u okviru Evropskih knjizevnih susreta" in *Oslobodjenje* (Sarajevo) May 22, 2005, http://www.oslobodjen-je.ba/index.php?option=com_content&task=view&id+45203&Itemi... (accessed on May 22, 2005.) Author's translation from Bosnian.
10. Marinko Culic, "Hrvatska obratnica," *Feral Tribune* (Split, Croatia), April 1, 2005, 8-9.
11. Marko Orsolic, "Biskupi iz srednjeg vijeka," *Feral Tribune*, April 4, 2005, 12, author's translation.

12. Jovan Janjic,"Vladika Lavrentije: Sedam susreta sa papom," in *NIN* (Belgrade) April 4, 2005, 61.

13. See Bishop Artemije Radosavljevic's essay, "Srpska Crkva protiv ekumenizma," delivered at a conference on ecumenism in Thessalonika, Greece, September 20-24, 2004, and printed in *Sveti knez Lazar* (Gracanica, Serbia and Montenegro), no. 47 (March 2004), 29-46. Author's translation.

14. Jelena Tasic, "Mitropolit Amfilohije: Nema haosa u SPC. To ste izmislili vi novinari" in *Danas* (Belgrade), April 2-3, 2005, 12-13. In this article, Amfilohije's denial of the chaotic situation is not very convincing.

15. Dragan Bujosevic, "Srbija, Bozija drzava," in *NIN*, (April 4, 2005), 16-20.

16. Jelena Lovric, "Papina ostavstina za Hrvatsku," in *Globus* (Zagreb), April 4, 2005, 30-31.

17. While many mainstream journalists welcomed Cardinal Bozanic's message, the right wing reacted very bitterly. See for example, Marko Juric, "Kardinal Bozanic krivo je protumacio Papu!" in *Hrvatski List* (Zagreb), April 7, 2005, 27.

18. See, for example, these newspaper articles: Davor Domazet-Loso, "Bez Hrvata u srednjoj Bosni i Hercegovini nema ni Hrvatske!" in *Hrvatski List* (Zagreb), April 7, 2005, 24-26; and Ivan Lovrenovic, "Pustos za prazninom," in *Feral Tribune*, April 1, 2005, 23.

19. Lovrenovic, "Pustos za prazninom." Translation and bracketed explanations are by the author.

20. Ivica Djikic and Igor Lasic, "Croats in Bosnia," in *Feral Tribune*, April 8, 2005, 10.

21. Gojko Beric,"Zlocin je nas prtljag" in *Oslobodjenje*, May 22, 2005. http://www.oslobodjenje.ba/pregled_fulltext_a.php?id=32939 (accessed May 22, 2005.)

22. Zija Dizdarevic, "Islamizacija po reisu" [Islamization According to the Reis] in *BH Dnevnik* (Sarajevo), August 22, 2005.

23. From an email received by Paul Mojzes on September 23, 2005, entitled "A Conversation with Dr. Mustafa Ceric" and copyrighted in 2005 by Nadeem Azam and Azam.com, Inc. New York and London. Text is in English.

24. For example, my interview with Bozidar Pantovic in *Osijek*, April 7, 2005, during which he told me of an incident in a bus where a Boshniak (possibly mentally deranged) loudly called for the slaughter of all Serbs.

25. See "Kardinal Puljic warnt von neuen Hass gegen 'andere'" in *Glaube in der 2. Welt* (Zurich), vol. 34, no. 6 (2006), 3.

26. Mirjana Kasapovic, "Asdownovo groblje hrvatsva," in *Globus* (Zagreb), April 8, 2005, 56.

27. Ivan Lovrenovic, "Strategija jadikovke," *Feral Tribune*, April 8, 2005, 13.

28. Kasapovic, "Asdownovo groblje hrvatsva," 56.

29. Dusan Kecmanovic, *Dometi Demokratije* (Belgrade: Cigoja stampa, Library Politea, 2005), 68, quoted in Vukasin Pavlovic, "Sumarni i sumorni ogled u balkanskom demokratskom corsokaku," in *Danas*, April 2-3, 2005, x.

30. Ibid.
31. Ina Merdjanova, *Religion, Nationalism, and Civil Society in Eastern Europe: The Postcommunist Palimpsest* (Lewiston, N.Y.: The Edwin Mellen Press, 2002), 100.
32. Ibid., 151.
33. Ibid., 152.

Summary of Combined Bosnia and Herzegovina Discussion and Final Comparative Discussion

After hearing about Bosnia and Herzegovina (B&H), the situation in Iraq looks brighter. The instrumentalization of religion and some of the extreme national features of religious expression have not been present in Iraq Shiite communities. Compared to the former Yugoslavia, the southern Iraqis have been fortunate in their leadership.

For example, a week before this conference in April 2005, a bomb was set off at a Shiite mosque in Baghdad. It killed 11 people and wounded 26 in a deliberate attempt to get the Shiites to go out and kill Sunnis. Hundreds if not thousands of Shiites have been killed all over the country in similar incidents. In almost every instance, a leader such as Grand Ayatollah Sistani or Ibrahim Jaafari has intervened with the local community. They have made the case to the Shiites that the process of building a new Iraq will give Shiites their rightful place and they run the risk of ruining it all, if they retaliate for the violence. Thus far, the Shiites have listened. How long can the Shiite leadership keep the lid on? There are no guarantees.[1]

The Shiite-Sunni split in Iraq does not have the same element of ethnic competition as Bosnia's ethnoreligious turmoil. When you hear Shiites talk about Sunni communities in Iraq, there is very little deliberate criticism on a religious basis. Shiites tend to talk about Baathists.

They welcome Sunni clerics onto provincial councils. Of course, they remember oppression and feel they have been economically excluded. Shiite clerics rarely complain about Sunni theologies, although in the Sunni community there are often strong theological critiques against the Shiites.

As well as some structural historical grounds for the lesser degree of explosiveness in Iraq as compared to Bosnia, is there something in the difference of the religions involved? Is there some particular structure or quality of Christian stories in the B&H case that served to mobilize the Croats? So much of what was at stake in B&H was the intersection of a set of social conditions with an emphasis on martyrdom, crucifixion, and blood. In B&H, a particular kind of religious remembering intersected with a particular set of social conditions.

The Husayn[2] analogy is the closest major international ritual to Christian Good Friday commemorations. It includes a similar notion of remembrance and physical atonement. With the exception of Muqtada Sadr and his army, in Iraq there has not been a strong appeal to the symbolic complex around the death of Husayn (and the notion of enemies as Yazid, responsible for the death of Husayn) as happened during the Islamic revolution in Iran. There the mourning during *Ashura* for the death of Husayn and his family and the curses on those who killed them became a curse on the Shah and on the Shah's backer, the United States, without ever having to be articulated. Later Khomeini did articulate this in sermon after sermon. It has been a surprise that *Ashura* has not been used in a political sense in protest in Iraq.

It may be that it takes some time for the creation of such theology. In Bosnia, there was first a period of change that then fed into the theological legitimization. If Muqtada Sadr becomes more powerful and if circumstances develop over the next 20 years so that his militia becomes imaginatively linked to the massacred followers of Husayn, then the rituals of the *Ashura* might be used with the same effect in Iraq as was the commemoration of the death of Prince Lazar in the former Yugoslavia.

In Pakistan, violence between Sunnis and Shiites is pronounced, particularly towards Shiites, sometimes in response to their mourning rites during *Ashura*. This divisive violence comes from a complexity of issues, one of which has to do with access to land and wealth. The tension between Shiite and Sunni in Iraq does not come near to that between them in Pakistan.

There has been a kind of anti-Baathist, guilt-by-association response on the part of the Shiites against the Sunnis. It has not been configured in ethnic terms, but as a vendetta against the Baath Party and people prominent in the Baath Party. It does not transfer to all Sunnis. However, as a practical matter, most upper- and middle-class Sunni Arabs in Iraq had some association with the Baath Party. For instance, if you were a high school teacher in Iraq in 1993 wanting to go on a summer training program to London, you would need a passport and to get one you would have to join the Baath Party. There were many people forced into that kind of position, all of whom have been fired at the insistence of the more vindictive anti-Baath elements among the Shiites. Shadowy accusations combined with guilt by association are worrisome. However, they are not being instigated on purely ethnic lines but in relationship to the Baath Party.

In the B&H case an important factor in building ethnonational fervor was a strong level of grievance by one group—for example, the Serb grievances against the Croat access to jobs. There seems to be those kinds of grievance in the Iraq case and yet they have not erupted with the same degree of intensity between the Shiites and the Sunnis so far. The allegiance of being Arab together overrides the grievances. Of course, if they want to manufacture these kinds of grievances, there are many elements in Shiite history on which they could draw.

In the North of Iraq, in Mosul, Arbil, and Kirkuk with the Kurds, strongly held grievances similar to those in Bosnia do exist with that kind of intensity. The Kurds think of Arabs as the people who gassed them. At the Middle East Studies Association Meeting in San Francisco in November 2004, the Kurds on a panel on the Kurdish situation expressed a frightening degree of anger, grievance, and hatred towards Arabs. There is somewhat of a reciprocal feeling among Arabs in the North. When Jalal Talibani became president of Iraq, a sheik in the North preached against him on the grounds that he was a Kurd and therefore should not be president. At the moment it has not gone further than a sense of grievance, partially because the Kurds still hope for a semi-autonomous Kurdistan in a loose federal framework.

Saddam Hussein and Marshall Tito both suppressed certain groups within each society. In the Bosnian case or the ex-Yugoslavian case, after Tito died, those groups rose up in a brutal form of ethnonationalism. There are some formal parallels in Iraq: suppression of Shiites and Kurds produced intense resentment. As a result of Saddam's ouster, one might think that kind of brutal ethnonationalism would emerge, but it has not as of yet. As Juan Cole pointed out in discussing the implications of Paul Brass's study of the subnationalisms in India, if there are two markers of identity that overlap, then it is easier to mobilize people effectively for these purposes. In the case of Sunni and Shiite, since they are both Arabs, there is only the one marker of difference. All of the Arabs are invested in Iraq as a national project. Each group would like to be in control of it, but Iraq as an entity is not questioned. That differs from the former Yugoslavia. Who was really committed to Yugoslavian nationalism after Tito? However, the situation with the Kurds in the North may be more comparable to B&H.

Another big difference between the cases is the horrendous events Yugoslavia experienced in World War II, in which each group claims to be the major victim of the others. Iraq has not had the same history of major communal atrocities committed by internal parties. As long as the focus in the former Yugoslavia was on an outside enemy, these groups could unite. The minute the threat from the Soviet Union and from American imperialism waned, they turned against each other. The presence of the United States in Iraq may similarly be a unifying factor.

Iraq does not have an extensive history of communal violence. The two big communal disturbances earlier in Iraqi history were a massacre of Syrian Christians in 1932, and then in the 1940s, the *farhud*, a persecution of Jews in Baghdad. After that, violence has not been primarily communal or ethnic. Saddam did not gas the Kurds because he did not like ethnic Kurds or because he had something against Indo-Europeans. He gassed them because they were making alliances with Iran to get more autonomy during the time when he was at war with Iran.

Within the Sunni world, the polarization between many in the

Sunni Islamic militant Salafi movement and the West is a global devel-opment over the last 40 years, acting like a tide underneath many con-flicts. It is changing things in a slow, incremental way. The invasion of Iraq by the United States serves to unite Iraq while Americans are there. That could turn into a Salafist construction of militancy against the United States, similar to that in other places in the Middle East. Those specific constructions could coalesce together. The Salafist movement has its own different set of symbolic dimensions that do not have the central ritual atonement of the *Ashura*. Salafists are operating in the Sunni areas in Iraq.

There are two points of comparison and contrast between the Sri Lanka and Bosnian cases and Iraq. First, on the question of a nation-wide nationalism, Iraq has an idea that unifies the Shiites and the Sunnis: Arab nationalism. In Sri Lanka, the Tamils definitely do not identify with Sri Lankan nationalism. The Sinhala majority identifies the mythical, glorious, legendary, imaginary state with the real geo-graphical place. The fact that it is an island has promoted this. The ocean makes a visible border around the island. People in the south think of the land within this border as theirs, completely ignoring the fact that the north and east have been occupied by a different ethnic group for a very long time.

On a different question, on the symbolic level that Michael Sells discussed, there are several parallels between the Bosnian and the Sri Lankan cases. For example, Paul Mojzes mentioned the use of the Serbian version of the Lord's Prayer. During the ethnic violence in 1983, some Buddhist monks asked people to recite Buddhist chants. If they did not, the immediate conclusion was that they were Tamils.

Another parallel is the use of various images to claim symbolic space, as Croat Catholics did with the cross. In the 1950s, Gananath Obeyesekere, an anthropologist from Sri Lanka, wrote about the Buddha in the marketplace. In Sri Lanka now, Buddhas are everywhere. They are massive images, and they are getting bigger and bigger. Similarly to the B&H case, they are being erected in very conspicuous places, such as on top of hills.

For example, a monk recently broke away from the monastic hier-archy in Kandy; claimed ownership of a thirteenth-century cave temple;

and started extracting money from tourists. What did he do with this money? He hired a Japanese contractor to make a Buddha statue, the biggest ever in a certain posture. It was brought in parts and assembled there.

A broad view needs to be taken in regard to the forming of identity, not just in relation to religion or religious elements. Language, for example, is a badge of identity. In Sri Lanka the language policies of the 1950s and 1960s have had a profound impact not only in terms of language as a designating identity, but also as they have expanded a space for political discourse in which politicians and other visible political agents can choose to function in different languages for different purposes. In the Sri Lankan case, some of the volatility comes from the fact that ideas can be articulated differently in different contexts even by the same person, which feeds fear, anxiety, and rumormongering.

In Sri Lanka there are the two markers that Paul Brass suggested may be determinative, for example, language and religion for Sinhala Buddhist identity. British racist attitudes, conditioned by European ideas of race, influenced Sinhala nationalism in British colonial times. Those attitudes continue to influence local conceptions of other people. Religion alone is not the issue, but the potent combination of religion, homeland, and language. This combination of indices fuels the fire of violence.

In the case of Sri Lankan Tamils, especially the LTTE movement, they have emphasized language and homeland. Why do they not include religion? Because the LTTE movement includes Hindus and Catholics. In Toronto the diaspora Tamil Hindu community is building Hindu temples, and the Tamil Catholics are going to Catholic churches. The way in which religious feeling enters for the Tamils as a whole is with the cult of martyrs for the Tamil cause. They celebrate their martyrs' deaths. There are Martyrs' Day performances in several places in Canada, England, Australia and other cities throughout the world. In Sri Lanka, they have many different graveyards for martyrs. The cult of the martyrs for the Tigers gives them a sense of dying for the cause, which is important to the Tiger resistance.

Diasporas have had an effect in most of the cases represented in this conference. In his presentation, Professor Sells discussed some positive initiatives that diasporas could take. There are some examples from other diaspora cases. First, the Ukrainian diaspora organization responded to the political crisis in Ukraine in late 2004 by sending observers to ensure that proper elections could take place. Second, the Afghan diaspora has been sending members, including women, to the *loya jirga*, the Grand Council. These countries are two examples in which there have been positive contributions from their diasporas. The Iraqi diaspora participated in voting and the election. About 220,000 of the million eligible to vote cast their ballots in the January 2005 election. Most of them voted for Sistani's list.

In the Sri Lanka case, some Sinhalas see human rights, minority rights, and NGOs as associated with the West, as part of what these groups consider a Judeo-Christian construct. This is also common in Iraq and in Palestine. The values associated with democracy and secularism are linked with the West. What kinds of effects does this rhetorical negative invocation of the West have?

In Sri Lanka, some scholars have shown how human rights and the rights of minorities are part of Buddhism and Hinduism. More work need to be done in this area. People develop rhetorical devices and ways of talking about human rights that help to indigenize the concepts, even when maybe they are not indigenous. For instance, the *fatwa* of Sistani, in which he demanded that there be one person/one vote elections echoed thought about popular sovereignty and democracy. By putting it in a *fatwa*, he made it unassailable. It is also common in Arab discourse to refer to the principles of humanity.

Is religion a constructive or destructive force in the situations addressed at the conference? For the most part, the discussion has focused on negative uses of religion. Religion in itself and religious principles not used instrumentally for political purposes have been largely absent, as has religion used for peace and reconciliation. In situations in which there is not a strongly developed sense of liberal secularism, there is a pragmatic turn towards engaging religious voices which can give meaning and enflesh certain principles that are also associated with liberal values.

Religious traditions do hold ideals such as peace, nonviolence, compassion, and brother- and sisterhood. It is important to find examples in which those ideals are embodied. H. L. Seneviratne's book, *The Work of Kings: The New Buddhism in Sri Lanka*, talks about the idealization of Buddhism in negative terms, but also as a perversion of a more authentic ideal. In postcolonial discourse the nation-state as an imagined community is viewed in negative ways, as an imperialistic imposition of a Western form. We need a new notion of imagined community that builds on the best of the elements in these states from their own traditions, whether they are Buddhist or Muslim or Hindu, those aspects that contribute toward building positive values of peace and nonviolence. What are the institutions where this might take place? In some of these situations, many of them are in a rudimentary form. Who are the individual leaders who are making a considerable difference in the sort of contrast that was drawn here between B&H and Iraq? What would Iraq be like today, if it were not for the Muslim clerics in the South?

As mentioned previously, religion has been playing a very positive role in southern Iraq. Despite all the chaos and violence of the occupation, southern Iraq is somehow calm because of the moderating effects of Islam. For the most part people are not assassinating their enemies or setting up protection rackets or smuggling diesel because of their religious beliefs. The clerical, scholastic Shiism represented by Grand Ayatollah Sistani is about moral order and justice. The Sadr people, although more radical and combative, often have the same effect. For instance, they did not let the libraries be looted in their areas. It was inconsistent with their idea of moral and social order. Many of these movements exist in conditions of slums, where the unemployment rate is enormous and the young men involved have nothing to do all day. A puritanical social order such as that in Sadr's group informs their world. It gives them a purpose in life.

Sistani returned early from heart surgery in London to stop the fighting in Najaf between the U.S. Marines and Sadr's Mahdi Army. From Basra, he dramatically announced a citizens' march on Najaf. Thousands of people came from all over the country, very peacefully. When thousands of civilians flooded into Najaf, the Marines and the Mahdi Militia could not fight anymore. There was something Gandhian about it. It was an admirable use of Sistani's moral authority, and of what Foucault calls "biomass," to address the disintegration of social order in Najaf.

When there is no fighting, the tradition will continue to impose a moral and social order, a kind of Puritanism: no liquor stores, no video stores, women covering up when they go out, and so on. That element of strict social order with which Westerners may be less comfortable comes along with all of the elements of order that Westerners see as "good." Religion plays this role in Iraq as it now is constituted.

It is important to understand the specific historical context that has emerged in Iraq: the disappearance of the Baath Party; the absence of other civil society organizations; and the collapse of various alternative traditional structures, like the tribal system. Therefore, religious leaders have naturally moved into that space. Only very recently have groups such as unions and youth centers begun to emerge.

As a footnote, all powerful political movements in southern Iraq trace their origins to efforts linked with the Shiite religion. They derive from the Dawa movement and are associated with various spiritual leaders. They are concerned with elements of theological debate, with *sharia* law, with social codes. They have similar types of leadership: leaders who were/are great scholars and have published a number of books; many have leaders who were assassinated; and many of them continue to refer to particular sources of emulation. The difference between these parties is much more a question of institutional history and leadership than it is of ideology. With the current preeminence of Sistani, it is difficult to get the parties to articulate any differences in manifesto or platform. As well as being religious parties, they have been secret parties for most of the last twenty years and, therefore, they are not comfortable talking about ideology, even when those differences exist. This will have consequences for the formulation of democratic policy in Iraq as will their connection to militia groups.

Another example of religion working for the good is that of the traditional Sufi orders in Sudan, which have been prodemocracy and opposed the dictatorship. Because they do not depend on the state, they are the traditional source of legitimacy. We also talked about the situation in B&H with the Croat Catholics where the Vatican has taken a pro-European stance and has disapproved of the manipulation of

Catholicism for nationalist purposes. Why can the Vatican do that? Because it is autonomous, it is not subordinate to the local political interests. The Shiite leaders in Iraq have the autonomy and legitimacy to stand up to power and have operated as a moderating force. In Morocco, where the king is simultaneously the head of state and the head of religion, where he does not need to inquire of any other Muslim authority what he can or cannot do, he has been extremely assertive in supporting human rights, democratization, and women's rights. These are all situations where religious institutions, when they have sufficient legitimacy, independence, and traditional authority, act as positive forces.

In the jargon of good governance traditions in places like the World Bank, "agencies of restraint" is a popular phrase. Those agencies can be both internal and external. A strong independent, central bank can ward off bad economic policy; checks and balances can ward off tyranny. What are the conditions under which religion provides pathways or inducements for violence or peace? The possibilities for both have been emphasized in a variety of ways in these cases. In one example, people have mobile reinforcing identities, and religion is one of them. Religion can then be used symbolically to empower people towards violence. In another example, individuals restrain themselves because of their belief system, or the priest or *imam* who invokes this restraint on behalf of the community.

When there is a general vacuum of power, for example, in Sri Lanka or Iraq, the lack of order generally may elevate the role of religion. It may also increase the prospects that religion may be used towards violence as, for example, in Rwanda, where now priests are being accused of actively engaging in a genocide project. There can be extraordinary extremes in religion: it can legitimate violence or restrain it.

When we talk about religion as a good or a bad influence, we need to be more specific: what religion? how it is engaging with various issues? and who are the people involved? The religious expression and religious thought which exists in Iraq after its long period of suppression may not be the kind of Muslim thought we find in other places. The Shiites in Iran, like Soroush and others, are actively thinking about Islam and its engagement with modernity. There are various opportunities that religion may offer, but the question is: what religion? and what are we talking about exactly when we refer to religion?

There is, obviously, no such thing as religion in general; it is always contextualized. In this broader comparative methodological conversation, we have been thinking about the conditions for certain kinds of outcomes, and how we might understand those in a comparative frame. Professor Sells' term, "concentric tensions," emphasized the plurality of elements in play in a rather complex frame and bears further thought. He and other speakers gave a very thickly described, robust picture of interconnecting conditions and possibilities for conflict. One could also give a thickly described, robust picture of conditions of possibility for more harmony. At times we might retrospectively look back to see what happened; at other times we might prospectively try to imagine certain kinds of positive outcomes.

Notes

1. Editors' note: Since the April 2005 conference, sectarian violence has increased between Sunnis and Shiites, yet it remains true that most Shiites have exhibited restraint.
2. Editors' note: Husayn, the Prophet Muhammad's grandson, was killed at Karbala in the seventh century. His death is mourned by Shiites during the Festival of Muharram, the culmination of which occurs on the tenth day, *Ashura*. To Shiites, Husayn was Muhammad's rightful heir and he is seen as having been martyred by the opposition led by Caliph Yazid. The question of the rightful successor to Muhammad is one of the main divisions between Sunnis and Shiites. See Juan Cole's paper in this volume as well. Helpful in writing this note was an article by James Browning, "Muslims Celebrate Ashura," on Ethics Daily.com, dated 02-07-06 http://www.ethicsdaily.com/article_detail.cfm?AID=6931 For more information about *Ashura* in Iraq, see Reza Aslan's article in Slate, "In the Footsteps of the Martyrs," http://www.slate.com/id/2095326/ February 16, 2004.

Appendix One: Sri Lanka Background

Christian Rice

The conflict in Sri Lanka between the Sinhala Buddhist majority and the ethnic Tamil minority has claimed over 60,000 lives. It erupted in the devastating 1983 riots in which Sinhala mobs targeted Tamil communities, using voter lists to identify and destroy property owned by Tamils, displacing hundreds of thousands, and killing many.[1] Not to be outdone, the Liberation Tigers of Tamil Eelam (LTTE), the main Tamil separatist group, has employed horrific ethnic cleansing in the territories it has captured in the north and east since 1983.[2]

As noted in the Sri Lanka papers and the summary of the discussion, the situation in Sri Lanka is complex, with a volatile mixture of religions, ethnicities, and territorial disputes. All Sinhalas are not Buddhists; all Tamils are not Hindu. Nor do all Sinhala Buddhists align with the strong Sinhala Buddhist nationalist movements, or all Tamils with the LTTE. The 1981 census identified the ethnic composition of Sri Lanka as 74 percent Sinhala, 18 percent Tamil, 7 percent Moor, and 1 percent other (including Malay and Burgher), with 2003 figures reflecting a similar makeup. There are many subgroups in these broad categories, with differing alliances. The 1981 census information identified religious affiliation as 69 percent Buddhist, 15 percent Hindu, 8 percent Muslim, and 8 percent Christian (figures have been rounded).[3]

Recent fervent Christian evangelical missions to Sri Lanka have increased tensions, with an equally fervent reaction on the part of some Sinhala Buddhists.

However, the cycle of violence has had its seeds in a recurring attitude of ethnoreligious chauvinism on behalf of the majority Sinhalas, followed by extreme ethnically oriented violence on the part of the main separatist Tamil group, the Liberation Tigers of Tamil Eelam (LTTE). While ethnic tension between the Sinhalas and the Tamils is reflected in ancient Sinhala mythology, the current cycle of violence should not be attributed to a mythologized historical precedent. Instead, Sinhala political and religious leaders in the modern era have made destructive choices that have initiated the downward spiral into ethnic violence. Such leaders have drawn selectively upon the history and mythology of Sri Lanka to promote the transmission of an ethnoreligious chauvinist ideology.[4] Tragically, other more positive aspects of Sri Lankan history could have been emphasized. This paper offers an introduction to the conflict, looking at historical aspects in relation to Buddhism in Sri Lanka, and provides a brief overview of its current status.

While modern Sinhala ethnoreligious chauvinism is in many ways a modern construction, owing much to postindependence politicians who instituted ethnically exclusionary policies in order to consolidate their own power, it is not entirely cut out of new cloth. In chronicles composed by Buddhist monks around 1,800 years ago, the Sinhala people are identified as the ethnic group entrusted with the preservation of the Buddha's teachings on the island of Sri Lanka. In the *Mahavamsa*, the Buddha himself is said to have visited the island and to have expelled the native inhabitants from Sri Lanka after frightening them off with supernatural acts of terror. This eventually paves the way for Vijaya, a North Indian whose descendents come to be known as the Sinhalas, to be established as the first king of Sri Lanka and protector of the Buddha's true doctrine,[5] thereby establishing the link of mutual protection and support between the Sinhala people and the religion of Buddhism. By their birthright, the Sinhalas are destined to be overseers of the island's territory, and all other ethnic groups in Sri Lanka assume a second-class status. The *Mahavamsa* notes the inferior status of the

Tamils specifically, while discussing the military conquests of Duttagamani. Duttagamani is the paradigmatic hero in the Sinhala tradition. As a young man, he becomes enraged by the Tamil domination of his homeland. With a relic of the Buddha on the tip of his sword, Duttagamani successfully vanquishes the Tamil king and reestablishes the primacy of Buddhism in Sri Lanka. As David Little has pointed out, the *Mahavamsa* chronicles show blatant disregard for fundamental Buddhist values such as nonviolence and peace. Instead, widespread slaughter of non-Buddhists is justified as part of the effort to defend Buddhism and assert Sinhala dominance over Sri Lanka.[6]

It is hard to imagine an ancient and authoritative text that could serve as a more effective warrant for ethnic exclusion than the *Mahavamsa*. While the Tamils are not targeted specifically on account of their religion (which is predominantly Hinduism), they nonetheless become the object of intolerance because their presence in Sri Lanka interferes with the manifest destiny of the chosen Sinhalas as a Buddhist people. The mindset of Sinhala ethnic superiority, reinforced through mythology and a selective reading of history, has had a devastating effect on the Sinhala imagination. As Sri Lankan historian K. M. de Silva has noted:

> In the Sinhala language, the words for nation, race, and people are practically synonymous, and a multiethnic or multicommunal nation or state is incomprehensible to the popular mind. The emphasis on Sri Lanka as the land of the Sinhala Buddhists carried an emotional popular appeal, compared with which the concept of a multiethnic polity was a meaningless abstraction.[7]

No one was more successful than Anagarika Dharmapala (1864-1933) in appropriating Sinhala mythology in the modern era. Dharmapala was a charismatic figure who at the turn of the twentieth century led a movement for Sinhala Buddhist revivalism in reaction to British imperialism. He drew directly on the legacy of Duttagamani's liberation of the Sinhala people from Tamil rule as his inspiration for a new modernized sense of Sinhala Buddhist nationalism. Dharmapala rallied the masses to oppose British imperialism and the Tamil influence by equating the moral welfare of Sri Lanka with the flourishing of Buddhism. Conversely, he understood the "slothfulness" of the

Sinhalas as a consequence of the vices introduced by the lax morality of Christianity and polytheism.[8] His rhetoric was thus a modern statement of the powerful ethnoreligious connection recovered from Sinhala Buddhist traditions.

Despite the obvious continuity between Dharmapala's ethnoreligious chauvinism and its antecedent located in the ancient Buddhist chronicles, it should be noted once again that it is misleading to describe the current ethnic conflict as simply the inevitable reoccurrence of primordial ethnic hatreds. Dharmapala and the ethnonationalist politicians who followed in his footsteps consciously aligned themselves with particular elements of history and mythology that could serve as warrants for contemporary Sinhala chauvinism. There is thus a strong element of imagined construction to the modern Sinhala nationalist identity. The eminent Sri Lankan anthropologist, Stanley Tambiah, has noted the contrast between the historical coexistence of the Sinhala and Tamil peoples and an ideology of ethnoreligious chauvinism that can be traced from the Buddhist chronicles to the present day. Tambiah emphasizes the historical fact that the Sinhalas were continually enriched by their interaction with the influx of Tamil migrants from South India. Both Tamil culture and its institutions were not rejected as alien, but rather, were incorporated into the Sinhala mainstream. Temples were constructed to Hindu gods, multiethnic trade unions were established, intermarriage was common, and, perhaps most surprising, intermarriage among the Sinhala and Tamil royalty in Sri Lanka made their royal lines virtually indistinguishable at times.[9] Clearly, the boundaries of ethnicity and culture were porous in premodern Sri Lanka. Tambiah acutely notes:

> The contemporary consciousness of ethnicity is a politicized product of post-independence 'democratic' politics, chauvinist rhetoric, and state-building . . . Deeply ignorant of their past, the young adults and youth of today, on both the Tamil and Sinhalese sides. . . have come to think and feel as two separate peoples, two ethnic species, locked in a man-made battle for survival.[10]

The modern phenomenon of nationalism has had the effect of consolidating hitherto porous identities into self-consciously distinct groups through the means of mass communication and the emergence of mass politics.[11] Tragically, Sri Lankan nationalism could have moved instead in an inclusivist direction, building upon the legacy of secularism and administrative rationality left behind, however imperfectly, by the British. Unlike India's postcolonial experience, which was fraught with ethnoreligious tension, Sri Lanka's transition to independence was relatively peaceful.[12] In other words, there was a genuine opportunity in Sri Lanka to move in the direction of a multiethnic liberal democracy. Politicians would see to it that such an opportunity would not last long.

Much of the blame for the contemporary conflict rests with state elites who have been genuine ethnoreligious chauvinists and have also found it in their political interests to employ divisive rhetoric in order to curry favor with the masses. One simply cannot ignore the unfortunate reality of misguided leadership in Sri Lanka as a major contributing factor to the genesis and escalation of the conflict. Shortly after independence, S. W. R. D. Bandaranaike rose to power in 1956 on a platform that advocated the legal favoritism of the Sinhala language. This proposal naturally enraged the Tamil minority, who felt that the elevation of Sinhala as the official language of Sri Lanka would create profound educational and economic disadvantages for them.[13] Bandaranaike, while clearly aware of the purely pragmatic benefits of pandering to the Sinhala majority, was also a Sinhala nationalist at heart who demonstrated quite early on in his career a commitment to illiberal nationalism for Sri Lanka. In the mid-1930s, he wrote that "nationalism based on cultural revival among the Sinhala-speaking Buddhists was the only solution [to colonialism]." His emphasis on cultural revival was to be coupled with ethnic chauvinism. Already in 1939 he claimed that a country could not progress "by embracing all communities and all cultures in their activities."[14] Once in office, however, Bandaranaike's pragmatism led him to agree to a pact with the Tamil leader, S. J. V. Chelvanayakam, that extended to the Tamil areas of the north and east a significant degree of regional autonomy, including the official sanction of the Tamil language in the Tamil regions.[15] Bandaranaike, however, reneged on the pact after pressure from Sinhala extremist groups, many of whose members were Buddhist monks traditionally committed to nonpolitical activity. Bandaranaike's change of mind initiated the first significant wave of widespread interethnic violence in 1958. Somewhat ironically, Bandaranaike, who had greatly contributed to the fanning of ethnic hatred, was assassinated in 1959 at the hands of an extremist Buddhist monk who viewed him as too conciliatory to the Tamils.[16] His widow, Sirimavo Bandaranaike, who took power after her husband's assassination and ruled from 1960 to 1965 and again from 1970 to 1977, only intensified Sinhala chauvinism by insisting that the "Sinhala Only" language policy be put into full effect and by adopting a geographical quota system intended to reduce Tamil entrance into the universities.[17]

An opportunity for peace was missed when the 1972 Constitution enshrined into law the primacy of Buddhism and did little to mollify the concerns of the Tamil minority. For the Tamils, their frustrations over the Constitution mounted to the point where many of them began to demand complete separation, abandoning their prior hopes for a multiethnic Sri Lanka. The main Tamil separatist paramilitary group, the LTTE, was founded around this time. While the election of J. R. Jayewardene in 1977 and the minority provisions of the 1978 Constitution offered some renewed hope for reconciliation between the two communities, the new government's failure to implement these provisions further enraged the Tamils, many of whom had already turned to guerilla action in order to fight for a Tamil homeland.[18] As the Tamils increasingly turned to violence, the Jayewardene government adopted extreme emergency provisions in order to head off civil war. The provisions contained in the Prevention of Terrorism Act (1979) gave the government broad extrajudicial powers to contain the Tamil threat. Unfortunately, these policies only further alienated the Tamil population, and Tamil terrorism increased. This cycle of violence reached its zenith with the brutal riots against the Tamils in 1983.

Since 1983, the conflict has taken the form of organized violence between the Sri Lankan military and the LTTE, each mounting offensives and counteroffensives into the other's territories with no ultimately decisive victory for either side.[19] The major military offensive launched by the Sri Lankan government in 1987 against Tamil positions in the north did have the effect, however, of bringing India into the conflict. Tamil Nadu politicians eventually prevailed upon Indian

Prime Minister Rajiv Gandhi to intervene to stop the shelling of the Tamil territories in the north by the Sri Lankan security forces. After the Sri Lankan navy turned away Indian ships carrying relief supplies for the Tamils in Jaffna, Gandhi eventually agreed to an airdrop of supplies, in clear violation of Sri Lankan air space, and put diplomatic pressure on Sri Lanka to halt the northern offensive.[20] The Sri Lankan government had rightly suspected that the Tamil insurgents were using the Indian state of Tamil Nadu, located across the narrow strait that separates India from Sri Lanka, as a safe haven, and had, in fact, launched the 1987 offensive to capture Vadamarachchi, a strategic point of traffic between India and the Tamil North.[21] Thus, although India had played an unofficial role in the conflict for years, it was now officially involved in the conflict. While India was not willing to accept the risks of direct military intervention on behalf of the Tamils, it did come to an "uneven bilateral agreement"[22] with the Sri Lankan government on July 27, 1987, and sent a peacekeeping force of 10,000 to disarm the LTTE and maintain peace in LTTE-occupied territories. While the LTTE initially accepted India's presence, their opinion toward the Indian Peace Keeping Force (IPKF) soon soured. India had taken for granted that the LTTE would call a truce and lay down their arms voluntarily. This, however, never occurred and India eventually found itself forced to abandon a completely failed mission after incurring 1,150 casualties of its own.[23]

Following India's withdrawal in 1990, fighting resumed between the LTTE and the government after a failed cease-fire, which lasted one year. The early 1990s saw a period of intense fighting. In late 1994, President Chandrika Kumaratunga, the daughter of the Bandaranaikes, came to power and soon extended an olive branch to the LTTE. In fact, she proposed a devolution plan that would have given substantial autonomy to the Tamil areas of the north and east. It was rejected by the LTTE as insufficient and sharply criticized by the Sinhalas as too concessionary to the Tamils. Peace talks thus once again collapsed and fierce fighting continued.[24] The tide of the war appeared to be turning in favor of the government with the capture of Jaffna in 1996, but the LTTE proved resilient, eventually recapturing lost territory and forcing the Sri Lankan government to end its offensive without control of the long desired Tamil supply routes.[25]

The conflict has long been punctuated by failed attempts at peace and periods of cease-fire (including the current fragile peace agreed to in 2002), but the fundamental issues motivating the warring parties have yet to be resolved. The current situation is depressingly but quite accurately characterized as a stalemate between the two parties. As Rohan Edrisinha notes in this volume, the last round of peace talks, mediated by the Norwegians, broke down in March 2003 after some initial optimism that the LTTE would abandon its commitment to a separate Tamil state and consider an asymmetrical federalist arrangement. Moreover, there is currently a sharp difference of opinion within the Sri Lankan government on pursuing peace with the LTTE. Since December 2001, political power has been split between Ranil Wickramasinghe, who, as prime minister has aggressively pursued an end to the war through negotiation, and President Kumaratunga, who has become a very outspoken critic of the peace process initiated by Wickramasinghe.[26] Their power struggle has effectively paralyzed the peace process, and Edrisinha suggests in this volume that a renewal of negotiations with the LTTE will likely not happen until after the presidential elections in 2006.

Though it is important not to boil down the conflict to two sides, an attitude among some Sinhala Buddhists of ethnoreligious superiority helped to create some of the conditions for civil war, as this historical summary highlights. It has also contributed to the inability of the Sri Lankan government to broker a lasting peace with the LTTE. Obviously the LTTE is not itself without blame for the perpetuation of the conflict. LTTE hardliners have either insisted on complete independence or the creation of a loose two-nation confederation—neither of which will be acceptable to the Sinhalas. As well, killings and political assassinations, such as the recent murder of the Sri Lankan Foreign Minister, Lakshman Kadirgamar, cast doubt on the LTTE's commitment to peaceful resolution of the conflict. Yet Sinhala chauvinism must also be seen as a formidable obstacle in the way of a workable federalist-style agreement with the Tamils and peace for all constituents in Sri Lanka. The election of Mahinda Rajapske as president in November 2005 has done little to change the dynamics described in this background piece.

As mentioned in the introduction, the government and the LTTE returned to peace talks in the spring of 2006, but are still at stalemate.

Notes

1. S. J. Tambiah, *Ethnic Fratricide and the Dismantling of Democracy* (Chicago: University of Chicago Press, 1986), 21.
2. Darini Rajaasingham-Senanayake, "Dangers of Devolution," *Creating Peace in Sri Lanka: Civil War and Reconciliation*, ed. Robert Rotberg (Washington, D.C.: Brookings Institution Press), 1999, 58.
3. 1981 figures from "Peace in Sri Lanka," official website of the Sri Lankan Government's Secretariat for Coordinating the Peace Process (SCOPP):http://www.peaceinsrilanka.org/peace2005/Insidepage/Facts and Figures/FactsandFigures.asp, accessed 9/12/05; 2003 figures from the website of the Sri Lanka Embassy in Egypt: http://www.lankaemb-egypt.com/SriLanka/facts.htm, accessed 9/12/05.
4. Tambiah, *Ethnic Fratricide*, 101.
5. David Little, *Sri Lanka: The Invention of Enmity* (Washington, D.C.: United States Institute of Peace Press, 1994), 27.
6. Ibid., 28.
7. Quoted in David Little, "Religion and Ethnicity in the Sri Lankan Civil War," in *Creating Peace in Sri Lanka: Civil War and Reconciliation*, ed. Robert Rotberg (Washington, D.C.: Brookings Institution Press, 1999), 42-43.
8. Little, *Sri Lanka*, 24.
9. Tambiah, *Ethnic Fratricide*, 94-95.
10. Ibid., 101-02.
11. Little, *Sri Lanka*, 31.
12. Ibid., 4.
13. Ibid., 69.
14. Quoted in Little, *Sri Lanka*, 61.
15. Ibid., 67-68.
16. Ibid., 71.
17. Ibid., 72, 74.
18. Ibid., 86-87.
19. Rajaasingham-Senanayake, "Dangers of Devolution," 58.
20. Chris Smith, "South Asia's Enduring War," in *Creating Peace in Sri Lanka: Civil War and Reconciliation*, ed. Robert Rotberg (Washington, D.C.: Brookings Institution Press, 1999), 19.
21. Ibid., 19.
22. Smith refers to the agreement with this description, 19.
23. Ibid., 20-25.
24. Ibid., 26-27.
25. Ibid., 28-29.
26. Gavin Thomas, *The Rough Guide to Sri Lanka* (New York: Penguin, 2004), 428.

Appendix Two: Sudan Background

Atalia Omer

"In the process of becoming a single political state," Francis Deng observes, "Sudan emerged as a deeply divided society in which ethnicity, region, and religion were frequently used to organize political competition."[1] Nowadays the predicament in Darfur, where government-supported Arab Janjaweed militia engage in a policy of ethnic cleansing against African tribes, highlights the complex nexus of ethnicity, religion, and nationalism, and the ways in which various leaders have manipulated those factors in perpetuating the Sudanese civil war since Sudan's independence in 1956. Fluctuating and conflicting interpretations of the politics of religion and ethnicity have fueled competing conceptions of Sudanese nationalism aimed either at the consolidation or the liquidation of state power. An exclusivist Arab-Muslim understanding of Sudanese nationalism that is designed to consolidate government control over the country is pitted against a religiously and ethnically neutral and inclusive ideal of citizenship on the part of the insurgents.

Indeed, as Deng notes, the civil war in Sudan which resulted in at least two million deaths and the displacement of approximately four million persons may be classified as a postcolonial nationalist conflict.

Its onset was conditioned by antecedent British colonial economic, cultural, and political arrangements intended to ensure geopolitical interests and to facilitate administrative control over the diverse Sudanese regions, peoples, and religions. The colonial infrastructure resulted in the systematic privileging of the North over the South, a pattern of discrimination with long-term ramifications. After independence, pre-existing political, economic, and religious advantages served to reinforce the Islamic-Arab ideal of Sudanese nationalism encouraged in the North. Favoring such an exclusive form of ethnoreligious nationalism naturally had the effect of disadvantaging Sudan's many other religious and ethnic minorities, the largest of which are the Dinka, Beja, Nuer, Nuba, Nubian, Fur, Bari, Azande, Moru, and Shilluk.

Religion and ethnicity have frequently been deployed as markers of political identification and controversy as well as ammunition for cultural, political, and economic conflict, primarily but not exclusively, between the northern and southern regions of Sudan. Nonetheless, northern and southern identities are subject to frequent reinterpretations and reinventions in relation to one another and to changing circumstances, opportunities, and interests. For example, the political understanding of religion and ethnicity in postcolonial Sudan differed from colonial times, even though the cultural and geographical divisions between the North and the South may be traced back to the period of British colonialism (1898-1955). It was the British who, after all, originally divided up Sudan, thereby delineating political as well as ethnic, religious, and cultural boundaries between the inhabitants of the North and South. This identification of geographical regions with specific ethnicities and religions, as if topographical barriers coincided with monolithic cultural entities, has had a lasting effect and is more than mere remnants of a colonial nomenclature. The equation of region and religion often assumed the rhetorical appearance of a religious war, especially when outsiders chose sides in the conflict, thereby strengthening the divisions. While such rhetoric clearly overlooks the complexity of religious, ethnic, and geographical factors, it does illustrate the connection between political domination and an appeal to religious, ethnic, or cultural superiority.

Since independence, Muslim Arabs have dominated Sudan's multiethnic and multireligious inhabitants on the political, cultural, and economic fronts, based on a claim to ethnoreligious superiority. This type of ethnic nationalism dates from the Turkiyya and Mahdiyya periods of the nineteenth century when northern economic domination was rationalized or legitimized by means of a belief in Islamic-Arab cultural, ethnic, and religious superiority.[2]

The Turkiyya (1821–1885) designates the period of Turko-Egyptian rule that dislocated and irreversibly transformed the life of many non-Muslim Sudanese, such as the Dinka and Shilluk as a result of slave trafficking. The Turkiyya regime was eventually overthrown by followers of Ahmad Ibn Abdallah who had proclaimed himself the Mahdi, a religious and political redeemer. Thus the so-called Mahdiyya period (1885–1898) has resonated in the northern national imagination as a golden moment of cultural, religious, and political liberation. On the other hand, southerners imagined the Mahdiyya period in an altogether negative way. Because of recurrent raids against the South during that time, the period became associated with the predatory policies of the slave-raiding Turkiyya.[3] Similarly, after independence, the disenfranchised South perceived the government in Khartoum as being no different from colonial rule. This divergence in the interpretation of the Mahdiyya and postindependence periods illustrates a recurring theme in North-South relations. What for the Arab-Muslim North stands as a glorious moment of redemption is for the African non-Muslim South nothing more than yet another instance of northern domination.

The period of British control which followed the Mahdiyya is known as the Anglo-Egyptian Condominium because the British pretended they wanted to reestablish Turko-Egyptian sovereignty in the region, although as de facto ruler of Egypt since 1882, Britain was in charge. Due to British encouragement and patronage, Muslim leaders of local northern Sufi societies such as the Khatmiyya were able to generate mass support for political movements that eventually would dominate the political landscape in Khartoum. Meanwhile, British policies in the South took a different course. Deeming the indigenous inhabitants of the South to be pagans, the British encouraged Christian missionary work in the area. Concomitantly, colonial officials prevented the establishment of a native administrative infrastructure, systematically eroding the scope of traditional tribal authority and isolating the two regions of Sudan under the pretense of protecting the South from Muslim influence.[4] The colonially-imposed boundaries together with the way the regions on either side were administered had devastating effects on the country. The South suffered from economic inequality and eventually from political underrepresentation,[5] conditions that contributed to the eventual onset of civil war.

The primary catalyst of the first phase of the civil war (1956–1972) was precisely the economic and political privileges enjoyed by the North after independence, which simply added insult to what the South perceived as an already long list of injuries. Some of the grievances were seemingly addressed in the Addis Ababa Agreement, which prevailed from 1972 until 1983. That agreement recognized the rights and individuality of the southern peoples after a prolonged period of disenfranchisement and cultural and religious domination by the North. Successive governments in Khartoum instigated policies of cultural, religious, educational, and legal homogenization as a means to consolidate and centralize control.

For instance, shortly after independence, General Ibrahim Abboud initiated the expulsion of Christian missionaries as well as the Arabization of the administrative and educational systems in the South. Abboud's policies as well as those of his successors aimed at a top-down assimilation of minorities into a particularly parochial Muslim-Arab interpretation of Sudanese nationalism. Concurrently, ethnic and religious minorities cultivated alternative criteria of citizenship, either pluralistic or secessionist.[6] The Addis Ababa Agreement reflected, if only dimly, these alternatives. Provisions against discrimination on the basis of religion, race, language, or gender were thereby included in the Sudanese constitution, signaling a more pluralist and inclusive form of nationalism, according to which, ideas of African and Arab identity might coexist instead of being dominated by the image of Arab-Islamic superiority and uniformity that the North had previously endeavored to impose upon the South.[7] The appearance of a more inclusive form of Sudanese nationalism suggested a departure from the inclination of northern and southern politicians to ignore the factor of ethnic and religious pride and thereby suppress the distinctive

interests and aspirations of each side, including their competing territorial claims.[8]

Undoubtedly, the Addis Ababa Agreement was intended to alleviate
some of the divisive effects caused by colonial policies and the attempts
of Khartoum thereafter to achieve cultural and political homogeneity
throughout an administratively unified Sudan. However, Jaafar
Nimeiri, having agreed to it eleven years earlier, unilaterally abrogated
the Addis Ababa Agreement in 1983, thereby scuttling ten years of rel-
ative domestic tranquility. Nimeiri, who took power in 1969, defined
his Revolutionary Command Council (RCC) as secular, socialist, and
pan-Arab, an orientation, which at the time propelled him initially to
endorse the 1972 peace accord. However, by 1977 Nimeiri's regime had
taken an authoritarian turn, with a strong commitment to
Islamization. Another more recent example of the same domineering
impulse, and with the same disruptive results, was the seizure of power
in 1989 by Omar al-Bashir, leader of the National Islamic Front (NIF).
Still in power, the NIF was originally dedicated to a program of
"Islamizing" and "Arabizing" the entire country. As the result of strong
southern resistance and continuing international pressure, gradually it
has had to modify or sublimate its objectives.

Nimeiri's abrogation of the Addis Ababa Agreement and the
revised constitution in 1983 inaugurated the second phase of the
Sudanese civil war. In their place, Nimeiri instituted *sharia* laws, also
known as the September Laws. These events brought into being the
Sudanese People's Liberation Movement/Army (SPLM/A), led by
Colonel John Garang, and the beginning of armed resistance against
the government's policies of cultural and religious coercion. In its place
the SPLM/A pursued a pluralistic and inclusive form of Sudanese
nationalism, one that eventually came to be endorsed by a variety of
northern political parties, such as the Democratic Unionist Party and
the National Democratic Alliance (NDA).[9] Despite Nimeiri's overthrow
in 1985 and the subsequent election of a relatively democratic government in Khartoum, the fighting persisted, displacing and eradicating
large numbers of the population. Further, the attempt in 1989 by Sadiq
el-Mahdi, the new prime minister, to neutralize the *sharia* laws and the
aggressive policies of the previous government was reversed following

the bloodless coup instigated by the NIF that same year.[10]

Beyond that, changes in the region seriously affected the course of the resistance against the Khartoum government. With the overthrow of the Ethiopian leader, Mengistu Haile Mariam in 1991, the SPLM/A lost its base and primary sponsor and, in addition, suffered internal division (mostly along ethnic lines) that weakened its role as exclusive representative of southern grievances and political demands.[11] This worsening state of affairs in Sudan prompted a response from Sudan's neighbors. Organizing themselves into what was called the Inter-Governmental Authority on Development (IGAD), they managed to work together with the Sudanese parties to produce in 1994 a Declaration of Principles for settling the Sudanese conflict. The declaration identified the cultivation of democratic practices, religious and ethnic impartiality, and respect for minority rights as necessary requirements for peace. The declaration also hinted at the importance of the right of self-determination for the South, which would become increasingly significant in the negotiations leading up to the January 2005 Comprehensive Peace Agreement (CPA) that marked the official end of the conflict. The declaration itself was somewhat tentative on the subject of self-determination for the South. It intimated the right of the South to hold a referendum on secession, but set rather unrealistic conditions for carrying it out. Despite a series of failed negotiations, an unambiguous provision was finally included in the recent agreement. It provides for a referendum on secession for the South following a six-and-a-half-year interim period.

Potentially, the result of such a referendum could be the declaration of an independent South. Because this act of secession by the oil-rich South would significantly diminish the economic revenues of the North, the political leadership of the latter has generally resisted a genuine reconfiguration of its conception of Sudanese citizenship whereby a perceived Muslim-Arab superiority legitimates the political and economic domination of the Southern regions and its peoples. Hence, the economic dimension of the conflict has indeed influenced the intensification of claims of religious and ethnic superiority as those transpired in the course of the civil war as well as its aftermath. However promising, the principles articulated in the CPA have inade-

quately materialized on the ground due to the old regime's unwillingness to accommodate the prospect of power sharing and elections
which would facilitate the eventual self-determination referendum.
This problem has been further augmented by a lack of a sufficient institutional infrastructure in the South.[12] While the nomination of John
Garang as vice president on July 9, 2005 signified a promising move
toward power sharing, his tragic death only twenty-one days later
instantly exposed the fragility of the CPA with an alarming increase of
unrest in Khartoum and the South. In a post-Garang Sudan as before,
the successful implementation of the CPA would have to depend on
the cultivation of democratic institutions and practices as well as a
reconsideration of the relation between Sudanese citizenship, on the
one hand, and religious-ethnic orientations, on the other. The swift
transition to a new first vice president, Salva Kiir, nominated by the
SPLM and taking office a few days after Garang's death,[13] does offer
some hope for continued peace between the North and the South.

The Sudanese civil war revolved primarily around the problem of
defining the parameters of citizenship in relation to the categories of
religion and ethnicity in postcolonial Sudan. The status of the Arab-
Islamic orientation as constitutive of a Sudanese national identity that
would override other ethnic and religious affiliations has been challenged by dissenting and previously disenfranchised ethnoreligious
minorities, the SPLM/A being the most vocal. The SPLM has, for the
most part, resisted an ethnocentric conception of national belonging in
favor of either secessionist platforms or inclusive and liberal forms of
nationalism. This vision involved a demand to de-monopolize a
parochial Sudanese national identity by redefining it along the criteria
of residence and birth rather than ethnic or religious identity. However,
the recurrence of Islamization campaigns and the devastating toll of a
continuous North-South polarization and cycles of violence have contributed to the diminishing appeal of such an inclusive model of
nationalism giving way increasingly, if not yet completely, to secessionist pressures.

In the year since April 2005, the CPA has started to become institutionalized. An interim constitution has been ratified for the entire
country. Power sharing is in place, with the southern rebels insured

30 percent of the seats in the National Assembly. There is a "Unified National Government." The government of southern Sudan also has a constitution, which the Sudanese Ministry of Justice has said is in conformance with the interim constitution and the CPA.[14] A major peace agreement was signed in Darfur as this publication was going to press in May of 2006. With both that agreement and the CPA the question remains: will these agreements hold, particularly in a country that has such a history of broken agreements and outbreaks of armed conflict?

Notes

1. Francis Deng, *War of Visions: Conflict of Identities in the Sudan* (Washington, D.C.: The Brookings Institution, 1995), 403.
2. Ann Mosely Lesch, *The Sudan: Contested National Identities* (Bloomington: Indiana University Press, 1998), 22.
3. Ibid., 26-29.
4. Ibid., 29-31.
5. Ibid., 36-37.
6. Ibid.
7. Ibid., 23.
8. Ibid., 26.
9. Ibid., 23.
10. See David Mozersky and John Prendergast, "Love Thy Neighbor: Regional Intervention in Sudan's Civil War," *Harvard International Review* 26, No. I (2004) http://hir.harvard.edu/articles/1220/2/.
11. Ibid.
12. International Crisis Group, "The Khartoum-SPLM Agreement: Sudan's Uncertain Peace" Africa Report No. 96 (July 25, 2005) http://www.crisisgroup.org/home/index.cfm?id=3582&l=1.
13. U.S. Department of State Department, Bureau of African Affairs, "Sudan Background Notes," January 2006, accessed online at http://www.state.gov/r/pa/ei/bgn/5424.htm
14. Ibid.

Appendix Three: Bosnia and Herzegovina Background

Kati Kargman

Different attempts at governing the area now comprising the country known as Bosnia and Herzegovina (B&H) were largely responsible for the development of the ethnoreligious tension and conflict that paved the way for the war there between 1992 and 1995. Moreover, the postwar government, when it has acted on its own, has done little to mitigate tensions and prevent future conflict. Without continuing international assistance, the present Bosnian state remains in serious jeopardy.

During Ottoman rule from the fifteenth to the nineteenth century, the *millet* system created autonomous ethnoreligious communities,[1] thereby providing the seedbed for the strong sense of ethnonational identity that developed in the region in the 1900s and finally helped ignite the Bosnian war. Ottoman favoritism toward Orthodox Christians and discrimination against Catholics heightened religious antagonism and tension between those two groups. In addition, resentment against the Ottomans on the part of the Christians extended to local Muslims who were often inaccurately identified by the disparaging term, "Turks," and frequently subjected to persecution.[2] Such hostility has typically been justified in reference to the Battle of Kosovo which took place between the Ottomans, or "Turks," and the Serbs in 1389. The Serbian army, led by Prince Lazar, was defeated at a place known as the Field of Blackbirds, thereby initiating 500 years of Turkish rule.[3] In a battle that has been described as the "centerpiece of the Serbian tradition,"[4] Prince Lazar was supposed to have chosen death, rather than betray his Orthodox faith by surrendering to the infidel Ottoman oppressor. What is regarded as Lazar's act of martyrdom has ever after served to rally Serbian resistance to Muslim influence in the south Balkans.

Ethnonationalist tendencies were further heightened during World War II. The fascist powers, Germany and Italy, supported a Croat government, known as the Ustasha, which tried to create, by means of a policy of ethnic cleansing, an ethnically pure Croat Catholic state, one that would have included B&H within its borders. The Ustasha's policies elicited a violent backlash from Serbian loyalists known as *chetniks,* and thereby intensified ethnic hostility in the region. In the 1990s fear that another Ustasha regime might arise under the leadership of the Croat chauvinist, Franjo Tudjman, fueled ethnoreligious tensions and contributed to the war fever of the period.

Tito's authoritarian regime also paved the way for ethnoreligious conflict. It was Tito's charisma and political dominance that held Serbs, Croats, and Bosnians together, along with Slovenians, Macedonians, Kosovars, and other members of the former Yugoslavia. Without him, there was no ideology or leader capable of consolidating all the different ethnic, religious. or regional groups.[5] After his death in 1980, the ensuing political and communal dissension paved the way for a severe ethnonationalist power struggle that would help ignite the war in Yugoslavia.

Important causes of the war include both the manipulation of existing ethnoreligious tension by nationalist politicians, such as Tudjman and Serbian strongman, Slobodan Milosevic, who sought to increase their own political power,[6] and the political and economic instability left behind by the collapse of Tito's regime. There was no stable system of mediating institutions that could contain the deepening divisions among the members of the former Yugoslavia as they took to fighting among themselves over the right to self-determination. The result was increasing chaos, violence, and devastation, most of all for those in B&H, but also in varying degrees for other Yugoslavs as well.

During the war, Bosnian Serbs, mobilized by their principal leaders, Radovan Karadzic and Ratko Mladic, allied with Serbian extremists with the goal of expelling all non-Serbs from the part of Bosnia that would then be annexed to Serbia. Analogously, Bosnian Croats, led by Mate Boban, joined forces with Croat chauvinists in an effort to remove all non-Croats from another section of B&H, and then make that a part of Croatia. Indeed, many thought that Milosevic and Tudjman secretly colluded to divide Bosnia between them.[7] By contrast, the Bosnian Muslims, led by Aljia Izetbegovic and Haris Silajdzic, sought to maintain the autonomy of Bosnia and protect its sovereignty within existing borders against the genocidal depredations of the Serbs and Croats.

At first, the international response to the conflict was limited to diplomatic action and humanitarian aid. However, when in 1995 it became self-evident that diplomatic efforts appearing to favor Serbian aggression did not end the violence, NATO intervened militarily, undertaking to reverse Serbian military gains and help create a multireligious and multiethnic state under the auspices of the Dayton Peace Agreement.

The Agreement was initialed in Dayton, Ohio, on November 21, 1995, and signed in Paris on December 14, 1995.[8] Participants in the negotiations included Richard Holbrooke, Slobodan Milosevic, Alija Izetbegovic, Franjo Tudjman, Carl Bildt, and members of the Contact Group.[9] The primary objectives included halting the fighting in B&H and creating a stable multiethnic state that would represent a compromise among the three warring factions and maintain the unity and territorial integrity of B&H.

The system of government prescribed by Dayton is a consociational federation, which allocates considerable power to each of the ethnic groups under a fairly weak set of national institutions. Though this model of power-sharing was acceptable enough to bring an end to the war, it has hardly succeeded in eliminating ethnic and religious tensions.

According to the Dayton arrangement, the central government has limited powers over two semi-autonomous "entities," Republika Srpska and the Federation of Bosnia and Herzegovina, which consists of the Bosnian Croats and the Bosnian Muslims (or Boshniaks). The central government is "dependent on budgetary transfers from the entities, [and] with neither an army, police force, nor judiciary of its own, it has relatively little leverage over lower levels of government."[10] This leaves the state government with little power to encourage unification or to enforce federally sponsored legislation. Republika Srpska is essentially a Serbian mini-state with its own president and national assembly, while the Federation of Bosnia and Herzegovina is a mini-federation of Boshniaks and Croats, with a presidency, bi-cameral legislature and canton governments.[11] As such, the system accentuates group-based ethnoreligious loyalties.[12]

Ideally, each entity is supposed to elect representatives on the assumption that they will find it necessary to establish coalitions across ethnic lines after realizing that dwelling exclusively on group interests makes it difficult to govern. Unfortunately, politicians within B&H have generally not been as far-sighted as some of Dayton's designers had hoped.

It is not just the politicians who are at fault. The consociational system of governance laid out in Dayton itself encourages ethnonationalism by favoring parties and candidates with narrow ethnocentric agendas rather than those who promote multiethnic interests.[13] This structural problem, innate to a consociational system of governance, serves to prevent the mitigation of tensions and reconciliation among ethnic groups in B&H.

To an important extent, the structure of the B&H government institutionalized ethnonationalist goals, and the policies of ethnic cleansing adopted by Milosevic and Tudjman were partially rewarded.[14] According to Sumantra Bose, this outcome was unavoidable since it was only this kind of compromise that could successfully end the war.[15]

In effect, Bosnia's consociational federation is a political system characterized by paralysis.[16] The battlefield was transferred from a military to a political context. Everything from the timing of meetings to their location as well as their agenda "has become an occasion for resistance."[17] The war shifted from physical violence to political action, or more often inaction, as a means of achieving one group's goals at the expense of another's. There has been so little progress that the Office of the High Representative (OHR) has had repeatedly to impose legislation and other measures in order to ensure that the Dayton Agreement was being implemented.[18]

The OHR is charged with overseeing and monitoring the implementation of Dayton.[19] By means of the so-called "Bonn powers,"[20] the OHR is authorized to "impose laws, to issue administrative decisions and to sack recalcitrant or corrupt officeholders whenever local institutions failed to do the job...."[21] In practice, this authority is a mixed blessing. It allows the OHR to push the B&H state towards stability, liberal democracy, and peace. On the other hand, it has also blurred the line between national and international jurisdiction. One critic asserts, "far from becoming a functioning democratic state, Bosnia is little more than a colony of the West run by increasingly arrogant and autocratic international officials."[22] This opinion is shared by many in B&H and has discouraged local inititiative.[23] The OHR's intrusiveness has made moderate politicians increasingly complacent, relying on the international community to take actions they ought themselves to take.[24] In addition, the OHR's continued unilateral action has deterred popular participation and encouraged apathy. At the same time, the OHR would never have had to become so active had the structure of government not made the achievement of the multiethnic goals of Dayton so difficult.

The various forms of government that have existed in Bosnia over many centuries have played a crucial role in setting the stage for conflict, either by heightening ethnoreligious tensions or by failing to go far enough toward eliminating them. Ottoman rule, the Ustasha government, and Tito's authoritarian regime all contributed in a variety of ways to the intensification of ethnic and religious tensions that set the stage for war in Bosnia during the 1990s. The post-Dayton political system of governance has had highly ambiguous effects. It did succeed in bringing an end to a bloody ethnic civil war, and in laying down some of the necessary political and legal conditions for interethnic harmony. On the other hand, consociationalism and the divisive ethnocentrism it tolerates combined with a system of international supervision does not constitute a just and stable solution to the problem of ethnoreligious nationalism. A major effort to change the situation for the good occurred in late November 2005 when Serbian, Croatian, and Boshniak leaders met in Washington and agreed to changes in the system. Instead of the current three presidents, each elected by a particular ethnic enclave, one president is to be elected by all in B&H. Plans also include a strong office of prime minister and parliamentary reform.

Notes

1. Under the *millet* system of governance, religious communities enjoyed a degree of semi-autonomy; each *millet* was ruled by a religious leader who was located on the lowest tier in a hierarchy of governance that reported to the Sultan and his officials.
2. Donald Quataert, *The Ottoman Empire, 1700-1922* (Cambridge: Cambridge University Press, 2000), 172.
3. Laura Silber and Allan Little, *Yugoslavia: Death of a Nation* (New York: Penguin Books, 1997), 71.
4. Silber and Little, *Yugoslavia*, 72.
5. Paul Mojzes, *Yugoslavian Inferno: Ethnoreligious Warfare in the Balkans* (New York: Continuum, 1995), 76.
6. Silber and Little, *Yugoslavia*, 29.
7. Richard Holbrooke, *To End A War* (New York: Random House, 1998), 10.
8. United Nations, *General Framework Agreement for Peace in Bosnia and Herzegovina: Dayton Accords* (New York: United Nations, December 14, 1995).
9. The Contact Group is comprised of representatives from Russia, France, Germany, the U.K., and the U.S.
10. Elizabeth M. Cousens and Charles K. Cater, *Toward Peace In Bosnia: Implementing the Dayton Accord* (Boulder, Colo.: Lynne Rienner Publishers, 2001), 103.
11. Cousens and Cater, *Toward Peace In Bosnia*, 103.
12. Sumantra Bose, *Bosnia After Dayton: Nationalist Partition and International Intervention* (Oxford: Oxford University Press, 2002), 63.
13. For the analysis in these two paragraphs, we are indebted to Timothy D. Sisk's book, *Power Sharing and International Mediation In Ethnic Conflicts* (Washington, D.C.: United States Institute of Peace Press, 1996).
14. International Crisis Group (ICG), *Is Dayton Failing?: Bosnia Four Years After the Peace Agreement*, (Sarajevo: ICG Balkans Report No.80, October 28, 1999), 2.
15. Bose, *Bosnia After Dayton*, 60.
16. Cousens and Cater, *Toward Peace In Bosnia*, 104.
17. Ibid., 104-05.
18. International Crisis Group, *Bosnia's Nationalist Governments: Paddy*

Ashdown and the Paradoxes of State Building (Sarajevo: ICG Balkans Report No. 146, July 22, 2003), 29.

19. United Nations, *General Framework*, Annex 11, Article II.
20. "In late 1997, the Peace Implementation Council granted the OHR its 'Bonn Powers,' which include the right to dismiss public officials and issue binding decisions by decree." Cousins and Cater, *Toward Peace In Bosnia*, 147.
21. International Crisis Group, *Bosnia's Nationalist Governments*, 1.
22. Timothy Donnais, *Division and Democracy: Bosnia's Post Dayton Elections*, Center for International and Security Studies Occasional Papers Number 61 (North York, Ont.: Center for International and Security Studies, York University, 1999), 10.
23. International Crisis Group, *Bosnia's Nationalist Governments*, 1.
24. Ibid., 2.

Contributors and Participants

Editors and Conference Organizers

David Little is T. J. Dermot Dunphy Visiting Professor of the Practice in Religion, Ethnicity, and International Conflict at Harvard Divinity School (HDS) and Faculty Associate at Harvard's Weatherhead Center for International Affairs. He joined HDS in 1999. Previously, he was senior scholar in religion, ethics, and human rights at the United States Institute of Peace (USIP) in Washington, D.C., where he directed the Working Group on Religion, Ideology, and Peace, which conducted a study of religion, nationalism, and intolerance in reference to the United Nations Declaration on the Elimination of Intolerance and Discrimination. From 1996 to 1998, he was on the State Department Advisory Committee on Religious Freedom Abroad. He is author with Scott W. Hibbard of *Islamic Activism and U.S. Foreign Policy*, and author of two volumes in the USIP series on religion, nationalism, and intolerance.

Donald K. Swearer is Distinguished Visiting Professor of Buddhist Studies at HDS and serves as Director of the Center for the Study of World Religions. Before coming to HDS in 2004, Donald Swearer taught at Swarthmore College as the Charles and Harriet Cox McDowell Professor of Religion. His primary research areas are: Theravada Buddhism in Southeast Asia, primarily in Thailand, and

Buddhist Social Ethics. His current research interests focus on sacred mountain traditions in northern Thailand as well as Christian identity in Buddhist Thailand. His recent books include: *The Buddhist World of Southeast Asia* (the 2nd revised edition in press); *The Legend of Queen Cama: Bodhiramsi's Camadevivamsa, a Translation and Commentary*; and *Becoming the Buddha: The Ritual of Image Consecration in Thailand* (Princeton, 2004). He serves on the boards of the Religious Pluralism Project and the Forum for Religion and Ecology.

Contributors and Presenters

Juan R. I. Cole is Professor of Modern Middle East and South Asian History at the History Department of the University of Michigan. He has written extensively about modern Islamic movements in Egypt, the Persian Gulf, and South Asia. His current research focuses on Shiite Islam in Iraq and Iran and the *jihadi* or "sacred-war" strain of Muslim radicalism, including al-Qaeda and the Taliban among other groups. His publications include *Sacred Space and Holy War* (IB Tauris, 2002), *Colonialism and Revolution in the Middle East: Social and Cultural Origins of Egypt's Urabi Movement* (Princeton, 1993), *Roots of North Indian Shiism in Iran and Iraq* (California, 1989), and *Shiism and Social Protest* (Yale, 1986).

Alex de Waal is a writer and activist on African issues. He is a fellow of the Global Equity Initiative at Harvard University, director of the Social Science Research Council program on AIDS and social transformation, and a director of Justice Africa in London. In his twenty-year career, he has studied the social, political, and health dimensions of famine, war, genocide and the HIV/AIDS epidemic, especially in the Horn of Africa and the Great Lakes. His books include *Famine that Kills: Darfur, Sudan* (Oxford, first edition 1989, revised 2004), *Famine Crimes: Politics and the Disaster Relief Industry in Africa* (James Currey, 1997), and *Islamism and Its Enemies in the Horn of Africa* (Hurst, 2004).

Rohan Edrisinha is a lecturer in the Faculty of Law, University of Colombo, Sri Lanka, specializing in Constitutional Law. He is also the founder, director, and head of the Legal Division, Centre for Policy Alternatives, an independent public policy institute engaged in research and advocacy on conflict resolution, constitutional and law reform, human rights and governance-related issues. In 2004–2005 as a Visiting Fellow at the Center for the Study of World Religions, he researched religion, ethnicity, and nationalism in the Sri Lankan peace process.

Phebe Marr is a Senior Fellow at the U.S. Institute of Peace where she is working on a project entitled "Envisioning an Alternative Future for Iraq." She has spent over 40 years as a scholar and analyst of southwest Asia and is a leading U.S. specialist on Iraq, frequently consulted by government and non government authorities. Dr. Marr is on the editorial board of the *Middle East Journal*, is a member of the Council on Foreign Relations and the Middle East Institute, and is a board member on the Middle East Policy Council. Her research has centered on problems of political and social development in the Middle East in general and the Gulf in particular. Her publications include *The Modern History of Iraq* (Westview, rev. ed. 2004).

Ann Elizabeth Mayer is an Associate Professor of Legal Studies at the Wharton School of the University of Pennsylvania. She has also taught at Georgetown, Princeton, and Yale. She earned her PhD from the University of Michigan; a Certificate in Islamic and Comparative Law from the School of Oriental and African Studies, University of London; and a JD from the University of Pennsylvania. In recent years her work has focused on cultural diversity and human rights. Her research areas also include Islamic law in contemporary Middle Eastern countries and problems of constitutionalism and the rule of law. She has published extensively in scholarly journals and edited collections, and her book *Islam and Human Rights* is now in its third edition.

Paul Mojzes is professor of religious studies at Rosemont College and until recently the Provost and Academic Dean. He is a native of Yugoslavia who came to the United States in 1957. Dr. Mojzes is the co-editor of the *Journal of Ecumenical Studies*, and founder and editor of *Religion in Eastern Europe*. He is the author of five books and editor of several more. He is the president of Christians Associated for Relationships with Eastern Europe and a member of the Europe Forum of the National Council of Churches.

Yitzhak Nakash is Associate Professor of Middle Eastern and Islamic Studies at Brandeis University. His contribution to the conference can be found in his latest book, *Reaching for Power: The Shia in the Modern Arab World* (Princeton, 2006). He is also the author of *The Shiis of Iraq* (2nd ed., Princeton, 2003).

Michael Sells is John Henry Barrows Professor of Islamic History and Literature in the Divinity School, University of Chicago. He formerly taught Comparative Religions at Haverford College. In 1993, he co-founded the Community of Bosnia, a nonprofit organization dedicated to resisting religious persecution, racism and genocide, and to working for a tolerant, multireligious society in Bosnia and throughout the world. His most recent book is *The New Crusades: Constructing the Muslim Enemy* which he co-edited and to which he contributed. His 1996 book *The Bridge Betrayed: Religion and Genocide in Bosnia* received the American Academy of Religion prize for the historical study of religion.

H. L. Seneviratne is a Professor at the University of Virginia. His specializations include religion and politics, socialism, classical social theory, human rights, democracy and free market economy, ethnonationalism, cinema, art and popular culture. His present research includes a critical examination of social change, emergence from colonialism, and the search for national identity and economic security in light of human suffering within the Sri Lankan context. He is the author of *Rituals of the Kandyan State* (Cambridge University Press, 1979), *The Work of Kings* (Chicago, 1999) and the editor of *Identity, Consciousness and the Past* (Oxford, 1989).

Other Participants

Rogaia Mustafa Abusharaf, fellow at the Royal Anthropological Institute and Durham University Anthropology Department and senior research associate at Brown University.

Leila Ahmed, Victor S. Thomas Professor, Harvard Divinity School.

Anne Blackburn, Associate Professor of South Asia and Buddhist Studies (South Asia, Southeast Asia, and Religious Studies Programs) and the director of the Sinhala Program in the Department of Asian Studies at Cornell University.

Hurst Hannum, Professor of International Law at The Fletcher School of Law and Diplomacy of Tufts University.

Raymond F. Hopkins, Richter Professor of Political Science at Swarthmore College.

Kati Kargman, BA, Harvard University.

Karim H. Karim, associate director, School of Journalism and Communication at Carleton University in Ottawa, Canada.

Omar Abdul Malik, Researcher, Islam in America.

Susan Lloyd McGarry, manager of planning and special projects, Center for the Study of World Religions, Harvard Divinity School.

Roy Mottahedeh, Gurney Professor of Islamic History at Harvard University.

Atalia Omer, PhD candidate in the Committee on the Study of Religion of Harvard University.

Robert A. Orsi, Charles Warren Professor of the History of Religion in America, Harvard University.

Emran Qureshi, Wertheim Fellow, Labor and Worklife Program, Harvard Law School.

John P. Reeder, Jr., Professor of Religious Studies at Brown University.

Christian Rice, ThD candidate in Christian Ethics at Harvard Divinity School.

John D. Rogers, associate editor of the *Bibliography of Asian Studies*.

Vijaya Samaraweera, consultant in law and development, with assignments in Sri Lanka, Cambodia, East Timor, Timor Leste, Yemen, and Iraq.

Rory Stewart, author of *The Places in Between* and the forthcoming book, *The Prince of the Marshes: And Other Occupational Hazards of a Year in Iraq*, formerly a fellow at the Carr Center for Human Rights Policy at the Kennedy School of Government, Harvard University.

Stanley J. Tambiah, Esther and Sidney Rabb Research Professor of Anthropology at Harvard University.